BLINDED
BY
THE
LIGHT

Harmony Books
New York

BLINDED BY THE LIGHT

THE SECRET LIFE OF THE SUN

JOHN GRIBBIN

Published by Harmony Books, a division of Crown
Publishers, Inc., 201 East 50th Street, New York, New York
10022. Member of the Crown Publishing Group.
Published in Great Britain by Transworld Publishers Ltd. in
1991.
HARMONY and colophon are trademarks of Crown
Publishers, Inc.

Manufactured in the United States of America

Library of Congress Cataloging-in-Publication Data
Gribbin, John R.
    Blinded by the light : the secret life of the sun / John
Gribbin.
        p.   cm.
    1. Sun—Interior structure—Popular works.   I. Title.
    QB539.I5G75   1991
    523.7′6—dc20   91-9941
                    CIP

ISBN 0-517-57827-1
10 9 8 7 6 5 4 3 2 1
First American Edition

CONTENTS

ACKNOWLEDGMENTS

This book has benefited from discussions with many astronomers at various scientific meetings over the past few years. In particular, it was John Faulkner's boyish enthusiasm for the WIMP theory that first made me aware that there was a story worth telling; Jack Eddy, Ron Gilliland, and Douglas Gough should also be singled out for mention, and thanks for their helpful responses to my requests for more information about their own work. Mick Kelly, Hubert Lamb, and Stephen Schneider share most of the credit for educating me on the subject of climatic change, which is featured in Chapter 6.

Douglas Gough also followed John Faulkner, more years ago than any of us care to remember, in the unrewarding task of acting as my supervisor when I was a research student at Cambridge. I hope they feel that my efforts here live up to their exacting standards, and I am grateful to them for not writing a better book on the subject first.

John Gribbin
December 1989

INTRODUCTION

The Sun has always kept its secrets well. Less than a hundred years ago, nobody knew, even in general terms, how the Sun maintained its heat. Less than a human lifetime ago, nobody knew what the Sun was made of. And it is scarcely fifty years since details of the nuclear processes that fire the Sun began to become clear. For centuries, progress toward an astronomical understanding of the deep workings of the Sun was painfully slow—and it was slow for an ironic reason.

Our Sun is simply a star, much like many of the other stars we see in the night sky. It looks so bright to us simply because it is so close, a mere 150 million kilometers away, quite a short distance in the cosmos. Because it is so close and its surface is so hot (roughly 6,000°C), it shines with dazzling brightness, and it is easy for astronomers to study the surface and the atmosphere of our neighborhood star. But studying the deep interior—the work I describe here—is naturally more difficult.

Not only would astronomers be blinded by the light from the surface of the Sun if they stared at it for long, but their sensitive instruments would be rendered useless as well. The very brightness of the surface helps to conceal the workings of the deep interior, telling us only that something deep inside the Sun is indeed generating enormous quantities of energy. Pioneers of astrophysics—the study of the workings of the stars—never dreamed that they would be able to see inside the heart of the Sun and make direct measurements of the conditions there. But in recent years two entirely separate and independent probes of the solar interior have been developed. They involve such bizarre developments as a telescope buried deep beneath the ground in a mine, and instruments so sensitive that they can measure vibrations that move patches of the solar surface in and out by a few tens of meters. Even stranger, some of these new studies of the conditions deep in the heart of the Sun may be telling us important things about the evolution and ultimate fate of the whole Universe.

As we move into the 1990s, astronomers are no longer completely blinded by the light from the surface of the Sun and are able to measure directly what goes on in its heart. This book tells the story of how the astrophysical pioneers began to unlock the secrets of the Sun—and points to the way they will be probing the solar interior in the years and decades ahead.

John Gribbin

BLINDED BY THE LIGHT

1 ANCIENT HISTORY

No other object has so stirred the imagination of mankind as the Sun. In earliest times, it was worshiped as a god, since our ancestors could clearly see that the Sun brings life to Earth and makes things grow. The ancients thought that the Sun was a ball of fire that traveled across the sky of our planet Earth by day and returned to its starting place, ready for the next dawn, through underground passages and caverns by night. The first recorded attempt to put these ideas on what we would nowadays regard as a scientific footing was made as long ago as the fifth century B.C. by the Greek philosopher Anaxagoras of Athens. His scientific reasoning was pretty good, as far as it went; but unfortunately the observational facts on which his reasoning was based were incomplete, so that his ideas about the Sun turn out to be very misleading. Nevertheless, Anaxagoras deserves pride of place for at least making the effort to understand the Sun as a physical phenomenon, subject to the same laws as the rest of the Universe, and not simply treating it as a supernatural object beyond mortal comprehension.

One of the things that started Anaxagoras thinking about the nature of the Sun was a meteorite that fell at Aegospotami. The meteorite was hot, so the philosopher reasoned that it must have come from the Sun. It contained iron, so he deduced that the Sun must be made of iron. As far as anyone knew in those days, a ball of red-hot iron, moving high over the land, could certainly provide the warmth of the Sun and the cycle of day and night. This description was what modern scientists would regard as a good "working hypothesis," a basis for further investigations. But like all good scientific hypotheses, this one raised new questions for the philosophers to puzzle over: How big would the ball of red-hot iron have to be? And how far above the Earth was it moving?

In those days, philosophers didn't really do much in the way of experiment and observation. They listened to reports of interesting phenomena, and they tried to fit the various pieces of hearsay evidence into a coherent picture. Anaxagoras himself, for example, had never traveled to the upper reaches of the Nile River, but he had heard reports from travelers who had. They said that in the city of Syene, which was located near the present position of the Aswan Dam, on the day of the summer solstice (the "longest day") the Sun was directly overhead at noon and cast no shadow. Now, Anaxagoras may not have been much of an experimenter or traveler, but he knew his geometry, and he also knew that at noon on the day of the summer solstice the Sun at the Nile Delta, about 500 miles north of Syene, made an angle of about 7 degrees with the vertical. Since he "knew" that the Earth was flat, Anaxagoras was quickly able to calculate the height of the Sun above the Earth, using the straightforward geometrical properties of right-angled triangles (Figure 1.1). He found that the Sun was just 4,000 miles above the heads of the observers at Syene. And because

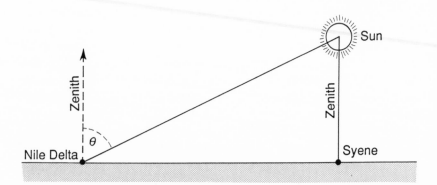

Fig. 1.1. Assuming that the Earth was flat, and using the geometry of right-angle triangles, Anaxagoras calculated in the fifth century b.c. that the Sun must be 4,000 miles overhead.

he also knew the *apparent* size of the Sun (its angular diameter is about half a degree), he was also able to calculate, from the geometry of triangles, how big the Sun must really be in order to appear the size it does to our eyes. His estimate, about 35 miles for the diameter of the Sun, suggested that it was very similar in size to the southern peninsula of Greece, the Peloponnesus.

This was a shocking and subversive suggestion to make in Greece in the fifth century B.C., where heavenly objects were regarded as gods. Anaxagoras was first arrested for heresy and then banished forever from his home city of Athens—treatment very similar to the fate Galileo Galilei suffered at the hands of the religious authorities more than 2,000 years later when he, too, dared to suggest that the Sun was a natural phenomenon. For all that time, from Anaxagoras to Galileo, nobody, as far as we know, attempted to understand the Sun in scientific terms—a dark age indeed. But even in the twentieth century, when we like to think that we are more open-minded and understand the Universe in which we live better than any of our predecessors, the example of Anaxagoras is worth taking to heart. Even his mistakes can teach us a great deal about science and about the hazards of complacency.

The speculation that the Sun might be a ball of red-hot iron was quite reasonable at the time. His geometrical calculation of the height of the Sun above a flat Earth was also impeccable. Where he made his big mistake was in taking for granted what "everyone knew" to be true—that the Earth was flat. Only a couple of hundred years later another Greek philosopher, Eratosthenes, used exactly the same evidence to calculate the diameter of the spherical Earth. Eratosthenes, by assuming that the Sun was so far away that rays of light from the Sun reach the Earth as parallel lines, used the measured angle of the Sun below the vertical at the solstice, as viewed from the Nile Delta, just as Anaxagoras had (Figure 1.2). Because the angle involved in the geometrical calculation is the same, he got the same "answer," 4,000 miles; but he interpreted this as the radius of the Earth, not the height of the Sun above the Earth. We now have an overwhelming weight of other evidence which shows that Eratosthenes was more or less correct in his reasoning.

But the moral of this tale is not that Anaxagoras was "wrong" and Eratosthenes was "right." Good scientists don't regard even their best theories as being "right" in any absolute sense. There are simply good theories and bad theories. Good theories enable you to make accurate

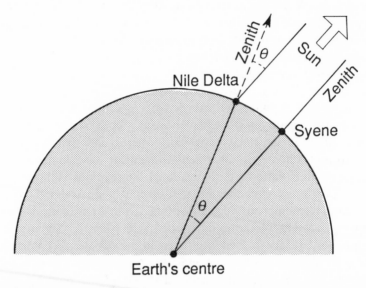

Fig. 1.2. Assuming that the Earth was round and that the Sun is at a vast distance, a later Greek philosopher, Eratosthenes, used the same geometrical calculation to infer that the radius of the Earth must be about 4,000 miles. Both *calculations* were correct; it was Anaxagoras's *assumption* that was wrong.

predictions about the way things will behave in the real world; bad theories make inaccurate, or unreliable, predictions. The best theories, such as general relativity, are so very good indeed that they have never been found to make an inaccurate prediction. But even lesser theories, such as Newton's theory of gravity, may be perfectly adequate for many purposes, provided their limitations are understood.

In that sense, the two ideas about the relationship of the Sun and Earth provided by the two Greek philosophers form a good set of hypotheses. The geometrical evidence obtained by observing the height of the Sun at the Nile Delta and at Syene tells us *either* that the Earth is flat and the Sun is 4,000 miles above it, *or* that the Sun is at a vast distance and the Earth is a sphere with a radius of 4,000 miles. The evidence available at the time was consistent with either possibility. Only further observations and measurements could reveal which hypothesis was correct. Together, the two interpretations of the one set of data make good science. But one lesson to be drawn from the tale is that even a radical and farsighted thinker, who was not afraid to fall foul of the established authorities of the day in his search for the truth, could not rid himself of the dogma of the flat Earth. Anaxagoras was so certain that the Earth was flat that he never questioned the assumption—otherwise he, and not Eratosthenes, might have been credited with the first accurate measurement of the Earth's radius. The history of science is littered with such unfortunate examples of theories that are argued with complete logic and perfect accuracy, but which start out from a basis of unquestioning faith in something that later turns out to be completely untrue. The true scientific method is to take nothing for granted; but some assumptions, like the flatness of the Earth in Anaxagoras's day, are so deeply ingrained that they are hard to eradicate.

Not surprisingly, the story of how astronomers developed an understanding of the Sun's internal fires is full of similar examples of assumptions that seem blindingly obvious to one generation and are totally rejected by the next. No theory is any better than the assumptions that are built in to it, and the only real test of a theory is its predictive power. By those criteria, the story I have to tell may lead in unexpected directions, but it follows an inevitable path. It is concerned primarily with the interior of the Sun—the secret Sun—and how it has maintained a steady supply of heat for thousands of billions of years. This only became a puzzle for scientists in the nineteenth century, when the discovery of the laws of thermodynamics revealed that nothing, not even the Sun, could stay hot forever. In terms of the history of astronomy, however, even nineteenth century science is ancient, so before we move on to the main theme of our story, I will explain why astronomers today are so confident that, unlike Anaxagoras, they really do have a good idea of how far away the Sun is, how big it is, and how hot.

○ VITAL STATISTICS

Distances to astronomical objects, including the Moon and nearer planets, can indeed be measured using the same basic technique, triangulation, that Anaxagoras used in his attempt to determine the distance to the Sun. This is exactly the technique used by surveyors and mapmakers here on Earth. If we want to know the distance to a landmark, such as a high mountain, we can simply measure out an accurate baseline, place surveying instruments at either end, and line them up on the landmark. By measuring the angle from each end of the baseline to the landmark, we can calculate the length of the sides of an imaginary triangle stretching out from the baseline with the landmark at its tip. The problem is that the farther away things are the more subtle the measurements become. Not surprisingly, the Sun is too far away for the technique to work—the difference in the angles measured at either end of the baseline is too small to detect. But it is fairly simple, using this technique, to establish that the distance from the Earth to the Moon is about 60 times the radius of the Earth.

Similar geometrical techniques provided the first estimates of the distances to the nearest planets, Venus and Mars. (In the second half of the twentieth century, such measurements have been improved by bouncing radar echoes off these planets and calculating the distances on the basis of the time it takes for the radio pulses, traveling at the speed of light, to travel there and back again.) The key measurement is the distance to Venus, because Venus orbits the Sun within the orbit of the Earth. Since the orbits are tilted slightly, we don't actually see Venus pass across the face of the Sun in every orbit. But on the rare occasions when Venus does pass across the face of the Sun, as viewed from Earth, it can be used to provide a measurement of the distance to the Sun (Figure 1.3).

This and other observations all give the same result. The average distance from the Earth to the Sun (''average'' because the distance varies slightly during the year) is 149,597,893 kilometers. In round terms, we can call it 150 million kilometers, or 93 million miles. Astronomers regard this as such a fundamental measure of distance that they also call it the Astronomical Unit, or AU, and measure distance to other stars in terms of the AU.

Putting this distance into perspective, it takes light, traveling at 300,000 kilometers per second, a full 8 minutes and 20 seconds to travel from the Sun to the Earth. Since the speed of light is too big to be familiar to us, consider this example: The fastest object any ordinary person is likely to encounter is a jet airliner, which might travel at a speed of 800 kilometers per hour. As a passenger inside such a vehicle, you could cross the Atlantic in a few hours, or travel from New York to Sydney, Australia, in little more than a day. But if you could keep airborne long enough to fly the equivalent of the distance from the Earth to the Sun, you would be flying nonstop for 21 years.

If the Sun is so far away, obviously it must be a lot bigger than the 35-mile diameter calculated by Anaxagoras when he thought it was just 4,000 miles above the Earth. In fact, in order to show as a disk

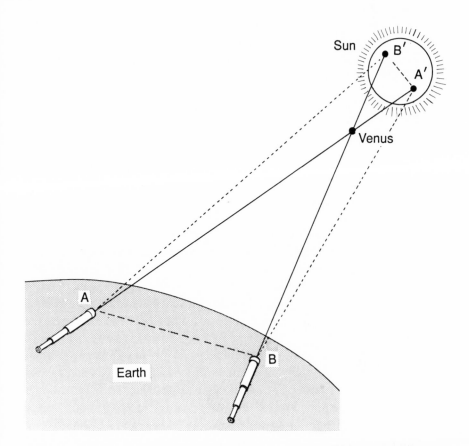

Fig. 1.3. Observers in different places on Earth see Venus against different parts of the Sun's face. The difference helps them calculate the distance to the Sun.

half a degree across at a distance of 150 million kilometers, the Sun must be 1,390,600 kilometers across, 109 times the diameter of the Earth. Now we know how far away the Sun is and how big it is. So how much matter does it contain?

The amount of matter inside the Sun determines the strength of its gravitational pull, which holds the planets in their orbits around the Sun. Isaac Newton's law of gravity says that the force pulling two bodies together depends on their masses, multiplied together and divided by the square of the distance between them, all multiplied by the gravitational constant, now written as G. In the eighteenth century,

Henry Cavendish carried out a series of painstaking measurements, using large and small masses in the laboratory, to find the force with which one mass tugs on another. In effect, he was measuring G, although this notation had not then been introduced. Once this was known, it was easy to calculate the mass of the Earth by measuring the force with which the Earth pulls on an object—its weight. The distance used in the calculation is simply the distance to the center of the Earth, the Earth's radius, which Eratosthenes showed us how to measure. Thus, the calculated mass of the planet is just under 6×10^{27} grams (that is, a 6 followed by 27 zeros).

With G and the mass of the Earth determined, astronomers can calculate the mass of the Sun. The Earth orbits the Sun once every year at a distance of 150 million kilometers, so astronomers know how fast it must be moving in its orbit. The force required to hold a planet in this orbit is known from basic physics. It doesn't matter whether the planet is being held in place by a long piece of string fastened at the center of the Solar System, or by the gravity of the Sun; the force must be the same. Newton's gravitational law says that in order to provide the right gravitational force the Sun itself must have a mass of just under 2×10^{33} grams, about a third of a million times the mass of the Earth.

Since we know that it has a diameter of just over a hundred times the diameter of the Earth, the Sun must be a million times bigger than the Earth (in the sense that a million globes the size of the Earth could fit within a globe the size of the Sun). Volume is proportional to the cube of the diameter of a sphere, and 100 cubed is 1,000,000. So the Sun has a mass of a third of a million Earths, occupying a volume of one million Earths. Therefore, its average density is only one third that of the Earth, just about 1.5 times the density of water. That may not sound particularly impressive, but remember that it is an *average*. As we shall see, although the outer layers of the Sun are composed of tenuous layers of gas, deep down inside the density, pressure, and temperature build up dramatically. But first we need some idea of how much heat the Sun is radiating at its surface.

In his book *Sun and Earth,* Herbert Friedman provides a beautifully simple example of the power of solar radiation. Friedman tells how C. A. Young of Princeton University used to put the point across to his students, starting with the observation, made by William Herschel in the eighteenth century, that the heat of the noonday Sun in summer would be able to melt a layer of ice one inch thick in 2 hours and 12 minutes.

This simple observation becomes more impressive when you realize that the Sun is pouring out radiation equally energetically in all directions. So if there is enough energy to melt a piece of ice one inch thick that quickly at the point where the Earth in its orbit happens to intercept the sunlight, there must also be the same amount of energy crossing every square centimeter of space at the same distance from the Sun. In other words, there is enough energy pouring out of the Sun to melt a whole shell of ice, one inch thick and 300 million kilometers in diameter, in 2 hours and 12 minutes. Young used to ask his students to imagine the shell of ice shrinking in diameter, closing in on the Sun so that its area got less and less, but with its thickness increasing so that it always contained the same total amount of ice. By the time the inner surface was touching the surface of the Sun, this imaginary layer of ice would be more than a mile thick, but it would still be thawed in exactly the same brief span of time.

The temperature at the surface of the Sun sufficient to achieve this feat is 5,770 K.* We can measure this today by measuring the amount of heat arriving at one square centimeter of the Earth's surface (or, indeed, warming the detectors on a satellite in space), and making suitable allowance for the distance to the Sun. Another way to measure the temperature of a hot object is by its color. Just as a white-hot piece of iron is hotter than a red-hot piece of iron, so a blue or white star is hotter than a yellow or orange star. This color-temperature connection follows a precise law, studied in detail in laboratory experiments, and can be quantified. The figure we end up with is still the same; the temperature of a yellowish star like our Sun is about 6,000 K.

This is not, in truth, a particularly remarkable figure. The glowing filament of an electric light bulb runs at about 2,000 K, and although it is a little hotter than red-hot iron, the *surface* of the Sun, at least, is not at a temperature that even Anaxagoras would have had any trouble comprehending. The trouble came in the nineteenth century, when geologists and evolutionary biologists began to appreciate the extreme age of the Earth and pointed out that the Sun must have been shining this brightly for many hundreds, probably thousands, of millions of years.

*Measured from the thermodynamic zero point of temperature, $-273°C$.

This posed a major problem for science, because it was also at about this time that physicists began to appreciate that the laws of thermodynamics and conservation of energy set very strict limits on how long the Sun could maintain its present-day output of energy. By all the known laws of nineteenth-century physics, there was simply no way in which the Sun could have stayed hot as long as geology and biology seemed to require. Were the geologists and biologists wrong? Or was the understanding of physics deficient? One of the greatest scientists of the day was convinced that if something had to give, it certainly was not going to be the laws of physics, and he mounted a determined attack on anyone who dared to suggest otherwise. And yet, the weight of geological evidence certainly had to be taken seriously.

○ THE FRENCH CONNECTION

As recently as the eighteenth century, it was widely accepted that the Earth was created about 6,000 years ago. In 1654, John Lightfoot had refined a famous calculation, originally made by Archbishop Ussher earlier in the seventeenth century. This refinement set the moment of the creation as 9 A.M., Mesopotamian time, on 26 October, 4004 B.C. on the Julian calendar. The estimate had no basis in scientific calculation or observation, but was arrived at simply by counting back the generations referred to in the Bible, from Jesus Christ back to Adam. Today, even theologians accept that the Bible should not be taken literally at that level and that the Earth, our Sun, and the Universe at large have been around for a vastly greater span of time than even our recent ancestors could have imagined. The first attempt to extend the time scale, the first real scientific estimate of the age of the Earth, only pushed this out to 75,000 years or so, still far short of the figure calculated today. But this still increased the age tenfold, and it flew in the face of established religious doctrine, just as Anaxagoras had rejected religious doctrine in his approach to the problem of the nature of the Sun. Georges-Louis Leclerc, Comte de Buffon, who made the calculation, did not suffer the same fate as Anaxagoras, however, and it took less time for the seed he planted to bear fruit.

Most of Buffon's work had no direct bearing on the puzzle of the nature of the Sun, but among his many interests he worried about the age of the Earth. Buffon was not convinced that the heat of the Sun was enough to keep the Earth warm, and he assumed that heat from inside the Earth was essential to provide conditions suitable for life. Since he knew of no way in which heat could currently be generated inside the Earth, he also assumed that the Earth had been formed as a molten ball of rock and had been cooling down ever since. The molten, primeval Earth, he suggested, had been torn out of the Sun by a collision with a passing comet. But how long would it have taken to cool to its present state?

Newton had pointed out in his *Principia* that a globe of red-hot iron as big as the Earth would take 50,000 years to cool down. Buffon actually carried out experiments with balls of iron and other substances of different sizes, observing how long it took for them to cool down from red heat. Armed with this information and the accurate knowledge scientists already had of the size of the Earth, he improved Newton's calculation, suggesting that if the Earth had been born in a molten state it would have taken 36,000 years to cool to the point where life could appear, and a further 39,000 years (75,000 in all) to cool to its present temperature.

Theologians of the day, naturally, attacked this extension of the time scale of Earth history. But at least Buffon wasn't sent into exile, and his ideas, breaking completely with religious dogma, had a lasting influence after his death, into the nineteenth century.*

The direct line of Buffon's influence on subsequent generations of scientists was through Jean Fourier, who is best remembered today for his development of the mathematical tool known as the Fourier series, developed as Fourier (or harmonic) analysis. In fact, Fourier was primarily a physicist and developed his mathematics as a means to an end, in order to be able to analyze interesting physical problems with accuracy.† In particular, he was fascinated by the problem of providing

---

*Buffon's son, born in 1764, came to a more sticky end. Although the boy showed signs of a brilliant mind, he was not interested in academic (or any other) work and became a spendthrift and wastrel, like so many members of the French aristocracy of the time. And, like them, he went to the guillotine, in 1794. There can hardly be a better example to young people of the importance of working hard at your studies!

†Primarily a physicist, that is, as far as his scientific interests went. He was also politically active at the time of the French Revolution and accompanied Napoléon on his expedition to Egypt. He was in charge of the publication of the 21-volume *Description de l'Egypte* which came out of that expedition and which established Egyptology as a branch of study. Back in France, Fourier became an able administrator, eventually rising to become prefect of the Rhône department and being appointed first a baron and then a count by Napoléon—but that didn't stop him from resigning during the last days of Napoléon's rule in protest against the excesses of the regime. Much of his scientific work was carried out as a hobby in his spare time—including what seems to have been the first scientific mention of what we now know as the greenhouse effect.

an accurate means of calculating the way in which heat is transferred through an object; and it was the attention gained by Buffon's estimate of the age of the Earth that led Fourier to his own study of heat conduction (and on to the mathematics he needed to describe the process). Buffon had simply measured the rate at which hot objects cooled, and tried to extrapolate this up to an object the size of the Earth. Fourier, on the other hand, tried to develop laws—mathematical equations—to describe the rate at which heat could escape from a body, and then used these to calculate how long it would have taken the Earth to cool. In this picture, the Earth must be coolest on the outside, but still at the temperature of molten rock at its center, even today (that means a temperature above 6,000 K, more than the temperature at the *surface* of the Sun). Of course, there is a steady fall in temperature—a thermal gradient—from the inside to the outside, and a steady flow of heat outward. Because the layers of cooler material surrounding the hot core act as an insulating blanket, holding heat in, it takes much longer for the Earth to cool, according to these estimates, than even Buffon had realized. In 1820, Fourier wrote down the formula for the age of the Earth, based on these arguments; but as far as anyone has been able to find out, he never wrote down the number that comes out of this formula. Perhaps he regarded the value he had derived for the age of the Earth as too big to be taken seriously—for, instead of Buffon's 75 *thousand* years, Fourier's equations implied an age for the Earth of 100 *million* years!

Fourier died in 1830, and it was to be another 30 years before essentially the same calculation was taken up and promoted widely as indicating the true age of the Earth. But by then the pace of change had been so rapid that the enthusiastic promoter of this time scale, William Thomson (who later became Lord Kelvin), was making the case that 100 million years was such a *short* time scale that it ought to be causing embarrassment to the geologists and evolutionists.

○ **THE GEOLOGISTS' TIME SCALE**

One of the most basic tenets of modern geological science is the idea that only the same sort of processes that we see at work on Earth today—erosion, volcanic activity, earthquakes, and so on—are needed to explain how the world got into its present state, provided that there has been enough time for the forces of wind and weather and the rest to do their work. The notion seems as natural to us as the notion of a flat Earth did to Anaxagoras, and would pass without comment as part of any introduction to geophysics. But this "obvious" idea only surfaced in the late eighteenth century, when it was put forward by the Scotsman James Hutton, a contemporary of Buffon; and it only became an established fact of scientific life in the nineteenth century, after a vigorous debate between the "uniformitarians," who held that the forces that shape the Earth have always been much the same as we see them now, and the "catastrophists," who argued that such dramatic features as mountain ranges and ocean basins could only have been created during epochs of great upheaval and turmoil, when the Earth was wracked in the grip of mysterious and perhaps supernatural forces.

Hutton, who was born in 1726 and was the son of a merchant, was intended by his family to follow a career as a lawyer but turned instead to chemistry. With a friend, John Davie, he invented a method for production of the valuable industrial chemical ammonium chloride and made enough money out of this, together with a modest inheritance, to set himself up as a gentleman farmer in Berwickshire. The farm, too, was successful, but while he was involved in agriculture Hutton became interested in the effect of running water on rocks and soil. He made several trips to the continent, ostensibly to study farming techniques, where he took advantage of every opportunity to learn more about rocks and minerals. In 1768, financially independent, Hutton returned to Edinburgh and spent the rest of his life in scientific work, mainly geology.

Although Hutton's uniformitarian ideas provoked a strong response from some critics when he first introduced them in the late eighteenth century, his rather impenetrable writing style meant that the ideas did not reach a wide audience until 1802, when his friend John Playfair published an edited version of Hutton's work. It was then that the ideas began to be taken seriously, and geologists began to divide themselves into two camps, for and against.

Uniformitarianism is so well accepted now that it may seem inherently obvious to us; but it is worth nothing that Hutton was the first person to point out, for example, that the heat of the Earth's interior could explain, without any supernatural intervention, how sedimentary rocks, laid down by water, could be fused into granites and flints. Heat from inside the Earth, he said, was also responsible for pushing up mountain chains and twisting geological strata. But he also realized that this would take a very long time indeed.

Hutton's writing may have been largely impenetrable, but he did come up with one particularly striking example. The forces of erosion work very slowly, and this is shown by the fact that Roman roads are still visible more than two thousand years after they were laid down. Clearly the time required for such slow processes to carve the face of the Earth into its modern appearance must be vastly longer, Hutton pointed out, than the biblical 6,000 years. He regarded the age of the Earth as beyond comprehension, writing that "we find no vestige of a beginning—no prospect of an end."

Hutton's pioneering idea was taken up and developed in the nineteenth century by another Scot, Charles Lyell, who was born in 1797, the year Hutton died. Like Hutton, Lyell was steered by his family toward a career in law. He was actually admitted to the bar in 1825; but, also like Hutton, his interest in science, especially geology, diverted him from a legal career. In the late 1820s, Lyell was able to travel extensively on the continent—his father was wealthy enough to support him—and everywhere he went he saw evidence of the way natural forces could mold the features of the Earth. The region around Mount Etna, in particular, provided striking reinforcement for the ideas he already held. The fruits of Lyell's travels appeared in his three-volume work *Principles of Geology*. The subtitle of volume one says it all: *Being an Attempt to Explain the Former Changes of the Earth's Surface by Reference to Causes Now in Operation.*

Lyell's books caused an immediate stir and made a particularly striking impression on a young naturalist just setting off on a voyage in HMS *Beagle*. Charles Darwin took volume one with him; volume two caught up with him during the voyage; and volume three was waiting for him when he returned to England in 1836. Darwin never failed to acknowledge his debt to Lyell, who showed him that the Earth was very old indeed and that all that was needed to explain its present appearance was the same set of forces that we see at work today. Evolution by natural selection required, above all else, a long time scale in which to operate, and Lyell gave Darwin that time scale.

Although Lyell was slow to come around to the idea of evolution, the two scientists became firm friends in later life. After the *Origin of Species* was published in 1859, Lyell gradually allowed himself to be persuaded by Darwin's evidence and lent his support to Darwin in a major new edition of *Principles of Geology*, published in 1865. This counted for a lot; Lyell was by then a knight and a friend of both the royal family and politicians. He held many professional honors and was widely known to the general public. By standing up to be counted alongside Darwin, at a time when opposition to Darwin's ideas was fierce, he persuaded many other people that there must be something in this evolution business, after all. Darwin was delighted, and commented, "Considering his age, his former views, and position in society, I think his action has been heroic."

Just at that time, however, both Darwin and Lyell were coming under attack, not from religious fundamentalists but from physicists who argued that no known natural processes could have provided conditions suitable for life on Earth for a long enough time for geological processes to have shaped the planet or for evolution to have produced the diversity of life we see today. There was no obvious answer to this criticism, which had to be taken seriously. Biology and geology seemed to be telling scientists that the Earth, and the Sun, were much older than seemed physically possible.

○ SOLAR THERMODYNAMICS

Fourier's work on the mathematics of how heat flows from one place to another became part of one of the greatest achievements of nineteenth-century science, thermodynamics. The realization that heat energy is exactly equivalent to mechanical energy (work), that heat only flows from a hotter object to a cooler one, never the other way (the second law of thermodynamics), and that the amount of disorder (entropy) in the Universe is always increasing (essentially the notion that, "things wear out," expressed in rigorous mathematical terms) revolutionized science and made it possible for physicists to investigate and quantify many phenomena that had previously been inexplicable in strictly scientific terms. Among those phenomena—at the time by no means regarded as the most important pieces of nature to be caught in the thermodynamic net—were the ages of the Earth and Sun.*

In the decades following Fourier's death, the realization that energy and heat could be quantified, and that the energy of even sunlight might be a limited resource, began slowly to spread. A few scientists began to worry about the profligate way in which the Sun pours energy out into space, and to wonder where the energy came from, and how long the supply might last. In those days, anyone who puzzled about such

*For more about the broad sweep of thermodynamics, see *The Omega Point* by John Gribbin and *The Second Law* by Peter Atkins.

things naturally thought in terms of the energy produced by burning coal, the basic power supply that was fueling the Industrial Revolution. Today we can update those calculations by thinking in terms of the modern successor to coal, gasoline. If the Sun were made entirely of gasoline, burning in the most efficient way possible, then it could maintain its present heat for only a few tens of thousands of years. In fact, no form of chemical energy can keep the Sun hot for more than 100,000 years.

It took some time for the message to sink in and for physicists to appreciate the importance of the message. The first two people known to have tackled the problem head-on were both largely ignored at the time, and although they have received some belated credit for their work, in view of the way they were treated it seems quite possible that some completely forgotten scientific hero may have been thinking along the same lines before either of them. As far as anyone now knows, however, the first person to express the law of conservation of energy, which says that energy can be converted from one form into another but can never be created or destroyed, was Julius von Mayer, a German physician living in Heilbronn.

In 1840 Mayer took a post as ship's physician on a vessel sailing to the East Indies. Those were still the days when bleeding a patient was an accepted part of medical routine, and when Mayer bled some of the crew of the ship during their sojourn in the tropics, he was surprised at the bright red color of the blood coming from their veins. Coming from Europe, Mayer was used to the different appearance of arterial and veinous blood. Arterial blood is bright red because it is carrying plenty of oxygen from the lungs to the muscles and other tissues of the body; veinous blood, returning to the lungs, is a much darker, purplish red because it is depleted in oxygen. Or so Mayer had always thought; when he opened the vein of a sailor in Java, however, he thought at first that he had cut an artery by mistake, because the blood was so red. When he realized that he had not made a mistake and found the veinous blood of all the sailors to be just as red, Mayer was alert enough to realize that this must mean, first, that the veinous blood was carrying more oxygen than it did in colder climates, and second, that this must be because the body needed less oxygen in order to maintain body temperature in warmer climates. He knew of the idea, pioneered by Antoine Lavoisier in the eighteenth century, that warm-blooded animals keep themselves warm by a form of slow combustion in the body, in which food is combined with oxygen; and he made the great intuitive leap to the conclusion that work (such as muscular exertion), heat (including the warmth of the body), and other forms of energy (such as the chemical energy released by oxidation of food or by burning coal) are all interchangeable, and that work or energy is never created but only transformed from one form to another.

Mayer returned to Germany in 1841 and settled down in Heilbronn as a general medical practitioner. He had a successful practice, but remained intrigued by these new ideas on the nature of heat, teaching himself physics, carrying out experiments (not very adroitly, it seems), and publishing the first scientific papers on such important topics as the way mechanical energy is converted into heat when air is compressed in a pump, and what should have been a key discussion of the energy source of the Sun. Yet his work was almost completely ignored at the time, and when the same ideas were discovered independently by other people, who began to get a great deal of publicity and credit, Mayer became so depressed that he attempted suicide in 1850 and spent several years in a mental institution. Later, however, his work began to be recognized, his health recovered, and he received many accolades before his death in 1878.

The other pioneer of solar thermodynamics fared even worse than Mayer, John Waterston was born in 1811 in Edinburgh, and as a young man he was allowed time off from his work as a civil engineer to study at Edinburgh University. He began publishing articles—scientific papers—in the research journals in 1830, and kept up his scientific activities after he moved to London in 1833 to work on the rapidly growing railway system. In 1839, Waterston went to India, where he worked as a teacher of the East India Company's cadets; by saving hard he was able to retire in 1857 and return to Edinburgh to devote himself to research. But he had increasing difficulty in getting his papers published, and became a bitter recluse; on 18 June 1883, he walked out of his home and was never seen again.

The turning point in Waterston's life had come as early as 1845, when he had sent a paper to the Royal Society in London, spelling out some important new ideas of what is now known as the kinetic theory of gases. Waterston showed how energy is distributed among the atoms or molecules of a gas, an important step forward in what became the branch of science know as statistical mechanics. The Royal Society, after consulting two experts, who were unimpressed by the efforts of this largely unknown teacher writing from half a world away, decided not to publish the paper and left it lying, forgotten, in their files. Waterston, in those days before the typewriter and the photocopier, had neglected to keep a copy of the paper himself and never reworked it fully for publication anywhere else. Although briefer summaries of his ideas were published and circulated, it took nearly 15 years for his basic discoveries in kinetic theory to be rediscovered, independently, by other researchers, who took all the credit. It was only in 1891, too late to do Waterston any practical good, that his paper was found in the vaults of the Royal Society by Lord Rayleigh, the secretary of the society at the time, who had it published in 1892, establishing Waterston's priority to the idea and adding a warning to young scientists about the reluctance of learned societies to accept new ideas.

During his time in India, probably in the late 1840s, Waterston had also developed his ideas about the thermodynamics of the Sun, and he did receive some credit for these after they were presented to a meeting of the British Association in 1853 and published shortly after. Ironically, however, the one piece of Waterston's work that did make a minor splash in the scientific community was itself at least partly predated by Mayer's work along similar lines, which had been carried out a few years before, but which was then virtually unknown. What both Mayer and Waterston realized was that if chemical energy was insufficient to maintain the heat of the Sun for more than a few tens of thousands of years, then it must be powered by the only other source of energy known to nineteenth-century science that might keep the Sun hot for a longer period of time: gravity. In terms of the conservation of energy, what they needed was some reservoir of energy that could be drawn on steadily for millions of years and converted into heat. Gravity might fit the bill, if a way of converting gravitational energy into heat could be discovered.

Both Mayer and Waterston suggested that the Sun might be kept hot if it were "fueled" by a continuous supply of meteors falling on it from space. This is a source of energy that comes directly from the gravitational field of the Sun. When a meteor—essentially, a lump of rock—falls toward the Sun, it does so, as Newton realized, because of the mutual gravitational attraction—or force—between the Sun and the meteor. Gravitational energy is converted into kinetic energy, energy of motion, as the meteor falls faster and faster. When the fast-moving rock hits the surface of the Sun and stops, all that energy has to go somewhere. In exactly the same way, when a fast-moving car is brought to a halt using its brakes, all the energy of motion of the car has to go somewhere. In the case of the car, the energy is converted into heat in the brakes and can easily be felt if you hold your hand near to the brake disks or drums just after the vehicle has stopped; in the case of a meteor falling onto the Sun (or, indeed, onto the Earth) the kinetic energy is also converted into heat, raising the temperature of both the meteor and whatever it happens to hit. When a meteor strikes the Earth, the impact can melt rock explosively, blasting out a huge crater with the power of many millions of tons of TNT—far bigger than any man-made explosion, including nuclear blasts. Because the Sun contains more mass than the Earth, it has a correspondingly stronger gravitational field, meteors fall that much faster when they hit the Sun, and the energy released is even greater than it would be if the same meteor struck the Earth.

In principle, you could, indeed, make the Sun hot in this way, if there were enough meteors around to fall onto it. There is nothing in the laws of physics which says that it is impossible to heat a star in this way. In the real Universe, however, there are nowhere near enough meteors around to do the job. Waterston himself realized this and later modified his argument to suggest that the Sun might maintain its internal heat by gradually contracting, shrinking down upon itself. This, too, would convert gravitational energy into heat, and this basic idea became the cornerstone of the arguments used by physicists in the second half of the nineteenth century to "prove" that the Sun could not have existed in its present form for more than 100 million years. Having given due credit to the pioneering efforts of Mayer and Waterston, however, the best way to appreciate the full impact of the calculations that provided such a contrast with the time scale required by Darwin and the geologists is to look at the work of the man who became the supreme advocate of this gravitational time scale: William Thomson, later Lord Kelvin.

○ VICTORIAN GENIUS

William Thomson was born with the scientific equivalent of a silver spoon in his mouth and had the ability to take full advantage of the unusual opportunities he was given. His father was the professor of mathematics at Belfast University, and both William and his older brother James were educated at home with the latest mathematical ideas, still new to university lectures (let alone students) at the time.

After graduating from Cambridge, Thomson worked in Paris for a time, but in 1846 the position of professor of natural philosophy became vacant at the University of Glasgow. Thanks to a careful campaign mounted by his father, and, of course, through his own obvious ability, Thomson was elected to the post—at the age of twenty-two. He stayed there for the rest of his career, retiring 53 years later in 1899. Although the puzzle of the age of the Earth and Sun was a lifelong fascination for Thomson, this was just one of the many facets of his glittering scientific career. In 1851, he put forward the second law of thermo-dynamics, that heat cannot flow from a colder object to a hotter one. He developed the scale of temperatures that starts from the absolute zero of temperature, $-273°C$, the temperature at which, thermody-namics predicts, all the thermal motion of the molecules and atoms in an object is stilled. It is in his honor that the temperature scale is now known as the Kelvin scale.*

The public knew him best as a great inventor, in the Victorian tradition, who worked on the design of the first successful telegraph cable laid across the Atlantic. But this eminently practical man of science had also been puzzling over the more esoteric theory of the age of the Earth, ever since he had formulated the second law of thermodynamics. For, as Thomson immediately realized, the second law tells us that the Earth is getting colder and cannot live forever—again, *things wear out*. In 1852, he wrote:

> Within a finite period of time past the earth must have been, and within a finite period of time to come the earth must again be, unfit for the habitation of man as at present constituted, unless operations have been, or are to be performed which are impossible under the laws to which the known operations going on at the present in the material world are subject.†

But Thomson did not immediately follow up this broad conclusion with any detailed calculations of the age of the Earth—partly because, as historian Joe Burchfield disarmingly expresses it, he was "diverted"

*In the Kelvin scale, degrees are the same size as degrees Celsius, but start from absolute zero. So 0°C, for example, is given as 273K (*without* the degrees symbol).
†Quoted in Joe Burchfield, *Lord Kelvin and the Age of the Earth* (Macmillan: London & New York, 1975), p. 22.

to the problem of solar energy.* It was at the annual meeting of the British Association in 1853 that Waterston's version of the proposal that the Sun might be kept hot by meteors falling onto it was aired. Thomson was immediately taken with the idea and set out to calculate how long the Sun could be kept hot by such means.

Thomson spent a lot of time trying to make the meteor idea work, but eventually he had to admit defeat. There is no need to go through all the painful steps, since the ultimate version of the "meteor" idea as developed by Thomson makes its deficiencies brutally plain. As it became clear that there were not enough small, rocky objects in the Solar System to provide the required input of energy to the Sun, Thomson toyed with the idea that the Sun might maintain its fires by consuming not mere meteors but whole planets, one by one. In this idea, Mercury, the innermost planet, might slowly spiral into the Sun, giving up its gravitational energy as heat—but this would only provide enough to keep the Sun hot for 7 years. Venus would do little better, providing enough energy to heat the Sun for 84 years, and even Neptune, the most distant large planet in the known Solar System, could contribute only enough energy, if it fell all the way into the Sun, to keep the fires hot for some 2,000 years. Even by gobbling up all of the planets in the Solar System in turn, the Sun still could not maintain its fires for more than a few thousand years. In the end, the "meteoric" fuel supply would be no better than the chemical one.

By the 1860s, Thomson was able to do better by invoking the idea of a shrinking Sun. But by then, in addition to Waterston's still little-known work, he had been preempted by a German researcher, Hermann Helmholtz, whose career had some curious parallels with that of the other unsung hero of the solar energy puzzle, Julius Mayer.

Helmholtz had been born in Potsdam in 1821. He was a delicate child and scarcely left his home for the first seven years of his life, but he was educated by his father, a teacher of philosophy and literature at the Potsdam Gymnasium (a school for pre-university students).† Young Hermann showed great academic ability, and when he was old enough, and well enough, to attend the gymnasium himself, he was particularly interested in physics. But since his father could not afford to pay for him to go to the university, he turned instead to medicine, taking advantage of an arrangement whereby his university fees were

*Burchfield, 1975, p. 23.
†On his mother's side, Helmholtz was a descendant of William Penn, the founder of Pennsylvania.

paid in return for a promise that he would serve eight years in the army after he qualified. During four years at the Friedrich Wilhelm Institute in Berlin, Helmholtz studied medicine, as required, but managed also to take courses in physics and mathematics and to become a skilled pianist. He obtained his M.D. in 1842, and by 1843 he was back home in Potsdam as surgeon to his regiment, which was stationed there. His medical duties were not too arduous, and Helmholtz was able to carry out experiments in a laboratory that he set up in the barracks.

The official biographies report that Helmholtz's skill and reputation as a scientist soon became so great that he was "released" from his military duties in 1848; there are suggestions, however, that after an official leave of absence to carry out scientific work he simply refused to return to army life and was actually dismissed from the service under something of a cloud. Either way, in 1849 he was appointed assistant professor of physiology in Königsberg and went on to a series of other academic posts in a long and distinguished career. It was also in 1848 that he had independently discovered the law of conservation of energy, from an investigation of the heat produced by muscles in animals—almost exactly the same course that had led Mayer to his discovery of the law several years earlier. This in turn led Helmholtz, as it had Mayer, to further work in thermodynamics, and to his contributions to the debate about the origin of the Sun's energy.

Helmholtz's first contribution on the subject appeared in February 1854, a few months before Thomson presented his own first paper on the meteor impact hypothesis to the British Association—Thomson probably saw Helmholtz's paper after his own paper was complete, but before it was read to that meeting. The brilliantly simple new idea that Helmholtz contributed was the suggestion that the whole mass of the Sun itself, not merely the planets, might provide the gravitational energy to make it hot. The argument is straightforward. If the whole Sun were made of rock, and it was broken into small pieces, and all the pieces were carried far out into space, then each piece would have a large amount of gravitational energy, and they would all fall toward the center of the cloud of stones. We can measure, or calculate, the energy involved in terms of the amount of work that would have to be done to spread the rocks apart. In the same way, if someone carries a heavy object up a flight of stairs it requires a lot of effort, because the heavy object is being raised in a gravitational field and given energy. If the object is now pushed out of a window, it drops, hitting the ground; and when it hits the ground, it stops and warms up. Gravitational energy has been converted first into kinetic energy and then into heat.

The kinetic energy provided by the mass of all the planets falling into the Sun could only keep the Sun as hot as it is today for a few thousand years. But the gravitational energy provided by the mass of the Sun itself, initially spread out in a cloud of rocks which then fall inward (converting gravitational energy into kinetic energy) and bash together in a molten ball of fire (converting kinetic energy into heat) would release as much energy as the Sun radiates in 20 *million* years. At the time, Helmholtz had not made the precise calculation, simply pointing out that a great deal of energy could be turned into heat in this way. Thomson soon put the numbers in, but didn't think much of the proposal; he considered that the idea that the original stuff of the Universe consisted of a spread-out cloud of irregular lumps of stone was rather implausible. Besides, what was the point of having 20 million times as much energy as the Sun radiates in a year produced all at once, long ago when the Sun formed? What was needed was a way to release energy slowly, over millions of years, not a means to generate a great cosmic explosion.

○ **KELVIN'S TIME SCALES**

In 1854, nobody took much notice of the contributions from either Helmholtz or Thomson, and Thomson was soon preoccupied with other matters. But in December 1860, a happy accident—for science, at least—left him with a broken leg and ample time to lie in bed thinking. This was just a year after the publication of Darwin's *Origin of Species*, and that may well have been the reason why one of the things Thomson thought about was the origin of the Sun's energy supply and the problem of the age of the Sun and Earth. The fruits of his thinking appeared in *Macmillan's Magazine** in 1862, and this time they did make a big impact.

At this time, Thomson based his arguments very much on the image of a mass of stony meteors coming together, distasteful though that had appeared to him earlier. He didn't worry too much about how the vast amount of energy available might be stored up and allowed to

*William Thomson, "Age of the Sun's Heat," *Macmillan's Magazine*, 5 March 1862, p. 288.

trickle out slowly over millions of years, but concentrated on the calculation of how much energy *was* available, and how long it could, if it were spread out, keep the Sun shining at its present brightness. In round terms, the theory showed that there was enough energy stored in the original cloud of rocks to provide for 10 million to 20 million years of solar output at present rates. Even allowing for the possibility of errors in the calculations or the assumptions on which they were based, Thomson could see no way in which this might be increased by more than about a factor of 10, and in that article he wrote:

> It seems, therefore, on the whole most probable that the sun has not illuminated the earth for 100,000,000 years, and almost certain that he has not done so for 500,000,000 years. As for the future, we may say, with equal certainty, that inhabitants of the earth cannot continue to enjoy the light and heat essential to their life, for many million years longer, unless sources now unknown to us are prepared in the great storehouse of creation.

It isn't giving too much of my story away to say that, with hindsight, these comments are remarkably prophetic. But Thomson surely did not expect that sources of energy unknown to nineteenth-century science would, in fact, turn up, as his attack on Darwin later in the article makes clear.

Building from Lyell's version of uniformitarianism, Darwin had, among other things, calculated how long it must have taken for erosion to have produced the present-day appearance of the chalk hills and valleys of the English Weald, from measurements which showed that chalk cliffs are now being eroded at a rate of one inch per century. He meant the calculation to illustrate the long time scale of the Earth; it wasn't a centerpiece of his story, and he carried it through rather carelessly, living to regret ever setting it down in print. But, although the number he came up with is a little on the high side, it isn't so ludicrously incompatible with the time scale envisaged today for the evolution of the Earth, which is several billion years. The figure he came up with—for one relatively recent phase of geological activity— was, however, longer than the figure Thomson had now calculated for the age of the Sun. Thomson was scathing in his rebuttal of Darwin's estimate:

> What then are we to think of such geological estimates as 300,000,000 years for the 'denudation of the Weald?' Whether is it more probable

that the physical conditions of the sun's matter differ 1,000 times more than dynamics compels us to suppose they differ from those of matter in our laboratories; or that a stormy sea, with possibly channel tides of extreme violence, should encroach on a chalk cliff 1,000 times more rapidly than Mr. Darwin's estimate of one inch per century?

With battle joined in such strong terms, Thomson initiated a debate which continued for the rest of the nineteenth century, during which he forced the uniformitarians back on the defensive. His article on the Sun's heat in 1862 was quickly followed by new calculations of the age of the Earth, based on the application of Fourier's equations of heat flow. Thomson assumed that the Earth had been formed in a molten state as a result of heat generated by colliding meteors—very much the same picture that astronomers have today. He knew that measurements made down mine shafts showed that the Earth's interior was still hotter than the crust, even today, and by using sound physics and known measurements of how long it takes heat to flow through an insulating blanket of rock he calculated how long it would have taken for the original molten planet to cool to the state it is in today. He came up with a figure of 98 million years for the age of the Earth, happily agreeing almost exactly with his calculation of the age of the Sun. Cautiously, allowing for a margin of error, he said that the calculations set limits on the possible age of the Earth. It might be as young as 20 million years, it might be as old as 200 million years, but there was no way (within the laws of physics known to Thomson) that it could be as old as Darwin and the geologists required. His calculations were impeccable, and his conclusions were correct—in the context of nineteenth-century physics. Thomson believed that the entire Universe could be described by the same set of physical laws that held in the laboratory and on Earth, and he held unshakably to that belief. The fact that his two age calculations, for the Sun and the Earth, independently came up with much the same number of years strengthened his position in the debate that followed.

In some ways, indeed, Thomson held more steadfastly to his views than Darwin did to his. Later editions of the *Origin of Species* show Darwin wriggling uncomfortably on the hook of Thomson's calculations of the age of the Sun and the Earth, and taking on board some now discredited ideas, essentially in an attempt to find a way to speed up evolution. This is why the first edition of his great work is still the best and clearest exposition of his ideas.

Although the uniformitarians were forced into some tactical withdrawals, the debate did continue, and Thomson continued to revise and improve his calculations. It wasn't until 1887 that he came up with the version that is enshrined in many student texts today, and which provides the complete description of how a star like the Sun does indeed get hot in the first place. The idea actually drew upon a suggestion made by Helmholtz in his own paper on the Sun's heat, back in 1854—though Thomson did not give Helmholtz any credit when he presented his calculations in a lecture at the Royal Institution in London in 1887, and may well have forgotten that Helmholtz had pointed the way.*

The important feature of this final step in Thomson's work on the heat of the Sun was the realization that as long as the same amount of matter—the same mass—is involved, it isn't important how big, or how small, the original "rocks" from which the Sun formed might be. Just two half-Suns, falling directly onto each other from far away would collide with as much kinetic energy as a cloud of meteors collapsing to its center. And the objects involved in the collision could also be much *smaller* than the kind of meteoric rocks envisaged in the earlier version of the theory. Tiny pebbles, gravel, a cloud of dust—as long as the *total* mass is the same, the energy available is the same. There is still, indeed, as much energy available if the original cloud from which the Sun formed was made of atoms and molecules—a cloud of *gas*, spread out initially over a huge volume and collapsing under the influence of its own gravity (under its own weight). By the time such a collapsing gas cloud had shrunk to roughly the size the Sun is today, the temperature at its core would be millions of degrees, and its surface would glow with a temperature of a few thousand degrees. Astronomers today accept this as the most likely explanation of how stars do indeed get going.

Once such a proto-star is hot inside, there is a great deal of pressure pushing outward, because the heat makes the atomic particles very energetic. The powerful jostling of the particles against one another tends to hold the star up against further collapse; as long as the star is hot inside, it can never collapse completely, and Thomson knew

*A nice irony, indeed, that Helmholtz, who had unwittingly upstaged Mayer and contributed to his depression, should now be upstaged himself, either by accident or design, by Thomson. Today, in the English-speaking world the credit is shared, with the final version of the thermodynamic age of the Sun called the "Kelvin-Helmholtz" age or time scale. German astronomers, unforgivingly, still often refer simply to the "Helmholtz" time scale.

that it would take a considerable amount of time for the heat liberated in the center to work its way outward. What would happen, however, when such a glowing ball of gas did cool a little? Thomson (and Helmholtz) had the answer. If the Sun were a glowing ball of gas and it cooled a little inside, it would begin to shrink. But what did shrinking really involve? All the atomic particles in the Sun would be moving closer to the center—they would be falling in a gravitational field. What happens when things fall in a gravitational field? They gain kinetic energy, which is converted into heat when they jostle against one another! All that was required to ensure that the gravitational energy stored up in the Sun was released slowly, over millions of years, was that the Sun should be shrinking slowly, at a rate of about 50 meters a year. This didn't provide any more energy—the total was still restricted to the 20 million years' supply that Thomson had estimated previously. But it did provide the means to spread the heat out over 20 million years, instead of releasing it in one huge blast. And the required shrinkage, at a rate of 50 meters a century, was certainly far too small to be measured by nineteenth-century astronomers, so the fact that nobody had noticed it was no problem at all.

As Thomson zeroed in on such a restricted time scale for the Sun, even though his physical reasoning improved at each stage, the uniformitarians became less inclined to accept it. Maybe they could have tried to live with 500 million years—but 20 million years was definitely insufficient to account for the changes wrought in the Earth and its living inhabitants since the time it had formed. In a sense, Thomson's time scale was a victim of its own success; the more clearly it pointed to a low age for the Sun and the Earth, the more clear it was that there was a real conflict between the physics and the geology.

In 1889, Thomson wrote, "It would, I think, be extremely rash to assume as probable anything more than twenty million years of the sun's light in the past history of the earth, or to reckon on more than five or six million years to come."* In 1892, the year he received his peerage at the age of 68, he repeated almost exactly the comment he had made as a young man of 28 in 1852, but now with the numbers to back it up:

> Within a finite period of time past the earth must have been, and within a finite period of time to come must again be, unfit for the habitation

*Burchfield, 1975.

of man as at present constituted, *unless operations have been and are to be performed which are impossible under the laws governing the known operations going on at present in the material world.*

And by 1897 Kelvin, as he then was known, had accepted the best estimate for the age of the Sun and the Earth as 24 million years.

All of his calculations, like those of Anaxagoras, were impeccable, given what he knew. Today, with the benefit of nearly a further century of observations of the Sun and stars, with more practice in the application of the laws of thermodynamics to the calculations, and with the aid of electronic computers to speed those calculations (though these are hardly necessary for solving so simple a problem), astronomers agree that a star like the Sun can keep itself hot by slow contraction for a few tens of millions of years, the Kelvin-Helmholtz time scale. This is all the energy that is available from the conversion of gravitational energy into heat. But it is nowhere near enough to satisfy the geologists' appetite. Well before the end of the nineteenth century, it was clear that this figure was incompatible with the requirements of geology and evolution. Something had to give, and the way ahead was pointed most clearly in 1899, neatly at the end of the nineteenth century, by Thomas Chamberlin, professor of geology at the University of Chicago. Thomson had always been careful to point out that the only way to provide a longer solar time scale was by invoking unknown sources of energy and new laws of physics, but the way he had done so made it clear that he was using this as an example of something too ridiculous to take seriously. Chamberlin, however, was prepared to contemplate the unthinkable. Writing in the journal *Science,** he commented:

> Is present knowledge relative to the behavior of matter under such extraordinary conditions as obtained in the interior of the sun sufficiently exhaustive to warrant the assertion that no unrecognised sources of heat reside there? What the internal constitution of the atoms may be is yet open to question. It is not improbable that they are complex organisations and seats of enormous energies. Certainly no careful chemist would affirm that the atoms are really elementary or that there may not be locked up in them energies of the first order of magnitude. No cautious chemist would . . . affirm or deny that the extraordinary conditions which reside at the center of the sun may not set free a portion of this energy.

*Volume 10, page 11, 1899.

Clearly, geology was fighting back; and it was right to do so. The scientific world was ready for a completely new explanation of how the Sun maintained its fires. Although hints of this "new" source of energy were already available when Chamberlin wrote those words, it was to be fully 30 years before the outline of what was going on in the Sun became clear, and more than 40 years before the details were worked out.

2

SEATS OF
ENORMOUS
ENERGIES

How much heat does the Sun produce? What are the "enormous energies" we need to unlock from the atom in order to prove Chamberlin right? In one sense, the energy production of the Sun is not so remarkable, compared with the rate at which energy is produced even by chemical reactions here on Earth. George Gamow, in his book *A Star Called the Sun*, came up with a striking analogy back in the early 1960s. If a coffeepot is advertised as producing heat at the same rate that heat is produced (on average) in the Sun's interior, he asked, how long will it take to start the water boiling?

The surprising answer to Gamow's question is that even if the pot were perfectly insulated so that no heat could escape, it would take many months for the water to boil. *On average*, each gram of the Sun's mass produces very little heat, as a simple calculation shows: 8.8×10^{25} calories of heat energy cross the Sun's surface each second and the mass of the Sun is 2×10^{33} grams; therefore, it is only necessary for each gram of material to produce, on average, 4.4×10^{-8} calories per second—less than half of one ten-millionth of a calorie per second. This is not only low by the standards of the average coffee percolator; it is much less than the rate at which heat is released in your body through the chemical processes of human metabolism.

The reason such a modest production of energy, compared with the mass or volume of the Sun, is enough to keep it so hot is because the heat from inside the Sun can only escape through the surface, an area that depends on the square of the radius. The mass, or volume, however, is proportional to the cube of the radius, so the mass and volume get bigger much more quickly than the surface area does when we compare spheres with bigger and bigger radii. Every time the radius is doubled, the surface area increases four times, but the volume of the sphere is eight times bigger.

We can see the effect at work, very clearly, in warm-blooded animals. A mouse has a very small volume, and a small mass, with a relatively large surface area. It loses heat quickly, and has to stay active and eat almost continuously in order to keep warm. An elephant, on the other hand, has a large mass and a proportionately smaller surface area. It has trouble losing heat, which is why it has evolved large ears, which act as radiators, and why it spends a lot of time, if it can, splashing about in water. No land mammal can be significantly bigger than an elephant, or it would cook inside through the heat generated by its own metabolic processes—which is one reason why, of course, the elephant is the largest land mammal that has evolved.

So, as the nineteenth-century astronomers appreciated, it is easy to make the Sun hot enough to shine, using a modest release of gravitational energy as it shrinks. Even burning coal would keep the Sun hot, for a time. The problem is explaining how it has been able to shine for so long. Which is where the new physics of the 1890s and the early twentieth century was able to lend astronomy a hand.

○ RADIATION REVEALED

The 1890s were exciting times for physics. It seemed new discoveries were made about the nature of matter and radiation almost daily. These discoveries were to lead the way to the development of the two great theories of the twentieth century, quantum physics and relativity, and thus to a completely new understanding of the nature of the physical world. As we move into the 1990s, many physicists are confident that they will soon be able to unite these two great theories into one package, a unified description of nature, completing a revolution that effectively began almost exactly 100 years ago, in 1895, with the discovery of X rays. It was this discovery that led directly to Henri Becquerel's discovery of the phenomenon we now know as radioactivity. His discovery led to the realization that the atom is not indivisible, and to the identification of the source of energy of the Sun and stars. But it came about partly by accident, and it took many years for the implications to be followed up and to become a cornerstone of physics and astronomy.

X rays were discovered by Wilhelm Röntgen, a distinguished, fifty-year-old professor of physics at Würzburg University in Germany. He had become interested in the investigation of cathode "rays" (we now know them to be streams of electrons), which are emitted from the negatively charged plate (cathode) of an electric discharge tube, a glass vacuum tube.* Röntgen made his discovery as a result of a chance observation in his darkened laboratory. Although the discharge tube was encased in a sleeve of thin black cardboard, Röntgen noticed that a paper screen lying nearby, which he had been using in another experiment and which was painted with barium platinocyanide, glowed whenever the tube was switched on. The fact that the screen could glow was no surprise—cathode rays striking the screen could make it glow, which is why Röntgen had it lying around. But cathode rays, it had already been established, could only travel a few centimeters outside the tube; the screen, which was not being used in the present experiment, was about a meter away. Something else must be making it glow—and, Röntgen soon discovered, the something else could make it glow when the tube was switched on even if the screen was taken into the room next door. He had discovered X rays, a previously unknown form of penetrating radiation.

When the news was announced on 1 January 1896 (including the dramatic discovery that X rays could be used to photograph human bones through the living flesh), it created a sensation, both in scientific circles and the press, on both sides of the Atlantic. Naturally, X rays were the main topic of discussion at a meeting of the French Academy of Sciences later in the month, at which Becquerel was present. He learned from his colleagues that Röntgen had identified the source of the X rays. They came from a bright spot where the cathode rays struck the glass wall of the vacuum tube and made it fluoresce. Becquerel immediately decided to investigate whether other phosphorescent objects could emit X rays. Among the crystals he set out to test were some uranium salts, including a sample of potassium uranyl disulphate that had been prepared fifteen years earlier.

---

*Such a vacuum tube is the direct antecedent of the picture tube in a modern television set, and the picture on the TV screen is painted by electrons, emitted from a cathode at one end of the tube, striking the phosphor-lined screen at the other end.

Becquerel soon found the effect he was looking for. The phosphorescent salts he was using became active when exposed to sunlight. After the sunlight had made the salts active, they would glow for a while before fading and needing a further charge of sunlight. Becquerel simply wrapped a photographic plate in two sheets of thick black paper and laid it out in the sunlight with a dish of the phosphorescent material on top of it. When the photographic plate was developed, he found the outline of the phosphorescent material on the photograph, and if he placed an object such as a coin between the dish and the photographic plate while it was sitting in the Sun the developed photograph showed the shadowy outline of the coin. In a paper he submitted to the Academy of Sciences in late February 1896, Becquerel concluded that "the phosphorescent substance in question emits radiations which traverse paper opaque to light."*

At this stage, it seemed that the phosphorescent activity, stimulated by sunlight, was radiation similar to X rays—perhaps, indeed, X rays themselves. Just a week later, however, Becquerel was back at the academy, reporting that the effect had nothing to do with sunlight or phosphorescence.

For the last few days of February 1896, Paris was overcast. Becquerel had prepared another experiment, in which a piece of copper in the shape of a cross was interposed between a dish of uranium salts and a wrapped photographic plate. As there was no Sun, he kept the experiment in a cupboard for several days. Then, perhaps tired of waiting, he developed the plate anyway and was astonished to find the image of the copper cross, clear and sharp. It seems to have been a total surprise, since Henri's son Jean later recalled that Henri was "stupefied" when "he found that his silhouette pictures were even more intense than the ones he had obtained the week before."

There was certainly an element of luck in the discovery, even if, as a good scientist, Becquerel planned to check out the "null result" that he expected, that the plate would be blank if the salts had not been exposed to sunlight. Becquerel himself, as Pais reports, felt that it was destiny, the culmination of sixty years of work by three generations of Becquerels working in the same laboratory on related problems in phosphorescence.

Unlike Röntgen's discovery, however, Becquerel's work made no

---

*From Abraham Pais's epic history of particle physics, *Inward Bound* (New York: Oxford University Press, 1986).

immediate impact outside a small circle of scientists. Perhaps the discovery seemed too much like that of X rays for the popular press to notice the difference. But the deep implications of the discovery quickly became clear, at least to a few cognoscenti. Becquerel himself soon showed that the source of the radiation was uranium itself, which, as a pure metal, is not phosphorescent at all, and by the end of 1896 he was already speculating about where the energy of the radiation came from, since it did not depend on sunlight after all. This was a mystery unique to his discovery, since the energy of X rays, of course, very clearly came from the electricity put in to the cathode ray tube. The uranium radiation, however, seemed to be something for nothing. In the journal *Comotes Rendus*, Becquerel wrote, late in 1896, "One has not yet been able to recognise wherefrom uranium derives the energy which it emits with such persistence."* But after the end of that year, he turned his attention to other scientific matters, and only published occasional short papers on radioactivity. It was left to two younger researchers to take up his discovery and carry its implications forward into the twentieth century.

○ **ENERGY FROM ATOMS**

In the wake of Becquerel's discovery of radioactivity, a young pair of chemists, Marie Curie and her husband Pierre, began investigating various radioactive substances. Marie analyzed several metals, salts, oxides, and minerals, and found that radioactivity (she introduced the term "radioactive substance" in a paper published in 1898), although rare, did not occur in uranium alone. She showed that the amount of radioactivity in a sample containing uranium depended on the amount of uranium in the sample; and, also, in 1898, she identified two previously unknown radioactive elements, polonium and radium. All of this work led to the Curies sharing the 1903 Nobel Prize for physics with Becquerel, for their pioneering work on radioactivity.†

*Volume 123, page 855, 1896.
†Their work also had tragic consequences. The dangers of radioactivity were unknown at the time, and the conditions under which Marie and Pierre labored would never be permitted in a modern laboratory. Marie's notebooks from the 1890s are so radioactive, as a result of contamination by the materials she worked with, that they are considered dangerous to handle even today; both Marie and Pierre suffered from what we now know as radiation sickness. This contributed to Marie's death in 1934; it probably also contributed, indirectly, to Pierre's death in 1906, when after a period of illness he slipped while crossing a road and fell under the wheels of a horse-drawn truck.

In 1911, Marie received a second Nobel Prize, this time in chemistry, for her work on radium. But in terms of unlocking the secrets of the Sun and its means for generating heat, although Pierre Curie (working with his assistant Albert Laborde) had measured the amount of heat generated by the activity of radium in 1903, Marie's work was now being overtaken by others. One of those was the young New Zealand physicist Ernest Rutherford. Rutherford was also involved, as early as 1903, in measuring the heat produced by radium; but it was his work in probing the structure of the atom and deciphering the rules of radioactive decay that made his name.

As a research student at Cambridge in the 1890s, Rutherford worked in the Cavendish Laboratory under J. J. Thomson, who was about to discover that cathode rays are actually the particles we now call electrons. Thomson's discovery was announced in April 1897 and provided the first evidence that atoms could be subdivided. It became clear from Thomson's work and that of other researchers at the time that electrons are literally pieces that can be knocked out of atoms. Working in Thomson's laboratory and with news of Becquerel's work coming from Paris, Rutherford naturally turned his attention to the study of atomic processes.

In a series of investigations, Rutherford showed that the radiation Becquerel had discovered was actually a mixture of two varieties of radiation, which he called alpha rays and beta rays. It has since been established by other researchers that beta rays are, in fact, fast-moving electrons, like cathode rays but carrying much more energy. Rutherford concentrated his efforts on the alpha rays, and after a long series of experiments, interlaced with periods of other work, he was able to show first that alpha rays are also streams of particles, and finally, in 1908, that each alpha particle has a mass roughly equivalent to the mass of four hydrogen atoms, but carries two units of positive charge. An alpha particle, he concluded, must be the same as a helium atom that has lost two electrons.* This conclusion rather neatly explained the discovery, made in 1895 and something of a puzzle at the time, that traces of helium gas are found in

---

*A hydrogen atom, later research showed, consists of one electron and one proton; a helium atom is composed of two electrons, two protons, and two neutrons. Protons and neutrons each have about the same mass; compared to a proton or a neutron, an electron has almost no weight. An electron has a single unit of negative charge, a proton carries a single unit of positive charge, and a neutron has no charge. Thus an atom of helium, with two neutrons and two protons, is four times as heavy as an atom of hydrogen, and if the two electrons are stripped from it the remaining core of the atom has two units of positive charge.

minerals that contain uranium. Helium had first been identified in 1868 by the British scientist Joseph Lockyer, who pioneered the study of the Sun using spectroscopy. In this technique, elements are identified by the characteristic patterns of lines they produce in the spectrum, as distinctive as fingerprints are for individual people. When Lockyer found spectral lines in sunlight that belonged to no known element, he claimed that they must be due to an element found only in the Sun, which he called helium from the name of the Greek Sun god Helios. Nobody expected to find helium on Earth; Rutherford's work showed how it could have been produced by radioactivity; alpha particles need only gain a respectable cloak of two electrons from their surroundings to become helium atoms.

Working with Frederick Soddy in Canada, Rutherford also explained that radioactivity is associated with the disintegration of atoms, when atoms of the radioactive element are converted into atoms of another element. And he showed that half of the atoms in a given radioactive sample will decay in this way in a certain amount of time (now called the "half-life") that is specific to each radioactive element. This is a very curious pattern of behavior. In a sample of radium, for example, after 1,602 years just half of the atoms will have decayed into atoms of the gas radon as alpha and beta particles are emitted. In the next 1,602 years, half of the rest of the radium (one quarter of the original) will decay, and so on. How does an individual atom "know" whether it ought to decay or not, and when? The answers to these questions came only in the 1920s, when the quantum theory of atomic behavior was developed.

Meanwhile, Rutherford himself soon went beyond studying alpha particles to using them to study atoms. He encouraged Hans Geiger and Ernest Marsden, in Manchester, to investigate the way alpha particles were scattered by gold foil, and they discovered that although most of the alpha particles in a beam would travel straight through the foil as if it were not there, a very few particles were bounced back as if they had struck something solid. It was this work that established that atoms are made of tiny dense nuclei, carrying positive charge, which are surrounded by tenuous clouds of electrons. A fast-moving alpha particle (now identified as a helium nucleus) can brush through the electron cloud like a rifle bullet through tissue paper, but if it happens to head directly for a nucleus, then the positive charge of the nucleus repels the positive charge on the alpha particle and bounces it back from whence it came.

It is hardly surprising, in view of all his groundbreaking work, that Rutherford received a Nobel Prize in 1908. It is surprising, though, that it was awarded for chemistry—for "his investigations into the disintegration of the elements, and the chemistry of radioactive substances." Rutherford had little time for anything except physics and had once even remarked that "all of science is either physics or stamp collecting." He accepted the prize with good grace, however, and commented in a speech at the Nobel banquet that he "had dealt with many different transformations with various time-periods, but the quickest he had met was his own transformation from a physicist to a chemist."* But Rutherford's work had by then also made a major contribution to astronomy, through the developing understanding of the sources of solar energy, and to the geological puzzle of the age of the Earth. No doubt he would have seen this as further proof that all of science derives from physics.

○ SOLVING THE ENERGY CRISIS

Although Rutherford's key contributions to our puzzle stemmed from the pioneering work on radioactivity in the 1890s, they were directly triggered by the work of Pierre Curie and Albert Laborde. When radiation was first discovered, researchers such as Henri Becquerel and Marie Curie speculated that the energy involved might come from outside, from some external energy source tapped by certain elements and converted into detectable radiation. But at the time they did not appreciate just how much energy was being released. Rutherford and R. K. McClung, at McGill University, showed as early as 1900 that the different kinds of rays actually carry enormous energy. Unfortunately, their paper pointing this out made little impact.

The next key step was taken by two young German schoolteachers, Julius Elster and Hans Geitel. As early as 1898, their research showed that the source of the energy in radioactivity could not come from the outside. They put radioactive substances into vacuum jars and down deep mines to shield them from the effects of any energy flowing in from outside the Earth, and they found no diminution of their radioactivity. The energy had to come from the atoms them-

*A. S. Eve, *Rutherford* (London: Cambridge University Press, 1939), page 183, quoted by Pais, 1986, p. 63.

selves.* Nobody was greatly worried at the time, although opinions differed on where the energy was coming from. In 1899, Rutherford commented that the origin of the energy in the radiation was "a mystery"; J. J. Thomson, on the other hand, always assumed that the energy was produced as a result of some internal rearrangement of the then unknown structure of the atom, and like most physicists was prepared to leave it to future generations to find out just how the trick was achieved.

By 1901, Elster and Geitel had shown that there is natural radioactivity present even in the air and in the soil, and before long other enthusiasts had found radioactivity everywhere, in snow, rain, lakes, and rocks. Here, at last, was a "new" source of energy, one that could keep the Earth, at least, hot inside for far longer than implied by Thomson's calculations of a cooling sphere. The first suggestion that radioactivity was at least partly responsible for the heat of the Earth and Sun came in 1903, from George Darwin of Cambridge and John Joly of the University of Dublin. Robert Strutt of Imperial College in London took up the idea and suggested that the presence of radium and other radioactive substances inside the Earth provided a source of heat that could extend the geological time scale indefinitely. And if the similarity between William Thomson's time scales for the age of the Earth and the Sun was broken, it was surely time to look again at how the Sun might get its energy.

The key was the realization of just how much energy is involved in radioactive processes. Rutherford's work on this topic with McClung might have been largely ignored, but once Rutherford and Soddy had established that radioactivity involves the conversion of atoms of one element into those of another, it seemed clear, as Rutherford put it in the first edition of his book *Radioactivity,* that "the continuous emission of energy from the active bodies is derived from the internal energy inherent in the atom." And just at that time, in 1903, the measurements made by Pierre Curie and Laborde brought the whole puzzle of the energy involved in radioactivity back to the forefront of

---

*For this reason, even though the existence of atoms was not fully established in 1898, Elster and Geitel are sometimes regarded as the discoverers of atomic energy. The actual term "atomic energy" was first used by Rutherford and Soddy in 1903, to refer to the energy stored in any atom. But the expression only became common currency in the 1940s, by which time, ironically, it was appreciated that the energy actually comes from the *nuclei* of atoms, which had not been identified in 1903. It seems that this misuse of the term was a deliberate decision by advisers involved with the political side of the "atomic bomb" project, who felt that the public would not be familiar with the term "nuclear" (see Pais, 1986, 116).

physics, demonstrating more dramatically what Rutherford and McClung had pointed out in 1900.

Before March 1903, scientists knew that elements such as uranium and radium released energy through their radioactivity, but most of them regarded the amount of energy involved as small enough not to worry about greatly. Then Pierre Curie and Laborde actually measured the heat released by a gram of radium and found that the amount produced every hour was sufficient to heat 1.3 grams of water from 0°C to the boiling point. Putting it another way, radium generates enough heat to melt its own weight in ice in an hour. This caused consternation. Such a productive release of energy simply could not be dismissed as a minor problem for future generations to solve, and some physicists even speculated that the law of conservation of energy, the most basic law of physics, might be violated in radioactive processes. Ignoring the work of Elster and Geitel, the former William Thomson, by now Lord Kelvin, said in 1904, the year of his eightieth birthday, "energy must be supplied from without. ...I venture to suggest that somehow etherial waves may supply energy to radium."*

Rutherford, meanwhile, had been working on the problem in Canada with Howard Barnes, who was to succeed him as professor at McGill when Rutherford returned to England in 1907. Six months after the work by Pierre Curie and Laborde, they were able to show that the amount of heat produced during radioactivity depends on the number of alpha particles emitted by a substance. These relatively massive particles are emitted by radioactive atoms (we now know, by radioactive *nuclei*) and collide with other atoms (nuclei) nearby, giving up their kinetic energy as heat. Rutherford himself soon turned the discovery of this new source of energy to the question of the age of the Earth. He later told of the occasion in 1904, when he presented these ideas to an audience at the Royal Institution in London:

> I came into the room, which was half dark, and presently spotted Lord Kelvin in the audience and realized that I was in for trouble at the last part of the speech dealing with the age of the earth, where my views conflicted with his.... [A] sudden inspiration came, and I said Lord Kelvin had limited the age of the earth, *provided no new source of heat*

*Quoted by Pais, 1986, page 113.

was discovered. That prophetic utterance refers to what we are now considering tonight, radium! Behold! the old boy beamed upon me.*

What Rutherford had realized was that radioactive events inside the Earth must be supplying heat, at a then unknown rate. The planet could no longer be regarded simply as a cooling body, and Kelvin's time scale for the age of the Earth could be no more than a minimum possible age. It was to take several decades for all the doubters to be persuaded and for the idea to be put on a firm footing following the development of quantum physics in the 1920s; but Rutherford's basic insight, that the interior of the Earth is kept hot—hot enough to be molten, even today—by radioactivity is now established as firmly as anything in science. The *surface* of the Earth, though, is kept warm today not by the relatively tiny trickle of heat leaking out from the interior, but by the heat of the Sun in the sky. In the early 1900s, it was already clear, at least to a few perceptive physicists, that radioactivity held the key to understanding the energy of the Sun, as well; but it was to take more than twenty years before that early insight could itself be considered on a proper scientific basis, since that, too, required the development of quantum physics. During those two decades, however, the age of the Earth, at least, was established on a secure basis at last, vindicating Darwin and the geologists.

○ MAKING A DATE WITH RADIOACTIVITY

Rutherford and Soddy's great realization is that radioactivity is a result of the transformation of atoms of one element into atoms of a different element. When alpha or beta particles are emitted by an atom (strictly speaking, by the atom's nucleus), then what is left behind is a different kind of atom (nucleus). One of the most important features of this process is that it occurs at a regular rate: again, in any sample of a particular radioactive element, exactly half of the atoms will "decay" into different atoms in a characteristic time, called the half-life of that element. It doesn't matter how much, or how little, of the radioactive element you have—just half of it is transformed into something else in one half-life. Half of the rest is transformed by radioactive decay in the next half-life, and so on.

Radioactivity; quoted by Burchfield, 1975 p. 164.

Another important feature of radioactive decay is that each radio-active element produces a characteristic mixture of elements—decay products—when it decays. Atoms of one radioactive element may decay into a stable element, or into another radioactive element. If the product is itself radioactive, then the process repeats until stable atoms are formed. And while some radioactive elements have such short half-lives, fractions of a second, that they never occur naturally on Earth, others, such as uranium, thorium, and radium have very long half-lives and are still found on Earth even though they have been decaying since the Solar System was born. By measuring the proportions of these characteristic decay products in rocks today and comparing these with the proportions of the parent radioactive elements such as uranium, physicists armed with a knowledge of the appropriate half-lives can infer the age of the rocks. What matters is not the actual quantities of each element present, but the proportions—the ratio of the quantities of stable elements like lead to unstable ones like uranium and thorium.

Of course, the trick of dating rocks by means of radioactivity depends on a thorough knowledge of the way radioactive elements decay and of what they decay into. This was pioneered by Rutherford and Bertram Boltwood in the first decade of the twentieth century. Boltwood, an American chemist, became interested in the problem after he heard Rutherford give a talk describing his work with radioactivity at Yale in 1904.

At that time, Rutherford already suspected that an alpha particle is exactly equivalent to a helium atom from which the two electrons have been removed. In 1904, Rutherford's old colleague, Soddy, working with Sir William Ramsay at University College, London, had established the rate at which a sample of radium produces helium—which, Rutherford realized, was simply a result of alpha particles released by the decay of radium picking up two electrons each from their surroundings and becoming atoms of helium. Using this rate as a guide, Rutherford calculated the ages of samples of rock simply by measuring the amount of helium they contained and assuming that all of it came from radioactive decay and (rather optimistically) that none had escaped since it was formed. This gave an age of 40 million years for a particular piece of rock Rutherford had in his possession—not yet a challenge to William Thomson's time scale, even though, assuming some helium gas had escaped over the eons, the real age of the rock was almost certainly more than this figure.

But Boltwood took the argument a stage further, looking at the overall products of radioactive decay, not just the helium. He knew in 1904 that the decay of uranium produces radium, and how quickly this happens; a year later he established that the further decay of radium ultimately produces lead. From measurements involving the uranium-radium-lead series, by the end of that year he had calculated ages ranging from 92 million years to 570 million years for different samples of rock. Unfortunately, however, these numbers were all wrong. They were based on measurements by Rutherford that turned out to have been inaccurate, and on a half-life for radium that was soon revised in the light of further studies.

By 1907, however, Boltwood and Rutherford were on the right track. Their figures were still not as accurate as modern estimates, but they were sufficient to show that something was seriously wrong with William Thomson's estimate of the age of the Earth. The new estimates (which involved, among other little problems, measuring a trace of just 380 parts per billion of radium, compared with uranium, in samples of rock) gave ages for different rocks ranging from about 400 million years to more than 2 billion years. Even with the remaining inaccuracies in the technique, they showed that the Earth must be about a billion years old—at least ten times older than Thomson's estimate.

Even so, the geological community was not persuaded overnight to take these age estimates seriously. The techniques involved were difficult and tedious, and nobody seems to have cared enough to try to duplicate the work immediately. Even after the new estimates for the age of the Earth appeared, many geologists continued to argue that radioactive heating could not really extend the lifetime of the Earth very much at all, and William Thomson's age estimate was still widely accepted.

Boltwood went on to other work, and Rutherford maintained only a desultory interest in the age of the Earth. It was left to the next generation, in the person of Arthur Holmes, to finally carry the radioactive dating technique through to universal acceptance.

During his time as a student at Imperial College, Holmes dated many rock samples using the uranium-lead method and decided that the oldest were about 1.6 billion years old. In 1913, he became the first person to use radioactive dating to determine the ages of fossils, putting absolute dates into the fossil record for the first time. Holmes further refined the radioactive dating technique, taking into account the new discovery that elements could come in different varieties (isotopes) with slightly different atomic weights. Eventually he built up such an impressive body of data that even the doubters were eventually forced to admit that the radioactive dating technique was revealing something significant about the age of the Earth.

By 1921, a debate at the annual meeting of the British Association for the Advancement of Science showed that there was a new consensus—geologists, botanists, zoologists, and physicists agreed that the Earth indeed must be a few billion years old, and that the radioactive technique is the best guide to its age. The final seal of approval came in 1926, in the form of a report from the National Research Council of the U.S. National Academy of Sciences endorsing the technique. Since then, further refinements have given an age of 3.8 billion years for the oldest rocks found in the Earth's crust; the oldest samples of rock from meteorites, which have fallen to Earth from interplanetary space, are 4.5 billion years old, and it is now widely accepted that the Solar System, including the Sun and Earth, formed roughly 4.5 billion years ago.

It was in the early 1920s that real progress at last began to be made in the search for the Sun's source of energy. Ironically, the way forward had been pointed out, in no uncertain manner, in 1920—at the meeting of the British Association for the Advancement of Science *before* the one at which Holmes finally persuaded his colleagues that he knew what he was talking about. To see why, we have to backtrack a little to 1903, and the sensation caused by the investigation of the heat output of radium by Pierre Curie and Laborde.

O **NUCLEAR ENERGY**

Gamow's coffeepot analogy shows just how little heat each gram of the Sun produces, on average; the experiment carried out by Pierre Curie and Laborde showed just how much heat a gram of radium produces. Four months after their results were announced, in July 1903 the journal *Nature* carried the suggestion, from the English astronomer William Wilson, that radium could provide the heat of the Sun. He showed that just 3.6 grams of radium in every cubic meter of the Sun's volume would be enough to supply all of the heat now being radiated from the solar surface.

Wilson's suggestion failed to make much of a splash in scientific circles. But a few months later the theme was taken up by George Darwin, the son of Charles. Hardly surprisingly, George Darwin had long had his doubts about William Thomson's chronology of the Sun and Earth, which seemed to conflict so strongly with the requirements of evolution. The younger Darwin also aired his views on radioactivity as a source of solar energy in *Nature*, but he was initially quite conservative in his claims, suggesting only that Thomson's time scale might be multiplied by ten or twenty. With the name "Darwin" attached to this speculation, echoes of the great debate between Thomson and the evolutionists in the nineteenth century were revived, producing a flurry of letters to *Nature*. By the end of 1903 there was a clear body of opinion that the Sun's heat must ultimately derive from radioactive energy. But even those researchers who held this opinion knew that it was based entirely on speculation and that the actual processes by which energy was released from atoms inside the Sun were unknown. In a sense, the claims were premature, and in the absence of a solid theory of solar energy production by any other means, William Thomson contraction hypothesis, and the short time scale it implied, lingered on—just as his time scale for the age of the Earth lingered on until the evidence against it was overwhelming. Thomson still had supporters ten years later.

The main objection to the idea of radioactive energy powering the Sun was that spectroscopy showed no trace of the characteristic "fingerprints" of elements such as uranium and radium in the light from the Sun. But the most prescient comment at this time came from the prolific pen of Rutherford, who suggested in 1913 that "at the enormous temperature of the sun, it appears possible that a process of transformation may take place in ordinary elements analogous to that observed in the well-known radio-elements," and went on to add that "the time during which the sun may continue to emit heat at the present rate may be much longer than the value computed from ordinary dynamical data."[*]

By then Rutherford knew, as Wilson and Darwin had not ten years previously, of Albert Einstein's proposal that mass and energy are interchangeable, through the relation $E = mc^2$, where c is the speed

---

[*]Rutherford's *Radioactive Substances;* quoted by Burchfield, 1975 p. 168.

of light. Einstein's first paper on special relativity, establishing, among other things, the mass-energy relation, was published in 1905. In the same year, in a second paper on the subject, Einstein specifically addressed the radioactive energy question and said, "If a body gives off the energy L in the form of radiation, its mass diminishes by L/c^2." He stated quite categorically that "the mass of a body is a measure of its energy" and speculated that "it is not impossible that with bodies whose energy content is variable to a high degree (e.g., with radium salts) the theory may successfully be put to the test."*

Einstein was too optimistic, by far, in his hope that anyone might be able to measure the reduction in mass of a radioactive substance as it released energy. In everyday terminology, we are used to measuring the flow of energy in watts, or kilowatts—such as the output of a hundred-watt light bulb. Using Einstein's equation, we can convert the amount of energy burned by such a bulb to its mass equivalent, a transformation of one trillionth of a gram of matter into energy each second. Such a tiny loss of mass cannot be measured.

Taking the argument out into space, the Sun radiates energy equivalent to the "loss" of four million tons of matter every second—but even if it has done so for four billion years, the amount of matter lost in this way represents only one five-thousandth of its original mass! Even if only 10 percent of the mass of the Sun can ever be converted into heat energy, it would still have a potential lifetime of almost 20 trillion years. "Atomic energy" can certainly solve the solar energy puzzle, and provide the time scale required by evolution. But how does it do the trick?

The next step toward understanding the seats of enormous energies in the Sun and stars was made by Arthur Eddington. A British researcher, Eddington was the first person to successfully apply the basic laws of physics to tackle the problem of what went on *inside* stars, and thereby invented the subject of astrophysics. He was also one of the best-known scientists of the time, since he had been responsible for organizing the expedition to measure the way light from stars was bent by the Sun during a solar eclipse of 1919 and had confirmed the prediction made by Einstein's general theory of relativity. (Popular folklore of the time even had it that Eddington was the only person, apart from Einstein, who really understood general relativity.) But he

*Annalen der Physik, vol. 18, p. 639; quoted by Pais, 1986, p. 104.

found time for a great deal more work besides this, and during the 1920s he speculated, at various times, that the source of energy in the Sun might be the total annihilation of matter to release energy, or the breakdown of heavy elements by radioactive decay (the process we now call fission), or the building up of heavy elements from light elements (now called fusion).*

Eddington had a clear idea which of these proposals was the best bet. "Annihilation of protons and electrons," he wrote in 1926 in his epic book *The Internal Constitution of the Stars,*† "or the disintegration of unknown elements of intense radio-activity are speculative hypotheses; these processes may or may not be capable of occurring. But in the formation of helium we have a process which *must* have occurred at some time and place—and where more likely than in the stars?" But why did Eddington single out the formation of helium, rather than any of the other elements? Largely because of a discovery made by Francis Aston, working at the Cavendish Laboratory in Cambridge.

Aston had developed an instrument, called a mass spectrograph, that could be used to determine the masses of atoms of a chosen element.‡ The technique, still used today, depends on measuring the way in which positively charged "ions" (atoms that have had one or two or a few electrons knocked off) are deflected by a magnetic field. His first mass spectrograph was operating by 1919, and one of the first discoveries he made with it was that an atom of helium has 0.8 percent less than the mass of four atoms of hydrogen.

The whole was less than the sum of its parts. In fact, other atomic weights were *nearly*, but not quite, multiples of hydrogen. The "not quite" gave Eddington his clue; the "nearly" resolved a puzzle dating back more than a century.

Back in 1816, the English chemist William Prout had suggested that

---

*Both fission and fusion can release energy, we now know, because the nuclei of atoms in the middle range of masses, with the lowest energies, are the most stable forms. The reasons have to do with details of quantum physics, which we won't go into here. The most stable nucleus of all is iron–56, and in energy terms all other nuclei would "like" to move toward this stable state, either by fission, in the case of heavier nuclei such as uranium, or by fusion, in the case of lighter nuclei such as carbon, oxygen, or hydrogen. A common analogy is to think of iron as being at the bottom of an energy valley, with lighter nuclei ranged up one side of the valley and heavier ones up the other side. Given the right conditions—and the inside of a star provides the right conditions—other nuclei will move down the slopes to the low point represented by iron.

†New York: Dover, 1959, p. 295.

‡The technique is so useful, and so important, that Aston received a Nobel Prize for his work in 1922.

the atomic weight of any atom is an exact multiple of the atomic weight of hydrogen, and although later research showed chemists that the rule did not hold precisely, the weights they determined for other atoms were tantalizingly close to whole multiples of the weight of a hydrogen atom.

Puzzlement over why this should be so persisted throughout the nineteenth century and into the twentieth. Chemists could only measure atomic weights by studying the behavior of large numbers of atoms in chemical reactions, comparing, for example, the weight of oxygen involved in reactions with a certain weight of carbon, or of hydrogen. The weights they found must always be the average of the weights of all the atoms involved in the reactions. In 1913, Frederick Soddy, who had worked with Rutherford in Canada and was by now at Glasgow University, explained the discrepancies by introducing the idea of isotopes, atoms of the *same* chemical element that had slightly different masses. If a sample of an element contained a mixture of atoms with slightly different weights but identical chemical properties, then chemical tests would indicate a single "atomic weight," which would be an average of the actual weights and therefore not necessarily a precise multiple of the atomic weight of hydrogen.

At the time, Soddy did not have the complete picture of isotopes and did not know how two atoms could have different weights but identical chemical properties. The key to that understanding came only in 1932, when James Chadwick discovered the neutron, a particle very similar to the proton but with no net electric charge.* Eddington, in 1920, knew nothing of neutrons and thought of what we know as the proton simply as the entire nucleus of the hydrogen atom.† But, like his contemporaries, he appreciated that Soddy's work had strongly reestablished the idea that all atoms could be thought of as multiples of the hydrogen atom, perhaps built up by somehow sticking hydrogen atoms together. He immediately seized on Aston's discovery that the nucleus of helium–4 weighed *less* than four nuclei of hydrogen "weighed" separately.

---

*We now know that, for example, there are two isotopes of helium: the rare helium–3, which contains two protons and one neutron in its nucleus, and the far more common helium–4, which has a nucleus made up of two protons and two neutrons (a helium–4 nucleus is an alpha particle).
†In fact, the proton itself wasn't named until 1920, by Rutherford, in a paper in *Nature* (vol. 106, p. 220). It is virtually impossible to tell the story of the development of astrophysics in the 1920s without slipping in concepts that actually became common currency only in later years!

○ SOLAR ENERGY

In August 1920, the British Association for the Advancement of Science held its annual meeting in Cardiff. Eddington chose to address the gathering on the subject of solar energy and began by knocking a few nails into the lid of the coffin of the contraction hypothesis:

Only the inertia of tradition keeps the contraction hypothesis alive—or rather, not alive, but an unburied corpse. But if we decide to inter the corpse, let us freely recognize the position in which we are left. A star is drawing on some vast reservoir of energy by means unknown to us. This reservoir can scarcely be other than the sub-atomic energy which, it is known, exists abundantly in all matter; we sometimes dream that man will one day learn to release it and use it for his service. The store is well-nigh inexhaustible, if only it could be tapped. There is sufficient in the Sun to maintain its output of heat for 15 billion years. . . .

Aston has further shown conclusively that the mass of the helium atom is even less than the masses of the four hydrogen atoms which enter into it—and in this, at any rate, the chemists agree with him. There is a loss of mass in the synthesis amounting to 1 part in 120, the atomic weight of hydrogen being 1.008 and that of helium just 4. I will not dwell on his beautiful proof of this, as you will no doubt be able to hear it from himself. Now mass cannot be annihilated, and the deficit can only represent the mass of the electrical energy set free in the transmutation. We can therefore at once calculate the quantity of energy liberated when helium is made out of hydrogen. If 5 percent of a star's mass consists initially of hydrogen atoms, which are gradually being combined to form more complex elements, the total heat liberated will more than suffice for our demands, and we need look no further for the source of a star's energy.

If, indeed, the sub-atomic energy in stars is being freely used to maintain their great furnaces, it seems to bring a little nearer to fulfillment our dream of controlling this latent power for the well-being of the human race—or for its suicide.*

---

*From *Observatory*, vol. 43 p. 353; quoted by Subrahmanyan Chandrasekhar, *Eddington* (New York: Cambridge University Press, 1983), p. 17. As Eddington himself acknowledged, the Frenchman Jean-Baptiste Perrin also pointed out the implications of Aston's discovery in 1920 (*Revue du Mois*, vol. 21, p. 113; cited by Eddington in his book *The Internal Constitution of the Stars*, 1959, p. 296). But he never developed as complete an understanding of stellar structure and the implications of this release of subatomic energy, as Eddington achieved.

Subrahmanyan Chandrasekhar, in his book *Eddington,* describes these comments as "some of the most prescient statements in all of astronomical literature." This comment has the benefit of hindsight but is at least partly true. Eddington himself did not always stand firmly by the idea of energy being produced by the conversion of hydrogen into helium, but also considered the possibility of the complete annihilation of protons and electrons into energy, following what we now know to have been a wrong turning. For years, the transmutation idea was just one possibility for consideration. On the social implications, however, he was certainly prescient. Eddington, a Quaker who had run into some difficulties with the authorities in Britain because of his pacifist beliefs during World War I, not only saw the implications of Einstein's equation for energy production in stars, but the mixed blessing that it implied for the inhabitants of planet Earth.

○ **SIMPLE STARS**

Eddington's astronomical work developed into one of the landmarks in science, a book called *The Internal Constitution of the Stars.* Even today, more than sixty years later, the volume is still essential reading for astrophysicists. In it, Eddington sets out the basic rules needed in applying physics to the study of stellar structure—how the inward pull of gravity is balanced by the outward pressure of the hot interior, how density and temperature vary from place to place inside a star, the relationship between the mass of a star and its brightness (luminosity), and more.

One of the most important of Eddington's insights, though, was the realization that in order to describe what he called "so simple a thing" as a star you *don't* need to know where the star gets its energy from. The laws of physics tell us that a ball of gas containing a certain amount of matter and held up by the pressure inside itself must have a certain size and radiate a certain amount of energy. It doesn't matter where that energy comes from—without an energy supply, as we have seen, the star will shrink slowly, but the way the material of the star behaves is the same whatever the source of energy in its heart. To nonphysicists, it is most surprising that the scientific laws that describe the nature of a star are the laws of behavior for a so-called perfect gas—even though the *average* density of the Sun is about one and a half times the density of water, and the density in its center is many times that of lead. This kind of structure is not what we usually think of as a "gas," but it does indeed behave like one. This is directly related to the way pressure holds the star up against the inward pull of gravity.

First, it is easy to understand why the inside of a star is hot. As we have seen, as the star is formed, gravitational energy is liberated as heat; also, it is a fact that anything that is squeezed gets hotter (like the air in a bicycle pump; and the opposite effect, that gas which expands gets cooler, is the principle on which your domestic refrigerator is based). But part of the pressure inside a star that holds it up is simply caused by the particles in its interior bashing against one another at high speeds—this is gas pressure. And if the particles are bashing together hard enough (if they are hot enough), negatively charged electrons get knocked off of atoms in the process and roam freely through the star. Atoms that have had electrons knocked off are called ions—they are left with a positive electric charge—and a mixture of ions and electrons is known as a plasma. It is this effect that makes the inside of a star behave as a gas.

The next thing to remember is that atoms consist of a tiny nucleus surrounded by a much bigger cloud of electrons. (To put the two components in perspective, if the nucleus of an atom were the size of a pea, the electron cloud would be the size of a concert hall.) In a solid, the electron clouds are touching one another and do not move about. In a liquid, the electron clouds of atoms are still just about touching one another, but the individual atoms have enough energy to slither past one another—and so a liquid "pours." But in a gas, the atoms have so much energy that they fly about freely through space, occasionally bumping into another atom. Atomic nuclei are so much smaller than atoms, however, that when the surrounding cloud of electrons is stripped from atomic nuclei to form a plasma, the nuclei are nowhere near touching each other and can be squeezed closer together, even to densities many times that of lead, while still flying free and behaving like gas particles. In other words, you can put a *lot* of peas in the Carnegie Hall without them touching each other. The nuclei fly freely through the interior of a star, occasionally colliding with each other. In doing so, they follow exactly the laws of physics describing ideal gases.

In a relatively small collection of matter, like a planet, atoms stay as atoms and the pressure in the center is enough to hold the outer layers up even without a plasma being formed; the matter behaves as a solid or, depending on what it is made of and the temperature and pressure, a liquid or a gas. But more interesting things start to happen, as Eddington realized, in larger globes of material with higher internal pressures and temperatures, where ionization becomes important. Once plasma forms, electromagnetic effects become important. Fast-moving charged particles convert some of their kinetic energy into the form of electromagnetic radiation, and this radiation in its turn interacts with other charged particles, especially electrons, being absorbed and re-radiated. The effect of all this on the plasma is an additional outward pressure, radiation pressure, which helps to hold the globe of material—what we must now think of as a star—up against the pull of gravity. So, a glowing, stable star is held up by a combination of gas pressure and radiation pressure.

But now look at the other extreme. Imagine a huge ball of gas that tries to form into a star. The temperature in the center will rise so high that there will be an enormous radiation pressure, which blasts the star apart.

So there are three possible fates for a ball of gas that collapses under its own gravity, depending on its mass. It can become a cool, small globe held up only by gas pressure; it can become a glowing star, held up by a mixture of gas pressure and radiation pressure; or it can become a short-lived, superhot gas globe that is quickly blown apart by radiation pressure. Stars only exist in the range of masses where gas pressure and radiation pressure contribute roughly equally to the support of the ball of gas against the tug of gravity. And this is only true for a very limited range of masses.

Exactly which range of masses depends slightly on what the star is made of, because that affects the number of electrons around to interact with the radiation. As we shall see in the next chapter, Eddington made a wrong guess about the composition of the Sun in his classic book; but this is a trivial mistake compared with the power of his discovery of the importance of applying the gas laws to stars. In *The Internal Constitution of the Stars*, Eddington asked the reader to imagine a series of globes of gas of various sizes, starting with 10 grams, then 100 grams, 1,000 grams, and so on. The nth globe contains 10^n grams of material. The *only* globes in which, according to the gas laws, radiation pressure and gas pressure combine to produce stable, glowing stars are numbers 32 to 35 in the series.* And this prediction

---

*I am using here the modern version of Eddington's calculation, with numbers appropriate to the actual composition of the Sun.

from basic physics is borne out when we look at the real Universe. Globe 31 has a mass about five times that of Jupiter, the biggest planet in our Solar System. Globe 32 has a mass of 10^{32} grams, just about one tenth of the mass of the Sun; and globe 35 is about a hundred times more massive than our Sun. A star cannot begin to glow until it is bigger than Jupiter and about one tenth of the Sun's mass, but if it has more than a hundred times the Sun's mass, gravity is insufficient to hold it together against the outward blast of radiation from its hot interior. Out of the infinite range of possible globes of gas that we can imagine, only globes 32 to 35 in Eddington's list correspond to stars. Eddington told astronomers, using basic physics, how bright stars of each mass should shine. And our Sun sits nicely at the lower end of this range, obeying the basic laws of gas physics, *whatever* its source of energy might be.

Eddington's calculations also fitted in with discoveries being made from observations of other stars. The discovery of a relationship between mass and luminosity (stars with low mass are dim; more massive stars shine more brightly) was particularly significant in developing an understanding of how stars work. But Eddington also found that all stars in the same family as our Sun (so-called main sequence stars), regardless of their mass and luminosity, must have the same central temperature. It happens that the figure Eddington worked out for this crucial central temperature, 40 million degrees, was rather too high. Since his pioneering work, the calculations of the physics of stellar interiors have been improved in several small ways, and today the accepted figure is about 15 million degrees.* But this relatively minor adjustment has no effect on his important discovery that all main-sequence stars "burn" energy in their hearts at the *same* temperature.

"Taken at face value," as Eddington pointed out when considering in his book the energy released by two specific stars, "it suggests that whether a supply of 680 ergs per gram is needed (V Puppis) or whether a supply of 0.08 ergs per gram (Krueger 60) the star has to rise to 40,000,000° to get it. At this temperature it taps an unlimited supply."† Later in the book he elaborated on the notion. A star will "contract until its central temperature reaches 40 million degrees when the main supply of energy is suddenly released. . . . A star on the main series

*These are, of course, degrees Kelvin (K), measured from the absolute zero of temperature, $-273°C$.
†Eddington, 1959, p. 179.

must keep just enough of its material above the critical temperature to furnish the supply required.''*

This is a beautiful example of a feedback process that maintains equilibrium in such a star. Suppose the star—any star—shrinks a little more. It would get hotter in the middle, as gravitational energy is converted into heat, and so more subatomic energy would be released, which would have the effect of making the star expand, restoring equilibrium. Or suppose that for some reason the star expanded slightly. That would make it cooler in the middle, slowing down the release of energy and making it shrink again. Stars have an inbuilt thermostat that keeps their centers just at the right temperature for subatomic energy to be released. In general terms, the physics worked out beautifully. But Eddington still had one major problem in trying to persuade his physicist friends that this was indeed the way stars worked. ''The difficulty is that from the physicist's point of view the temperature of the stars is absurdly low. He regards the stars as practically at absolute zero, because in regard to nuclear processes 40 million degrees is a small quantity which it is scarcely worth while to take notice of.''†

The problem was that in the mid-1920s physicists were able to carry out calculations which showed that the energy required to make nuclei interact with one another in the first place was much more than the energy of motion of particles inside the Sun at the temperature Eddington calculated. There was plenty of nuclear energy available in principle, but how could the stars release energy at so low a temperature? This was the main objection, in the mid-1920s, to Eddington's theories of stellar energy generation; but he stuck firmly to his guns. ''The helium which we handle must have been put together at some time and some place,'' he pointed out. ''We do not argue with the critic who urges that the stars are not hot enough for this process; we tell him to go and find *a hotter place*.''‡

Even as these words were going through the printing presses, however, a new understanding of physics that would solve the problem was being developed. In his preface dated July 1926, Eddington mentions that ''as we go to press a 'new quantum theory' is arising which may have important reactions on the stellar problem when it is more

---

*Eddington, 1959, p. 299.
†Eddington, 1959, p. 300.
‡Eddington, 1959, p. 301. Eddington, stressing his faith in the laws of physics that unambiguously revealed the temperature at the heart of the Sun was, in fact, telling his critics to ''go to hell.''

fully developed.''* He was right. The first great revolution in physics in the twentieth century, relativity theory, had provided an understanding that mass could be converted into energy, in principle, and opened up the possibility of a star like the Sun living for billions of years. The second great revolution in physics in the twentieth century, quantum physics, showed how the trick could be achieved in practice, and that the conditions of temperature and pressure at the heart of the Sun, calculated by Eddington, were indeed exactly right to permit a series of interactions that effectively converted hydrogen nuclei (protons), four at a time, into helium nuclei (alpha particles).

The message was one that Chamberlin would have appreciated, and one that recurs throughout science. When observations tell you that something is happening but theory says it is impossible, it is time to change your theory, not the observations! But it took well over ten years for the hopes expressed by Eddington in July 1926 to become reality, with the development of a full understanding of the way energy is produced inside the Sun and stars.

*Eddington, 1959, p. xi. For a discussion of the quantum revolution of the 1920s, see *In Search of Schrödinger's Cat*, by John Gribbin.

3

AT THE
HEART OF
THE SUN

In his address to the British Association for the Advancement of Science Eddington made a particularly prescient comment about the source of solar energy. He referred to the possibility that "sub-atomic energy is actually being set free in the stars." Transmutation of elements could, if it occurred, set free energy corresponding to the difference in mass, and "if 5 per cent of a star's mass consists initially of hydrogen atoms, which are gradually being combined to form more complex elements, the total heat liberated will more than suffice for our demands, and we need look no further for the source of a star's energy."

The only doubt, at that time, seemed to be that transmutation of the elements might not actually be possible inside stars. But Eddington had an answer to that. Rutherford, he told his audience, had recently been breaking down atoms of oxygen and nitrogen, driving out an isotope of helium from them; and "what is possible in the Cavendish Laboratory may not be too difficult in the sun." Eddington was tantalizingly close to the truth, but his intuitive speculation had run ahead of scientific understanding. Before the real importance of the transmutation of hydrogen into helium could be established and astronomers could come to appreciate that hydrogen makes up far more than 5 percent of the bulk of a star like the Sun, the quantum revolution had to provide physicists with a new set of tools to describe the way particles interact under the conditions found at the heart of the Sun. The most important of these was "uncertainty."

○ A QUANTUM OF UNCERTAINTY

I have told the story of the quantum revolution in detail in my book *In Search of Schrödinger's Cat*—the story of the strange quantum world of particles like electrons and protons, where particles have to be regarded as being waves as well as particles, and waves, like light, must also be regarded as particles (in the case of light, photons). One of the strangest aspects of quantum reality, closely linked to this wave/particle duality, is known as uncertainty. In the quantum world, you can never be quite sure exactly where a particle is—not simply because of the difficulty of measuring the position of something as tiny as an electron, but because it *does not have* a precisely defined position. This is because the particle is also a wave—and a wave is, by its very nature, a spread-out thing (Figure 3.1). It was this feature of the quantum world that explained how alpha particles—what we would now call helium nuclei—could escape from the nuclei of radioactive atoms.

By the 1920s, it was clear that atoms consist of a cloud of negatively charged electrons surrounding a tiny kernel, the positively charged

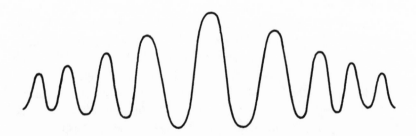

Fig. 3.1. A wave packet. Fundamental "particles," such as electrons and protons, are best thought of as tiny wave packets, not mathematical points. A wave packet is, by its nature, a spread-out object with a finite size.

nucleus. In a normal, neutral atom, the number of electrons in the outer cloud is exactly balanced by the number of protons in the positive nucleus—but the nucleus also contains particles, similar to protons but with zero charge (thus they are neutral and don't affect the atom's charge), called neutrons.* A nucleus of the most common isotope of radium contains 88 protons and 138 neutrons, and when it decays 2 protons and 2 neutrons are ejected together as an alpha particle, leaving a less massive atomic nucleus behind.

Since like charges repel each other, and the alpha particle carries a positive charge as does the nucleus being left behind, it is no surprise that, once the alpha particle is outside the nucleus, it should be repelled strongly and rush away from the nucleus. Yet all nuclei beyond the hydrogen atom contain more than one positively charged proton and they don't blow apart as the like charges repel one another. This is because there is another force at work inside the nucleus. It is called the "strong nuclear force," and over very short distances—just across the nucleus of an atom—it overwhelms the electric force repelling the protons from each other and glues the mixture of protons and neutrons together. The strong nuclear force only has a very short range, but it completely dominates the electric force over that range. One of the puzzles that quantum physicists had to solve at the end of the 1920s was how the escaping alpha particle from a radioactive nucleus could overcome this attractive force long enough to make its getaway.

The answer came from uncertainty, and it was found by a young Russian, George Gamow, who was visiting the University of Göttingen in 1928 (and who later moved to the United States and became an American citizen). Gamow realized that the strict rules of quantum uncertainty allowed—indeed, *required*—the alpha particle in some nuclei to be smeared out over a short distance, extending out of the nucleus proper and beyond the range of the strong nuclear force. Together, the combined influence of the strong nuclear force and electric repulsion produced the energy equivalent of a hill surrounding the nucleus, a barrier that the alpha particle had to climb over in order to escape. Measurements of the energy of escaping alpha particles showed

---

*Neutrons were not discovered until 1932 and so it was that Eddington talked, in 1920, of helium atoms containing two extra electrons, bound up in the nucleus to cancel out some of the positive charge possessed by four hydrogen nuclei (four protons). In fact, a helium-4 nucleus, or alpha particle, consists of two protons and two neutrons, not four protons and two electrons. But a neutron left on its own for more than about 10 minutes will "decay," spitting out an electron and turning into a proton, so Eddington's description wasn't really so wide of the mark, after all.

that they did not have quite enough energy to climb over this hill; Gamow's work showed how quantum uncertainty would allow them, in effect, to "tunnel through" the hill. When the numbers from Gamow's work were put into the equations, they matched precisely; quantum uncertainty and the tunnel effect exactly explained how alpha particles with the measured energy got out of radioactive nuclei (Figure 3.2).

But what has this to do with "the transmutation of hydrogen into helium," effectively sticking a couple of hydrogen nuclei together to make helium? The relevance is that the tunnel effect also works the other way around. If a proton is approaching a positively charged nucleus, it "ought" to be repelled by the positive electric charge in the nucleus and bounced away. If it is moving fast enough—with enough kinetic energy—it can get close enough to "touch" the nucleus, and then the strong nuclear force can grab hold of it. The nucleus has

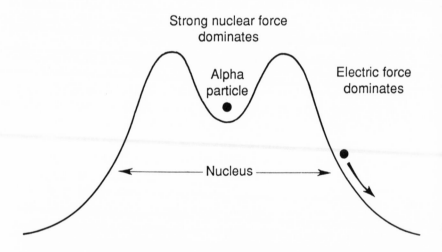

Fig. 3.2. The interplay between the strong nuclear force and the electric force makes a "potential well" in which particles in the nucleus of an atom are trapped. An alpha particle inside the well that does not have enough energy to climb over the barrier ought to be trapped forever. But quantum uncertainty, related to the fact that the particle is really a wave packet that extends beyond the confines of the nucleus, allows some alpha particles to "tunnel through" the barrier and escape. In a similar way, during fusion reactions some particles from outside can tunnel in to the nucleus through the barrier.

gained a proton and been transmuted. But the energy needed for the incoming proton to get close enough for this to work is very high— far higher than the energy possessed by protons at the temperatures that, simple physics told Eddington, exist inside the Sun. The tunnel effect, however, changes the picture. Because of its wavelike character, the proton only has to get near enough to the nucleus for its wave to overlap with the wave of the nucleus before it is grabbed. In effect, it tunnels through the electric barrier holding it at bay. And *that* is why there is no need of "a hotter place" than the heart of the Sun to transmute hydrogen nuclei (protons) into helium nuclei. This was the key insight that set astrophysicists on the trail of the processes that keep the Sun, and other stars, hot. Still, though, it took them ten more years to sort out the details.

○ TUNNELING INSIDE STARS

Gamow's insight, and the discovery of the tunnel effect, set physicists off along two separate but related trails. It gave astrophysicists a chance, at last, to understand where the enormous energies that powered the stars came from; and it opened up the possibility of achieving the alchemists' dream and changing one element into another in laboratories on Earth. The astrophysicists were quicker off the mark but took longer to achieve their goal.

The first steps were taken astonishingly quickly after Gamow came up with the idea of tunneling in 1928. By the next year, the physicists Robert Atkinson and Fritz Houtermans had taken up the idea and used it to demonstrate that in principle solar energy could be produced by sticking atomic nuclei together—the process now known as nuclear fusion. Their calculations showed how hydrogen nuclei (protons) could indeed get close enough to other nuclei for fusion to take place even at the kind of relatively low temperature that straightforward physics said must exist in the heart of the Sun.

The key to an understanding of how the tunnel effect does make the energies of protons inside the Sun adequate to do the job is that a little fusion goes a long way. So much energy is released each time four protons are converted, by whatever means, into one alpha particle that the reaction can be quite a rare one and yet (given that the Sun is made up of many billions of particles) provide enough energy to keep the Sun hot. Even at the temperatures at the heart of the Sun—

about 15 million K by modern estimates—*most* protons are not moving fast enough to tunnel through the electric barrier. Although the temperature of anything, including the Sun, is a measure of how fast the particles it is made of are moving and jostling against one another, that doesn't mean that all the particles have exactly the same energy, or exactly the same speed. There is a particular average speed that is most common, and which is appropriate for that particular temperature. But some particles will be moving faster than average, and others more slowly, in a very well-defined way that obeys a precise statistical law. At any temperature, it is possible to calculate not only the average speed but also what fraction of the particles will be moving 10 percent faster, 50 percent faster, twice as fast as the average, or whatever speed you are interested in (Figure 3.3). These rare fast particles are said to lie in the "high-speed tail" of the distribution of velocities.

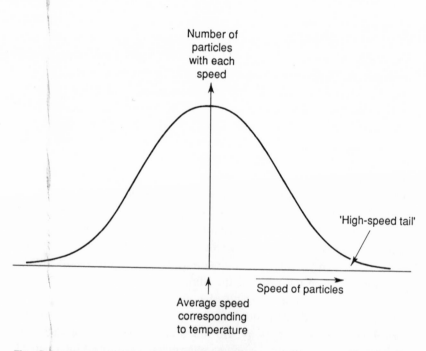

Fig. 3.3. Even with the aid of the tunnel effect, only a few particles are moving fast enough for fusion to occur inside the Sun. They belong in the "high-speed tail" of the distribution of velocities that corresponds to the temperature at the heart of the Sun.

The triumph of the application of Gamow's tunnel theory to the conditions inside the Sun was that it showed that at the right temperature just enough particles from the high-speed tail (by no means every proton) could tunnel through the electric barrier. But the 1929 paper by Atkinson and Houtermans* was only a first step along the road to unlocking the secret of what keeps the Sun hot, because at that stage not only did nobody know exactly which fusion reactions were at work inside the Sun, they had completely the wrong idea about what the Sun was made of.

Anaxagoras, remember, had thought that the Sun must be a ball of red-hot iron. In 1929, astrophysicists' ideas about the composition of the Sun hadn't really moved very far from that idea. It was natural to guess that the composition of the Sun might not be so very different from that of the Earth, and the idea that the Sun's energy might come from the radioactive decay of elements such as radium, which are heavy metals, encouraged the view that most of the Sun's bulk consisted of heavy elements. So, although Atkinson and Houtermans had shown that protons could penetrate other nuclei of heavier elements and fuse with them under the conditions that existed inside the Sun, at the end of the 1920s nobody guessed that what kept the Sun hot was, in fact, the fusion of protons with other protons to make helium— the most efficient energy source of all.

Atkinson went on to develop these ideas in more detail in the 1930s, while Houtermans turned to other work. Meanwhile, in 1928, Albrecht Unsöld had shown for the first time, using spectroscopic evidence, that hydrogen is not only the most abundant element in the atmosphere of the Sun, but that there are roughly a million times more hydrogen atoms there than anything else. This was confirmed, using evidence from a completely different spectroscopic technique, by William McCrea in 1929. But it took a long time for astrophysicists to appreciate that hydrogen is comparably dominant *throughout* the Sun and stars. Even in the 1930s, less than a human lifetime ago, the Sun still kept the basic secret of what it was made of. Nevertheless, there was clearly ample hydrogen available to provide energy by fusion, and in the early 1930s Atkinson developed the idea that heavier nuclei might absorb protons one after another until they became unstable and, as a result of a kind of nuclear indigestion, spat out alpha particles instead—a way of turning hydrogen into helium through an intermediary. He was

*Zeitschrift für Physik, vol. 54, p. 656.

nearly right—as we shall see, some stars do get their energy in this way, but this is not the main fusion process at work inside the Sun. But Atkinson did show, by 1936, that the single most likely fusion reaction under the conditions prevailing at the heart of the Sun would be the simple fusion of two hydrogen nuclei to form a deuteron. (The deuteron is also known as heavy hydrogen. It is a nucleus consisting of a single proton and a single neutron held together by the strong nuclear force.) In this process, one of the protons is converted into a neutron by spitting out a positively charged counterpart to the electron, known as a positron. But all this talk of one particle changing into another and spitting out still a third in the process shows how much the world of physics had changed by 1936. In 1929, when Atkinson's work with Houtermans was published, nobody knew that either neutrons or positrons existed. They were to become part of the laboratory version of the story of twentieth-century alchemy.

○ ALCHEMY IN THE LAB

In 1928, when Gamow came up with the idea of the tunnel effect, physics only knew of two "fundamental" particles, the proton and the electron. The alpha particle seemed to be a group of four protons and two electrons bound together in one unit, and all atoms could be envisaged as built up from protons and electrons alone. But there was still a long-standing puzzle about the nature of radioactivity, involving these particles and dating back to the distinction Rutherford had found in 1898 between alpha and beta "rays." Although beta rays had been firmly identified with electrons at the turn of the century, at the end of the 1920s it was still far from clear how the electrons got out of atomic nuclei. In particular, measurements made in 1914 had shown that when a radioactive atom (we would now refer to it as a radioactive nucleus) emitted beta rays (electrons) some energy seemed to be lost. This is related to the way mass is converted into energy, or the other way around.* In nuclei that are prone to beta decay, the mass of the nucleus before it emits the electron is not quite the same as the mass of the nucleus plus the electron after the decay. An energy equivalent

---

*The discussion here, and elsewhere in this chapter, often uses ideas and names that were not common until much later; I give what is essentially the modern version of beta decay (and other processes) at work in order to avoid confusion. Some of the historical byways that led to the modern understanding—often by devious routes—are explored in my other books.

to about one and a half times the mass of an electron is released in the decay, and this energy ought to be taken up by the electron, giving it a very specific speed—the *same* speed for all beta decay electrons. But the statistics of many measurements of electrons produced by beta decay showed that they emerged from the nucleus with a whole range of energies, always less than the magic figure corresponding to 1.5 electron masses. Energy seemed to have vanished into thin air.

In 1930, Wolfgang Pauli explained the discrepancy by invoking the presence of another kind of particle, with no electric charge and very little mass, that had never been detected in any experiment. The sole raison d'être for this particle was to carry away the missing energy in beta decay. The hypothetical particle was later given the name "neutrino," and later still neutrinos were actually detected (we shall hear much more about them in Chapter 4). But in 1930 it was an act of daring in the physics community to suggest that there might be another kind of fundamental particle besides the proton and the electron.

Just two years later, in 1932, the discovery of the neutron confirmed that there was more going on inside atoms than just interactions involving protons and electrons. This helped to give the neutrino idea respectability, and very soon beta decay was explained in terms of the workings of another kind of force, called the "weak nuclear force," which describes how a neutron can convert itself into a proton by emitting both an electron *and* a neutrino. In beta decay, the radioactive nucleus loses a neutron but gains a proton, being converted into a nucleus of a different element in the process. With neutrons and neutrinos added to the list, the number of known fundamental particles had doubled in a couple of years. But where do positrons come into the story?

At about the same time that people were beginning to think seriously about the implications of tunnel theory, in 1929, the British physicist Paul Dirac came up with an idea that at first seemed outrageous. Working with the new equations of quantum physics (which he had developed himself), he had found that the equations that describe the behavior of the electron (including its curious wave-particle duality) seemed to have two sets of solutions. This is rather like the way in which a simple equation such as $x^2 = 4$ has two solutions, $x = 2$ and $x = -2$. Both 2×2 *and* $(-2) \times (-2)$ are equal to four. Of course, Dirac's equations were rather more complicated than that, but they did have two solutions, and only one solution was needed to describe electrons. Dirac suggested that the "extra" solutions to his equations described a particle like the electron but with positive charge. Very few people (if any) took the idea seriously until 1932, when studies of cosmic rays (high-energy particles from space) revealed the existence of positive electrons—positrons. Dirac's chutzpah was vindicated, and by 1933 all the main players in the game of solar alchemy were known, even if the neutrino, in particular, was not yet taken fully seriously by all physicists.

We now know that just as there is a kind of mirror-image particle for the electron, so there are mirror-image "antiparticles" for the neutron, proton, and neutrino. We can imagine whole planets and stars made of this mirror matter—but there is very little of it around in our part of the Universe, because any antiparticle that meets one of its particle counterparts annihilates in a blast of pure radiation, with all of the mass from both particles being converted into energy. Almost certainly, the entire Universe is, in fact, made almost entirely of matter, not antimatter. But that doesn't stop antiparticles like positrons from being created in nuclear reactions and taking part in other nuclear reactions during their brief lives. Which brings us back to the modern alchemists.

While other people were worrying about what the quantum equations meant and "inventing" new particles to explain where the missing energy from beta decay was going, some of the more pragmatic physicists were still indulging in the kind of experiments that had started the particle physics revolution in the first place—essentially, bashing atoms (or nuclei) as hard as possible and watching to see what happened to them. This particular phase of atom bashing was a direct result of the development of new quantum ideas—it stemmed from Gamow's tunnel theory.

Early in the 1930s, physicists developed the first machines that could accelerate beams of protons, using electric fields, to fairly high energies. The energy of the beams produced by these particle accelerators is usually measured in terms of the energy that an electron would gain by being accelerated across an electric potential of one volt (1 eV). The old-fashioned equations that described collisions between protons and atomic nuclei said that the protons could only approach close enough to "stick" to the nuclei—to come within range of the strong nuclear force—if they had energies of millions of electron volts (several "MeV"). Just as the heart of the Sun was too cold for such reactions to occur according to the old theory, so, in the late 1920s, particle accelerators that might be built on Earth were, physicists knew, not energetic enough to make protons stick to nuclei in the lab. But Gamow's tunnel effect equations apply just as much in laboratories on Earth as they do inside the Sun.

In the late 1920s, one of the junior members of Rutherford's research team at the Cavendish Laboratory was John Cockroft, a physicist who had made rather a late start in his eventual speciality (he had been born in 1897) because his education had been interrupted by army service during World War I. He had a background in electrical engineering, related to his army work in signals, and this was to stand him in good stead in the work that was to make his name famous. At that time, the only particles physicists had available to bombard atomic nuclei with in atom-bashing experiments were alpha particles produced by radioactive decay. These had produced the first successful transmutations of elements when Rutherford discovered in 1919 that when a fast-moving alpha particle strikes a nucleus of nitrogen the nitrogen is transformed into oxygen, while a hydrogen nucleus, to which Rutherford gave the name "proton," is ejected. Even before Rutherford identified the proton as a fundamental particle, physicists had discovered that positively charged hydrogen nuclei could be produced by stripping the electrons off the atoms electrically. Ten years after his first transmutations of nitrogen into oxygen, they knew how to produce protons in profusion. But there seemed little point in trying to develop a proton accelerator if the protons would not have enough energy to penetrate the electric barrier around nuclei. In a conversation with Gamow in 1929, however, Cockroft learned that protons with energies of only a few hundred keV could penetrate the nuclear barrier—and he knew that a machine to accelerate protons to such energies could be constructed using the technology of the time. But it wouldn't come cheap.

Cockroft persuaded Rutherford to use his influence to obtain what was then a very large sum of money to begin work on the particle accelerator project—one thousand pounds. Working with a research student from Ireland, Ernest Walton, Cockroft developed the first particle accelerator in a couple of years of intensive work, producing a beam of protons with energies of more than 700,000 eV (700 keV). The rationale behind the project was, in fact, a neat reversal of one of Eddington's quips from his 1920 British Association for the Advancement of Science lecture, although no latter-day Eddington seems to have pointed this out. Eddington had said that "what is possible in the Cavendish Laboratory may not be too difficult in the sun." Gamow had pointed out that the way in which fusion could work inside the Sun at the relatively low temperature of 15 million K meant that fusion should be possible in the laboratory using protons with energies of a few hundred keV—in effect, that "what is possible inside the *Sun* may not be too difficult in the Cavendish Laboratory." It is entirely fitting that the first particle accelerator was indeed built in the Cavendish Lab—and that it produced nuclear fusion reactions as early as 1932 (the work for which Cockroft and Walton received the Nobel Prize in 1951).

This may be a surprise to anyone who knows that researchers today are still struggling to obtain energy commercially by reproducing on Earth the kind of fusion reactions that take place inside the stars. But their problem is somewhat more difficult—to produce a stable, sustainable reaction that can be used safely in power stations on a regular day-to-day basis. All that Cockroft and Walton had to do was bombard nuclei of a chosen substance with protons and test to see if any of those nuclei were absorbing protons and being converted into other elements in the process. That's all—but it achieved the age-old dream of the alchemists, transmutation of elements, and it took physics a crucial step further toward unlocking the secret of how the Sun stays hot.

The target that Cockroft and Walton chose to bombard with their proton beam was a thin layer of lithium. This is the third lightest element, after hydrogen and helium, and is the lightest solid that exists under everyday conditions. Each lithium nucleus carries only three units of positive charge. Obviously, the smaller the positive charge on the chosen nuclei the easier it would be for the protons in the beam to tunnel through the electric barrier. We now know that the nucleus of a stable lithium atom consists of three protons and four neutrons held together by the strong nuclear force. Most of the protons in the beam from Cockroft and Walton's accelerator passed through the almost empty spaces between the lithium nuclei, brushing aside electrons like armor-piercing shells bursting through wet Kleenex. But just a few protons hit their nuclear targets head-on and, in accordance with Gamow's prediction, tunneled their way into the nuclei. In each case, the result was a nucleus containing four protons and four neutrons— an isotope of the element beryllium. But this isotope is highly unstable, and whenever it is formed it almost immediately splits into two alpha particles (helium nuclei) each containing two protons and two neutrons.

Mass is converted into energy in the process, and the two alpha particles hurtle out of the lithium layer and can easily be detected.

In the popular press of the day, and almost always since, the Cockroft-Walton experiment was described as "splitting" the atom, as if the flying protons simply blasted the lithium nuclei apart, like a cannonball demolishing a brick wall. But there is much deeper significance in the fact that the atomic nucleus that splits is actually an unstable *beryllium* nucleus, created, if only fleetingly, by the *fusion* of a proton with a lithium nucleus. The tunnel effect could be seen to be at work in the Cavendish Laboratory, and nobody could doubt any longer that it was also at work in the heart of the Sun. But which atomic nuclei did it operate on?

○ **THE SOLAR PRESSURE COOKER**

Because of their misconceptions about what the sun is made of, astrophysicists were hamstrung throughout the 1930s in their efforts to pin down the exact cycle of fusion reactions that keeps the Sun hot. Unsöld and McCrea had convinced them that there was a lot of hydrogen in the Sun (at least in its atmosphere), and so they knew that there were probably many protons available inside the Sun with the right kind of energies to participate in the kind of reactions that Cockroft and Walton had demonstrated in the Cavendish Laboratory (and which were very soon being demonstrated in other laboratories, in the United States and elsewhere). The approach pioneered by Eddington, using the standard equations of physics that describe how heat is transmitted outward from the interior of a globe of gas like the Sun, showed how the flow of heat, and therefore the stability of the globe of gas, depended on the composition of the star. Electromagnetic radiation interacts strongly with charged particles, such as electrons and protons, and according to these calculations a star like the Sun could only be stable provided that there was the right mixture of electrons and nuclei inside it. Too many charged particles, and they would hold the radiation in, making the star swell up as it pushed them out of the way; too few, and the radiation would escape too easily, so that the star would deflate like a pricked balloon. And it makes a difference whether the protons all roam about freely, as hydrogen nuclei, or whether they are packed together, 26 at a time (plus the appropriate number of neutrons, 30 in the most stable form of iron), into nuclei of iron, as Anaxagoras had supposed. For the same total mass of the Sun, the number of electrons is always the same as the number of protons. The most electrons are present if all of the nuclei are simple protons, and there are far fewer electrons if a large fraction of the mass is locked up as neutrons. (For a Sun made of pure iron, less than half the mass would be protons, and the rest neutrons, so there would be less than half the number of electrons as in a Sun made of pure hydrogen.)

Unfortunately, as it turned out, the calculations showed that a globe exactly the size of the Sun, with the Sun's temperature and measured rate of energy generation, could exist as a stable star provided that the proportion of hydrogen in its interior was *either* about 35 percent *or* at least 95 percent (at least 95 percent made of hydrogen *and helium*, in fact, with very little scope for any heavier elements). Once again, what "everybody knew" would only color ideas about the Sun and hold back progress. Until Unsöld and McCrea showed otherwise, "everybody knew" that the composition of the Sun was rather like that of the Earth. Once somebody discovered that unlike the earth, there was a lot of hydrogen inside the Sun and the laws of physics said that "a lot" meant either 35 percent hydrogen and 65 percent heavy elements, or less than 5 percent heavies, it was "obvious" that the lower figure for hydrogen, closer to what "everybody knew" before, must be correct. So theorists began to look for ways in which protons could combine with heavier nuclei to produce unstable nuclei that would spit out alpha particles and liberate energy, just like the "atom splitting" of lithium carried out in the Cavendish laboratory by Cockroft and Walton.

This misconception colored the work of Robert Atkinson when he developed the ideas he had first put forward in collaboration with Houtermans. In 1931, he suggested that the proportions of different elements inside stars and the energy generation process might both be explained if heavier nuclei absorbed successive protons and spat out helium nuclei—but he thought then that a star like the Sun contained only 35 percent hydrogen. Even handicapped by these misconceptions, by 1936 Atkinson had established that the single most common nuclear reaction occurring in the heart of the Sun is the collision of two protons to form a deuteron (a nucleus containing one proton and one neutron) and a positron. The next step was to establish the way in which some stars, at least, really do extract nuclear energy.

Once again, George Gamow comes into the story. In April 1938, he organized a conference in Washington, D.C., bringing astronomers and physicists together to discuss the problem of energy generation inside stars. One of the young nuclear physicists at that meeting, who had a thorough understanding of the conditions required for protons to penetrate more massive nuclei, but had not been aware of the astrophysical problems, was Hans Bethe. Bethe was born in Strasbourg (then in Germany, now part of France) in 1906 and worked at several German universities before moving to Britain in 1933 (when Hitler came to power) and then to the United States in 1935, where he worked at Cornell University in New York.

By 1938, astrophysicists knew that the energy of the stars must originate from nuclear processes, but they didn't know which nuclear processes. The problem is fairly simple to sum up, using a couple of examples. A reaction like the classic interaction between hydrogen nuclei and lithium nuclei—the Cockroft and Walton "atom-splitting" process—is far too efficient to explain how the Sun stays hot. Even at a temperature of 15 million degrees, if there were very much lithium in the Sun's core it would all be rapidly converted into helium nuclei, releasing so much energy so quickly that the Sun would blow itself apart. On the other hand, reactions between protons and (for example) oxygen nuclei are far too slow, at these temperatures, to produce the right amount of energy on their own. If the Sun depended on those reactions, it would fizzle out (in fact, it would shrink until it got hot enough in the center to make the reactions go faster). Bethe, and the other participants in the conference, were asked which nuclear reaction, or set of reactions, would go at just the right rate at the temperature inside the Sun to produce the amount of energy the Sun actually does radiate.

In his book *The Birth and Death of the Sun*,* written just after these events, Gamow describes how Bethe decided that this shouldn't be a very difficult problem to solve, and how he set out to find the secret of stellar energy on the train back to Cornell. According to legend, Bethe promised himself he would solve the problem before the steward called the passengers to dinner—and did so with seconds to spare. At the same time, early in 1938, another German, Carl von Weizsäcker, had identified the same solution to the stellar energy problem, back in

*New York: Viking, 1940.

Berlin. But he lacked the presence of an ebullient Gamow to make the discovery memorable by spreading the (possibly partly apocryphal) news of a hasty calculation while waiting for dinner on a train.

○ STELLAR ALCHEMY

In its modern version, only slightly improved since 1938, this energy generation process is called the carbon cycle, or the carbon-nitrogen-oxygen (CNO) cycle. It works like this:

First, a proton tunnels into a nucleus containing six protons and six neutrons (a nucleus of carbon-12). The nucleus that is produced, nitrogen-13, is radioactive and emits a positron and a neutrino, converting into carbon-13. If a second proton now tunnels into this nucleus, we get a nucleus of nitrogen-14, and if a third proton tunnels into the nitrogen-14 nucleus it is transformed into oxygen-15, which is also radioactive and spits out a positron and a neutrino, transmuting into nitrogen-15 (in every case, the *name* of an isotope depends on how many protons it contains; its *number* is the combined total of neutrons plus protons). But now, if yet another proton tunnels into the nucleus of nitrogen-15, it ejects an alpha particle—two protons and two neutrons bound together to form a helium nucleus. What is left behind is a nucleus of carbon-12, just what the cycle started with; along the way, four protons have, in effect, been combined to make one helium nucleus, with a couple of positrons, two neutrinos, and a lot of energy released along the way. A relatively small amount of carbon-12 in the heart of a star will act as a catalyst for many cycles of this kind (Figure 3.4), steadily converting hydrogen into helium and releasing energy to keep the star hot—even though, overall, the amount of carbon, nitrogen, and oxygen in the star is unchanged. (And if Bethe really did work all that out on the train before dinner, he deserves all the credit Gamow gave him.)

The process explains beautifully how many stars stay hot. But it turns out that it is *not* the most important process for generating energy inside the Sun. As astrophysicists improved their calculations, and their observational colleagues obtained more accurate estimates of stellar masses and luminosities, it became clear that the carbon cycle is the dominant energy source in stars with more than about one and a half times the mass of the Sun, and correspondingly higher internal temperatures, but that it can only produce a modest amount of energy

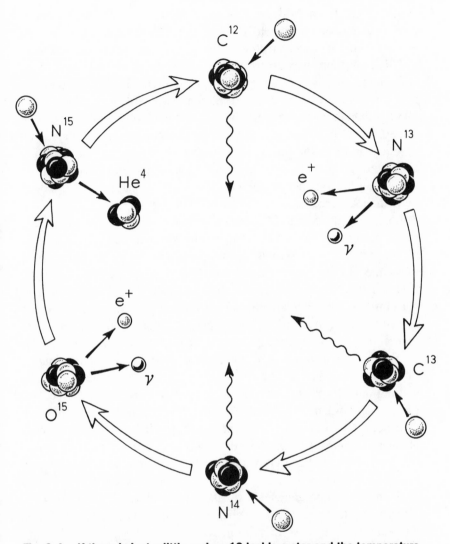

Fig. 3.4. If there is just a little carbon-12 inside a star and the temperature is just right, then hydrogen can be converted into helium and energy can be released by the carbon-nitrogen-oxygen cycle. Start at the top of the diagram and follow the arrows clockwise; each incoming particle from outside the ring is a proton, and the net effect is to convert for protons (hydrogen nuclei) into one alpha particle (helium-4 nucleus), while the carbon nucleus is reformed. Wavy lines indicate gamma rays.

at the temperatures inside the Sun itself. By the time this was realized it was no embarrassment to the astrophysicists, because Bethe had already found the nuclear process that really does keep our Sun hot.

This time there was no train ride involved, just steady work back at Cornell, with his colleague Charles Critchfield. Their work on what is known as the proton-proton (p-p) chain was also first published in 1938, although it was not until the 1950s that astrophysicists were able to say for certain that it is the p-p chain, not the CNO cycle, that produces most of the Sun's energy. (One of the main reasons it took so long to sort this out was the confusion about the Sun's composition; everything fits together neatly once it is realized that the Sun is indeed more than 95 percent made of hydrogen and helium. In fact, the modern estimate sees the Sun as 70 percent hydrogen, 28 percent helium, and just 2 percent for everything else, the heavy elements.)

The p-p chain starts with the reaction that Atkinson had pointed to as the starting point for nuclear fusion inside stars, a collision between two protons (p) in which the tunnel effect allows them to get close enough together to fuse into a deuteron (d), spitting out a neutrino and a positron in the process. Another proton can then tunnel into the deuteron, producing a nucleus of helium-3 (He^3), containing two protons and one neutron. Finally, when two nuclei of helium-3 collide they form a stable nucleus of helium-4 (He^4), spitting out two protons as they do so (Figure 3.5). About 95 percent of the helium-3 nuclei do suffer this fate; the other 5 percent have a choice of two slightly different fates, which we shall learn more about in Chapter 4. Just as in the CNO cycle, the net effect is that four protons have been converted into one nucleus of helium-4, and energy has been released. But whereas, we now know, the CNO cycle needs temperatures above about 20 million degrees to work effectively, the p-p chain is an efficient energy source even at a temperature as low as 15 million K.

It is very hard to put all of this in any kind of everyday context. Temperatures like 15 million K and densities many times that of lead are simply not part of our everyday experience. But there are some slightly mind-boggling features of these nuclear reactions that are worth trying to take in (and which, if nothing else, will make you appreciate what engineers are up against in trying to reproduce fusion processes as a source of energy for power stations here on Earth).

First, the tunnel effect calculations show that even at a temperature of 15 million K the basic proton-proton interaction that starts the

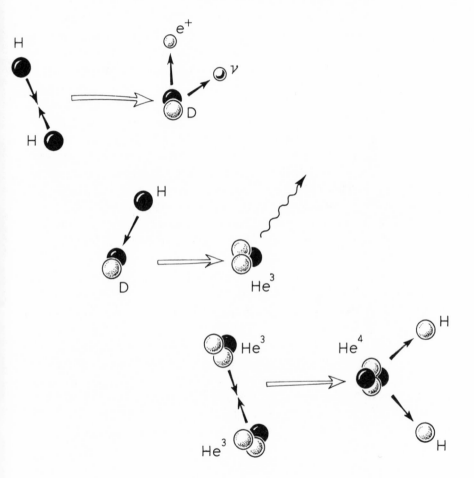

Fig. 3.5. **Our Sun is not hot enough to be powered by the CNO cycle, al-though other stars are. It gets its energy from another fusion process, the proton-proton chain. Thanks to the tunnel effect, two protons can combine inside the Sun to form deuterium, from which first helium-3 and then helium-4 is formed. But even in the heart of the Sun, only rare fast-moving particles are able to take advantage of the tunnel effect and fuse in this way.**

chain off only occurs if one of the colliding protons is traveling five times faster than average, way out in the high-speed tail of the velocity distribution. And even then, the collision has to be almost exactly head-on—a fast-moving proton that strikes another proton only a glancing blow will not be able to tunnel through the electric barrier. Inside the Sun, just one proton in a hundred million is traveling fast enough even for a head-on collision to do the trick. And unless one of the two interacting protons spits out a positron during the tiny split second that they are within tunneling range of each other, they will still not form a stable deuteron—a "nucleus" consisting of just two protons is not stable in its own right. Each proton in the heart of the Sun is involved in a collision with other protons millions of times in every second. But even so, the quantum calculations show that on average it would take an individual proton 14 billion years to find a partner able to join it in forming a deuteron through a head-on collision. Some will take longer than average; some will find their partners more quickly. The Sun is only about 4.5 billion years old—which is why most of its protons have not yet found such partners. But there are so many protons inside the Sun that, even at this incredibly slow rate of reactions, with just one collision in every ten billion trillion (1 in 10^{22}) initiating the p-p chain, and just 0.7 percent of the mass of each set of four protons being converted into pure energy when a helium-4 nucleus is formed, about 5 *million* tons of mass is converted into energy every second inside the Sun. And so far, the Sun has processed only about 4 percent of its initial stock of hydrogen into helium, although the p-p reactions have been going on steadily for 4.5 billion years.

Strictly speaking, these mind-blowing statistics bring us to the end of the story I set out to tell at the start of this chapter, the secret of how the Sun stays hot. But it would be a pity to move on to other secrets of the Sun without mentioning, if only briefly, how more complex nuclear reactions inside other stars explain our presence here on Earth today.

○ STARDUST

Astronomers now have good evidence that the clouds of gas from which the first stars formed, after the Big Bang in which the Universe was born, contained only hydrogen and helium (about 25 percent helium), with just a tiny trace of a few other light elements.* Everything else has been made inside stars.

The first stage is the processing of hydrogen into helium. This affects the nature of the star in which the hydrogen is being "burnt" and has, astrophysicists calculate, already changed the size and appearance of our own Sun over the past 4.5 billion years. Because each single nucleus acts like an individual particle in the "gas" at the heart of the Sun, every time four protons are combined to make one helium nucleus there are three less particles to contribute to the gas pressure holding the Sun up. As the gas pressure slowly decreases as a result, the core of the Sun shrinks slightly and gets hotter, so that extra radiation pressure exactly makes up for the deficiency. But shrinking and getting hotter in its heart means that the Sun's *outer* layers actually expand slightly, as they become hotter in response to the increased flow of energy out from the core. Over its life so far, the Sun's brightness has increased by about 40 percent. In another 1.5 billion years, when it is 6 billion years old, it will be 15 percent brighter still. This has interesting implications for life on Earth—the climate of Norway will then, other things being equal, be like that of northern Africa today, and there will be no polar ice caps. But at least the Sun will still be recognizable.

In 6 billion years from now, when the Sun is rather more than 10 billion years old, it will no longer be recognizable. By then, almost all of the hydrogen in its heart will have been converted into helium, and although plenty of hydrogen will remain in the outer part of the star, those regions are not hot enough for the proton-proton process to operate. Without hydrogen fusion in its heart, the Sun's core will shrink in upon itself and get hotter still. Hydrogen burning will take place in a shell around the burnt-out core, making the surface layers expand until the Sun swells to more than three times its present size. Although a lot of energy will be flowing out through this large star, it will have a vast area of surface to flow through, and so the surface itself will be cooler than today, and dark red in color. The Sun will be a red subgiant and will continue to swell slowly for the next couple of hundred million years. Eventually it will become a true red giant, reaching a size 100 times bigger than its present diameter and engulfing Mercury, the innermost planet.

But then, according to astrophysical calculations, another dramatic

---

*See my book *In Search of the Big Bang* (London: Heinemann, and New York: Bantam, 1986).

change will occur. Over all this time, the temperature in the core has been rising, and when it reaches about 100 million K a new kind of nuclear fusion, *helium burning*, begins. Helium burning starts almost literally in a flash, releasing so much energy that the outer layers of the giant star are blown away into space, sweeping past the planets and probably taking the earth's atmosphere with it. Then the core settles down to a new life as a helium-burning star—which takes us the next step along the road of stellar alchemy.

But helium nuclei—alpha particles—cannot combine in pairs to form another stable nucleus. The nucleus that corresponds to two helium-4 nuclei combined is beryllium-8—and as Cockroft and Walton noticed, beryllium-8 is *extremely* unstable. The only way helium-4 nuclei can be used to build something more complex is if a *third* alpha particle collides with the beryllium-8 nucleus during its very brief lifetime—within ten millionths of a billionth of a second after the first two alpha particles collide. Ridiculous though it may seem, this does happen, just often enough for helium burning to be a major source of energy in stars farther along the evolutionary trail than our Sun. The end product is carbon-12, a respectable, well-behaved, and stable nucleus.*

Other fusion processes occur at higher temperatures in correspondingly more evolved stars (more massive stars go through their life cycles, or evolve, more quickly than less massive stars, so many stars in our Galaxy have already died, even though our own Sun is barely middle-aged). Once carbon-12 has been produced inside a star, it is relatively easy for another alpha particle to tunnel into the nucleus, making oxygen-16, so the end product of helium burning is a mixture of carbon and oxygen nuclei. *Carbon burning* occurs at a temperature of around 500 million K (after the core has shrunk appropriately), when pairs of carbon nuclei interact to produce a mixture of products including neon, sodium, and magnesium nuclei. *Oxygen burning*, at around a billion K, produces silicon, sulphur, and other nuclei. The most important product of the combined transmutation of oxygen and carbon is silicon-28, which is the key element in the last, and most complex, version of the fusion energy-generation process.

Silicon burning is, in fact, rather more complex than the simple

---

*The story is even more surprising than it seems from this simple outline. Three alpha particles can only form a stable carbon-12 nucleus because of a striking quantum coincidence involving the energy levels of the carbon-12 nucleus. This coincidence (among others) is discussed in *Cosmic Coincidences*, by John Gribbin and Martin Rees (New York: Bantam, 1989).

addition of two silicon-28 nuclei together to make one nucleus of iron-56. In effect, alpha particles break away from one nucleus and join the other one, one at a time. But the end result is the same—silicon is converted into iron. All the way from helium to iron, the elements that are produced in large quantities by this stellar alchemy are, in effect, combinations of alpha particles, with masses roughly a multiple of four times that of a proton (only roughly—remember that the whole point is that at each stage some mass is converted into energy). Some of these nuclei spit out a positron as a proton is converted into a neutron to make a more stable configuration; but that doesn't change the mass number significantly, since the mass of a positron (or an electron) is only about one two-thousandth of the mass of a neutron or proton. Elements with mass numbers that are not multiples of four form when these nuclei capture stray neutrons from their surroundings; they may then spit out electrons to convert some of those extra neutrons into protons. But everything stops at iron-56. Nuclei of iron-56 have the most stable arrangement of protons and neutrons that any nucleus can have. In order to make more massive nuclei—things like lead, or uranium, or gold—energy has to be put *in* to force extra particles into the nucleus. Instead of each nucleus being lighter than the sum of its parts, now the addition of an extra alpha particle or neutron makes the new nucleus even heavier than the sum of its parts, as the energy needed to force the particles together is converted into mass.

The extra energy is only available in the last stages of the life of a few heavy stars. When such a star runs out of nuclear fuel, its core collapses, pulling the floor from under the outer layers, which are no longer supported either by radiation pressure or by gas pressure. As they hurtle inward onto the burnt-out core of the star, so much gravitational energy is released that not only are nuclei of elements lighter than iron-56 forced together to make more massive nuclei, but the whole star then explodes outward, scattering the elements it has created across the space between the stars. Such an exploding star is called a supernova; some idea of the energy involved is indicated by the fact that a supernova may shine, temporarily, as brightly as a whole galaxy of stars—and a galaxy contains tens of billions of stars like our Sun. The Sun itself is too modest a star ever to suffer this fate. When its nuclear burning options are exhausted, it will settle down quietly into a cooling lump of star stuff, basically white-hot iron, fading away into old age as a so-called white dwarf. Anaxagoras's guess about the composition of the Sun would have been right—if he'd been born a few billion years later. But even Anaxagoras never imagined that he was himself made of stardust.

All the elements except hydrogen and helium (and even some of the helium) have been manufactured inside stars. But the only stars that these elements ever escape from are supernovas.* The mass of our Milky Way Galaxy is about 100 billion times the mass of our Sun; astronomers estimate, from studies of the spectra of stars, that just 1 percent of this matter, only a billion solar masses, is in the form of heavy elements ("heavy" meaning anything except hydrogen and helium). Since the Galaxy is about 10 billion years old, this means that just one tenth of a solar mass of material is processed into heavy elements each year. Allowing for the fact that there were probably more supernova explosions when the Galaxy was younger, this requires about one supernova explosion, each releasing two solar masses of processed material into the void, roughly every thirty years today. Supernovas make stardust, and some of that stardust eventually gets into clouds of gas collapsing to form new stars and planets. That is where the heavy elements in the Sun, a relatively young star, and on Earth came from. The silicon in the computer I am using to write these words was formed inside a star at a temperature of a billion degrees and was later shot out into space when that star exploded. Our Sun will never turn itself inside out in this way—it isn't massive enough. But by the 1960s, it seemed to astrophysicists that even without being able to see inside the Sun, they could describe its structure from the inside outward.

○ THE SUN INSIDE OUT

The structure of the Sun, inferred from astrophysical calculations in the 1950s and 1960s but never probed directly at that time, is described in terms of a series of layers, or shells. The heart of the Sun—the *core,* in which nuclear processes generate energy—extends just one quarter of the distance from the center of the Sun to the surface and

---

*This has recently been confirmed by studies of a supernova that exploded relatively near to us, literally in the galaxy next door to our Milky Way, and was first visible from Earth early in 1987. Even though the Sun itself is *not* destined to become a supernova, this is such an important and exciting development in astronomers' understanding of the way stars work that I have included a detailed discussion of the event, known as SN 1987A, in Chapter 9.

represents only 1.5 percent of the Sun's volume. But this is the region where electrons are stripped from atoms to leave nuclei that are packed together at a density 12 times that of solid lead, even though they behave like the particles of a perfect gas. And half of the mass of the Sun is concentrated in this inner core (the total mass of the Sun is, in round terms, 330,000 times the mass of the Earth, while its radius is 109 times that of the Earth). The temperature inside the core, according to the standard astrophysical models, is 15 million K (the temperature at the outer edge of the core is about 13 million K), and the pressure is three hundred billion times the pressure of the atmosphere at the surface of the Earth. Under these extreme conditions, even a photon (a quantum of radiation, the particle component of light) only travels a fraction of a centimeter before it collides with a charged particle. The photons produced by the nuclear reactions are gamma rays—created out of the mass that is "lost" when four protons form an alpha particle. When these photons are absorbed by charged particles, the energy is promptly reradiated as X rays, and it is as X rays that the energy produced by nuclear fusion in the core begins to make its way outward through the Sun.

It does so very slowly, in one sense, even though each X ray travels at the speed of light. When a photon is absorbed and then reradiated by a charged particle in the hot plasma outside the core, it may be radiated in any direction, at random, including back the way it came. The result is that it moves in an erratic, zigzag path known as a "random walk," with each step in that walk just about one centimeter long, on average. Over a range of one centimeter, there is very little difference in temperature in this part of the Sun, called the *radiation zone*. But that tiny difference ensures that just a few more photons work their way outward than inward at each distance from the center. If a photon could fly in a straight line from the core of the Sun to the surface, its journey would take just 2.5 seconds; in fact, on average it takes a photon 10 million years to get from the core to the surface. During all that time, it has been traveling at the speed of light—so its zigzag path is actually 10 million light-years long. If the zigzag could be straightened out, it would stretch five times farther than the distance to the Andromeda Galaxy, a neighbor of our own Milky Way. Looking at this another way, it means that the conditions on the surface of the Sun today are the conditions that correspond to what the core of the Sun was doing 10 million years ago. We cannot, simply by looking at the Sun's surface, be sure that nuclear reactions have not, in fact, stopped converting hydrogen into helium in the Sun's core sometime during the past few million years.

The radiation zone extends out to about one million kilometers, 85 percent of the distance from the center of the Sun to the surface. All the way out, the plasma is getting cooler and thinner. Halfway from the center of the Sun to the surface, the density is the same as that of water, and two thirds of the way out it has dropped to the density of the air that we breathe. At the outer edge of the radiation zone, the temperature is only about half a million K, and the density of the solar material is just 1 percent that of water (because the dense core is so small, incidentally, the *average* density of the Sun, from the center to the surface, is just one and a half times the density of water). Under these conditions, nuclei can cling to a cloud of electrons, and at the same time the energy of each photon has been degraded, shifting the radiation to longer wavelengths, which interact less violently with the particles. At this point, the atoms of gas are able to absorb the energy of the photons and hang on to it without immediately reradiating it in all directions. The energy they absorb makes the atoms hot—they seethe with energy, dumped at the bottom of the shell known as the *convection zone* by radiation that has, almost literally, run into a brick wall.

The material of the convection zone, heated from below in this way, responds like the water in a pan that is heated from below on a stove. The hot material rises upward through the zone and is replaced by colder material from the surface sinking down into the depths—in other words, living up to its name, it convects (the cooler material that sinks down to complete the convective cycle and replace the rising hot gas has lost its energy by radiating away photons at the surface). This seething activity extends over the last 15 percent or so of the Sun's radius, from a depth of 150,000 kilometers up to the visible surface of the Sun. The convection zone is a bit less than half as thick as the distance from the Earth to the Moon and is thought to consist of three main layers of convection, one on top of the other (Figure 3.6).

The top of the convection zone corresponds to the visible bright surface of the Sun. In this very thin zone called the *photosphere*, the temperature is a mere 5,800K, the pressure is down to one sixth of the atmospheric pressure on Earth, and the density is less than a millionth of the density of water. Under these conditions, atoms can no longer block the flow of radiation outward, and photons stream freely

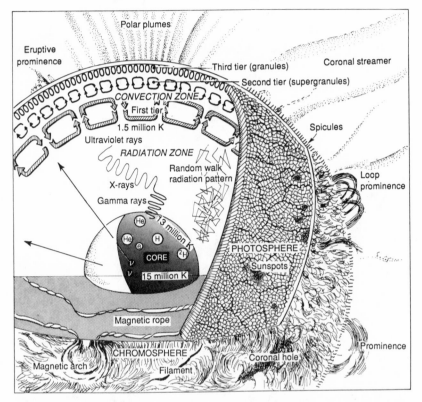

Fig. 3.6. The structure of the Sun, from inside to outside. Adapted from an illustration in *Sun and Earth*, by Herbert Friedman (New York: Freeman, 1986), with permission of the publishers.

out into space. The light we see all comes from this layer, no more than 0.1 percent of the Sun's radius (500 kilometers) deep. The energy in that light has traveled for millions of years at the speed of light on its zigzag journey through the radiation zone, then been carried up in the form of hot gas through the convection zone (at a modest 75 kilometers an hour, but essentially in a straight line) in about 90 days. It then speeds, once again in the form of light, across the 150 million kilometers to the Earth in just over eight and a half minutes.

Until recently, light from the photosphere provided all the information we had about the interior of the Sun. In effect, it told us what the Sun's core was doing ten million years ago. But in the 1970s and 1980s two new techniques were developed, one probing the core itself to find out what it is doing today, and the other "looking" down into the Sun from its surface layers. Those new techniques have shown that the astrophysicists were very nearly right in their calculations of conditions in the solar interior—but they have also revealed new secrets about the workings of the Sun and stars, and provided new mysteries for researchers to puzzle over.

4 TOO FEW
GHOSTS

The cozy picture of steady progress toward a thorough understanding of the way stars work, which had prevailed since the 1920s, was shattered in the second half of the 1960s. It turned out that astronomers might not, after all, understand "so simple a thing," in Eddington's words, as a star—and the embarrassment was compounded because the observations that showed their understanding to be flawed were not made on some distant, faint star that might be expected to be hard to understand, but on the Sun itself, our nearest star and the one we ought to understand best. The first problem, which emerged in 1968 and has remained for twenty years, is that the Sun is producing too few of the ghostly particles called neutrinos—too few, that is, if the standard models of how stars work are correct.

The implications seemed to spread wider the more seriously physicists took the problem, and the longer the experiments continued to show this paucity of solar ghosts; today, this difficulty in understanding what goes on in our own astronomical backyard is seen as part of a major difficulty in understanding the evolution of the Universe at large. Both problems, local and cosmic, may, as we shall see, be solved in one neat package. But first we have to go back sixty years or more, to the late 1920s, when atomic physicists were grappling to understand a puzzle mentioned briefly in Chapter 3—the phenomenon known as beta decay.

○ **THE NEED FOR NEUTRINOS**

In beta decay, the nucleus of an atom emits an electron, which is also known as a beta ray. We now know that in the process a neutron inside the atomic nucleus is converted into a proton—but in the 1920s nobody knew of the existence of neutrons, which are particles with roughly the same mass as the proton (2,000 times the mass of an electron) but which carry no electric charge. Part of the puzzle of beta decay was that it seemed possible for electrons to emerge from atomic nuclei in all kinds of directions, at all kinds of energies, without this being balanced by the recoil of the nucleus itself. This seemed to conflict with the law of conservation of momentum—if an electron shot out of the nucleus in one direction, something else ought to shoot out on the other side, just as a rifle "kicks" when a bullet is fired from it. Nobody could find the missing "other particle" that ought to be carrying momentum away from the nucleus in beta decay, and for a time physicists seriously considered the possibility that the laws of conservation of energy and momentum might not work in atomic nuclei—just as their not so distant predecessors had speculated that energy might not be conserved in radioactive processes. An alternative explanation came from an Austrian-born physicist in 1930 and gradually became accepted as the right answer to the puzzle.

Wolfgang Pauli, born in Vienna in 1900, had a reputation as one of the leading theorists of his day. He obtained his doctorate in 1922 at the University of Munich, and he worked with both Max Born and Niels Bohr in the pioneering days of quantum physics. By 1930, he was professor of physics in the Federal Institute of Technology in Zurich and later he became a Swiss citizen. Pauli was known for his clear thinking—he had made his name as a nineteen-year-old student by producing what was then the clearest account of Einstein's two theories of relativity—and he saw how to cut through the Gordian knot of the beta decay problem. In a letter to Lise Meitner (one of the physicists whose work led to an understanding of nuclear fission), he made the straightforward proposal that the "extra" energy was indeed being carried off by another particle which must be emitted from the nucleus at the same time as the electron observed in beta decay, but which was unobservable by the technology of the day and might never be detected.

This idea was published formally in 1931, but it did not gain much immediate support, in spite of Pauli's reputation. Of course, it looked like too convenient a solution, and we must remember that in 1931, only two fundamental particles, the electron and the proton, were known. "Inventing" a new one was a much bigger step then than it became in later decades when particles seemed to proliferate like rabbits. We can easily imagine other physicists of the day thinking that if theorists invented a new particle every time the experimenters couldn't balance their books, where would physics end up? Besides, Pauli's hypothetical particle seemed too odd to be believed. Not only would it have to have zero charge, it would also have to have scarcely any mass—otherwise it would have been detected already. The only property it was allowed to have, said Pauli, was "spin," a quantum property that is quite different from the concept of spin in everyday life (for example, a quantum object has to rotate completely *twice* to get back to where it started).

He called the particle the "neutron." But the idea had so little impact at first that this name was hijacked in 1932 when the particle we now know as the neutron was discovered. A year later, however, Pauli found an ally in the Italian physicist Enrico Fermi, who suggested the name "neutrino" ("little neutral one") and made the particle respectable by developing a new theory of particle interactions in which the neutrino played an integral part. (It also helped, of course, that the neutron itself had been discovered. If one neutral particle was known to exist, physicists were more willing to accept the possibility that another one might exist as well.)

Fermi's description of beta decay is essentially the same as the modern interpretation. When a neutron decays, it emits both an electron and a neutrino (strictly speaking, an antineutrino), and becomes a proton. The scientific accounting books were kept in balance, and the new understanding of the particle world developed in the wake of Fermi's interpretation of Pauli's insight helped in the development of an understanding, in the late 1930s and beyond, of the nuclear fusion reactions that keep the Sun and stars hot. In all of this theoretical work, the neutrino played a key role and became indispensable.

The existence of the neutrino was not finally proven by experiment until 1956. The reasons are not hard to see—indeed, the surprise is that neutrinos were ever detected at all. Pauli himself considered it so unlikely that in 1931 he offered a case of champagne to any experimenter who successfully took up the challenge, and he seemed to have a safe bet. According to the original concept of the neutrino, it has zero charge, zero mass, and travels at the speed of light (later refinements suggest that it may have a tiny mass and travel at very nearly the speed of light). A neutrino does not interact with other particles through the electromagnetic force that holds molecules together, or through the strong nuclear force that holds nuclei together. Apart from gravity, which has little effect on a particle with so little mass, neutrinos only interact with the rest of the world through what is called the weak nuclear force, introduced by Fermi to explain the behavior of nuclei during decay. This is a very weak interaction indeed—if a beam of neutrinos like those thought to be produced by nuclear reactions inside the Sun were to travel through solid lead for 3,500 light-years, only half of them would be absorbed by the nuclei of the lead atoms along the way.

If the standard theory of how stars work is correct, the nuclear processes going on in the heart of the Sun produce roughly 2×10^{38} neutrinos each second. About one tenth as much energy as we observe in visible light actually emerges from the Sun in the form of neutrinos. But, unlike the visible light, the neutrinos come directly from the heart of the Sun. Only one in a thousand billion of them is absorbed on the way out through the Sun itself, and the Earth, and our own bodies, are virtually transparent to neutrinos. Billions of these ghostly particles are zipping right through you every second, as you read these words, without your body noticing them, or them noticing your body.

So how do you catch a neutrino? You need a big detector (one with lots of atomic nuclei in it, for the neutrinos to have a chance of interacting), and you need a lot of neutrinos (so that even though the chance of any one neutrino interacting is small, out of the billions passing by just a few of them will be stopped by nuclei in your detector). The trick was first achieved beyond any reasonable doubt in 1956 by Frederick Reines and Clyde Cowan. They used a tank containing 1,000 pounds of water placed alongside the Savannah River nuclear reactor in the United States. According to theory, the flood of neutrinos from the nearby reactor crossing the tank of water should have been 30 times greater than the amount of solar neutrinos reaching the detector across 150 million kilometers of space, so there would be just a chance of catching one or two of them in the tank every hour. The reaction that Reines and Cowan actually looked for, during a series of tests they called "Project Poltergeist," was the reverse of beta decay. In this reaction, an antineutrino strikes a proton and converts it into a neutron, while a positron (the antiparticle counterpart of an electron) carries away the positive charge. It was the positrons that the Savannah River experiment actually detected. Hints of the anticipated "neutrino signal" came in 1953, and full confirmation that Pauli's idea was correct came in 1956. Reines and Cowan sent Pauli a telegram informing him of their success; Pauli, in turn, duly paid up on his 25-year-old bet by giving them a case of champagne.

The successful discovery of the neutrino put nuclear physics on a firmer footing than ever before, and gave theorists renewed confidence. It also suggested a new challenge, if any experimenter were brave enough to take it up. If neutrinos—or, at least, events directly attributable to neutrinos—could be detected coming from a nuclear reactor here on Earth, maybe it might be possible, after all, to capture a few of those billions of solar neutrinos that pass by us, and through us, every second. The idea of a "telescope" that would not look at the surface of the Sun, but would provide a direct probe of conditions in the solar interior, caught the imagination of one man, who has since devoted his working life to the hunt for solar neutrinos.

Many theorists dismissed his efforts as a waste of time. They knew how stars worked—the standard model of the Sun told them how hot it was inside, what pressures were encountered there, and what nuclear reactions were going on. It hardly seemed worth the enormous effort of catching a few neutrinos just to prove the theories right. But they were wrong.

○ THE DAVIS DETECTOR

The man who took up the challenge was Raymond Davis, Jr., of the Brookhaven National Laboratory on Long Island. But New York is no place to build a solar neutrino detector. Davis and his colleagues had to build a detector where it would be shielded from everything except solar neutrinos. (There are many other things that can interact with atomic nuclei to make them transmute, notably the cosmic rays—protons, electrons, and other particles striking the Earth from space.) Paradoxically, because only neutrinos pass unaffected through the Earth, that meant burying the new solar telescope deep down a mine,

Fig. 4.1. The neutrino detector deep underground at the Homestake Gold Mine. 400,000 liters of cleaning fluid fill the tank of the "telescope." Photograph supplied by Ray Davis.

where light from the Sun is never seen. Then the detector had to be big, in order to have any hope of capturing even a few out of the enormous number of solar neutrinos passing through each cubic centimeter of its bulk every second.

Beginning in 1964, the experiment was installed 1,500 meters below the ground in the Homestake Gold Mine at Lead, South Dakota. Seven thousand tons of rock had to be removed to make room for the detector, a tank the size of an Olympic swimming pool (Figure 4.1), containing 400,000 liters of perchlorethylene (C_2Cl_4, commonly used as a cleaning fluid in so-called dry cleaning processes). It was the chlorine in the cleaning fluid that Davis planned to use to detect solar neutrinos.

Davis's reasoning behind the choice of detector was as follows. About a quarter of all the chlorine atoms that occur naturally on Earth are in the form of the isotope chlorine-37, each nucleus of which contains 17 protons and 20 neutrons. With four chlorine atoms in every molecule of perchlorethylene, that means that in round terms there is one atom of chlorine-37 for every molecule of cleaning fluid in the tank—about 2×10^{30} potential "targets" for the neutrinos to hit. On the very rare occasions that a neutrino from the Sun does interact with a nucleus of chlorine-37, one of the neutrons in that nucleus is converted into a proton, and an electron is emitted—a kind of forced beta decay. The resulting nucleus now contains 18 protons and 19 neutrons, and "belongs" to the element argon—specifically, the isotope argon-37 (Figure 4.2). This interloper is released from its place in the former perchlorethylene molecule, and as more neutrinos strike their targets argon-37 builds up in the tank of cleaning fluid as a dissolved gas. If the Brookhaven team could count the number of argon-37 atoms in the tank, they would know how many neutrinos have interacted with chlorine nuclei in the tank.

But that is easier said than done, and because argon-37 is itself unstable and decays back into chlorine-37 by capturing an electron, you can't wait forever to let the argon build up in the tank. The half-life of argon-37 is about 34 days, so the tank has to be swept clean of argon, and the atoms counted, every few weeks.

Davis's experiment, and the technique for counting the argon atoms in particular, is one of the most beautiful pieces of work in the whole of physics. People have certainly received Nobel Prizes for less, and even the brief summary that we have room for here is enough to inspire

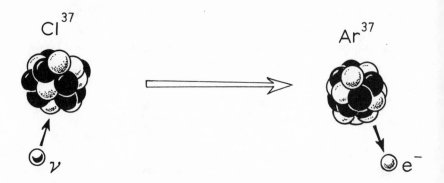

Fig. 4.2. When a neutrino from the Sun interacts with a nucleus of chlorine-37 in the tank at the Homestake Mine, it is turned into a nucleus of argon-37. The Davis detector actually counts the number of argon nuclei produced in this way.

awe. First, the huge tank of cleaning fluid has to be "purged" of argon-37 by bubbling helium gas through the tank. In fact, some inert argon gas, either argon-36 or argon-38, is also added to the fluid to help flush the argon-37 out. The argon atoms (including the argon-37 atoms) mingle with the helium and are carried out of the tank with the gas. They then have to be separated from the helium (a fairly simple technical feat, compared with the rest of the work). Then the Brookhaven team takes advantage of the fact that argon-37 decays back into chlorine-37. When this decay takes place, the atom involved releases a characteristic, precisely defined burst of energy. Automatic counters, shielded from cosmic rays, record every flicker of activity from the argon over a period of up to 250 days and record each pulse that has the appropriate energy "signature." After all that effort, an average of 12 counts are actually recorded in each run of the experiment. It is an astonishing tour de force.

The first results from the experiment emerged in 1968 and seemed to disagree with the predictions of standard solar theory. At that time, nobody was very worried, since it seemed hard to believe that the difficult experiment was really being carried out with sufficient accuracy to be a reliable guide to what was going on inside the Sun.

Confidently, the astrophysicists waited for the experimental figures to "improve" and come in line with the predictions of their theories. But over the past 20 years the experiment has been repeated time and again, and every step of the experiment has been repeatedly tested (for example, by adding a known quantity of argon-37 to the tank and seeing how the detectors respond). Always, the answer is the same. Davis and his colleagues detect only one third of the number of solar neutrinos that theory says they should detect. On average, only one argon-37 atom is produced in the tank every two or three days. The far-reaching implications of this can only be seen by looking at how the theorists made their confident predictions that Davis would actually detect three times as many neutrinos.

○ FORECASTS THAT FAILED

I described in Chapter 3 how energy is produced in stars in general and in the Sun in particular. According to the standard model, less than 2 percent of the Sun's energy is produced by the carbon-nitrogen-oxygen (CNO) cycle; the Sun simply is not hot enough for this process to dominate, even though it happens, through an accident of history, to have been the first stellar nuclear energy source to have been "discovered" in 1938. Most of the Sun's energy, astrophysicists are convinced, comes from the fusion process known as the proton-proton (p-p) chain. It's worth recapping on just how this works, with emphasis on the ways in which this step-by-step fusion of hydrogen nuclei (protons) into helium nuclei (alpha particles) releases neutrinos along the way.

The Sun is made chiefly of hydrogen, and in the heart of the Sun the nuclei of the hydrogen atoms (the protons) are separated from their electrons and travel at high speeds, constantly colliding with and ricocheting off other protons. Occasionally in such a collision two protons will stick together, with one proton releasing a positron and becoming a neutron. The neutron-proton pair is a deuteron, the nucleus of an atom of deuterium, an isotope of hydrogen. Along with the positron, a neutrino is released and passes virtually unhindered out of the Sun and into space. Such neutrinos are referred to as p-p neutrinos, to remind us of their origin; they are no different from other neutrinos, to remind us of their origin; they are no different from other neutrinos produced when protons are converted into neutrons, but have a characteristic energy. The next step in the fusion process occurs when a proton combines with a deuteron to make a nucleus of helium-3; no neutrino is involved in this reaction.

Helium-3 nuclei cannot combine directly with protons, but when two helium-3 nuclei collide, a more complex interaction can take place. *Two* protons are released in the interaction, leaving behind a nucleus of helium-4, which contains two protons and two neutrons. Overall, four protons have been converted into one helium-4 nucleus, with the release of part of the energy that keeps the Sun hot, and two positrons, each accompanied by a neutrino. These are *not* the neutrinos that Davis can detect (they have too little energy to convert Cl-37 in Ar-37).

In all the activity at the heart of the Sun, a helium-3 nucleus and a helium-4 nucleus will occasionally collide to make a nucleus of beryllium-7 (Figure 4.3). Under the conditions in the solar interior, beryllium-7 can do two things. The nucleus might capture an electron and give off a neutrino, becoming an isotope of lithium (the isotope lithium-7) as one of its protons is converted into a neutron by inverse beta decay. Lithium-7 can then capture another proton and split into two helium-4 nuclei (the Cockroft-Walton reaction). Alternatively, the beryllium-7 nucleus might capture a proton first, becoming a nucleus of boron-8, which then decays, in less than a second, giving off a positron and a neutrino to become beryllium-8 and then splitting into two helium-4 nuclei. The neutrinos produced in these reactions (mainly the boron-8 neutrinos) are the ones that Davis can detect. They are only produced rarely, compared with the p-p neutrinos, but they carry much more energy.

The p-p neutrinos do not have enough energy to trigger the conversion of chlorine-37 into argon-37. The beryllium-7 neutrinos have enough energy so that some of them can do the trick; the boron-8 neutrinos have ample energy to make the transmutation take place.

So how many neutrinos should be produced by each process inside the Sun, and how many should Davis detect, according to the standard model? At this stage, theory and experiment combine. Astrophysicists tell the particle physicists what the conditions at the center of the Sun are like, according to the standard model. Experimenters—notably, in this particular story, researchers working at the Kellogg Radiation Laboratory at the California Institute of Technology—accelerate beams of protons, deuterons, and helium-3 and helium-4 nuclei in particle accelerators and watch as they interact, measuring

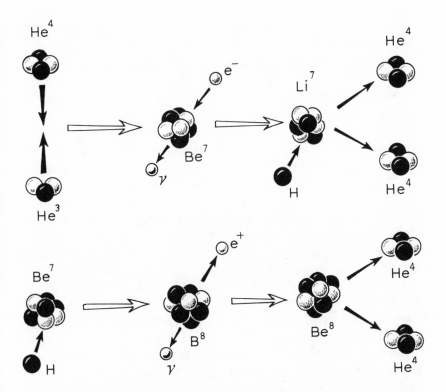

Fig. 4.3. **The neutrinos that Davis detects actually come from a side-reaction to the proton-proton chain. Sometimes in the heart of the Sun a helium-4 nucleus will fuse with a nucleus of helium-4, not another helium-3. This produces beryllium-7, which can follow two different routes, shown here, to becoming two nuclei of helium-4. It is the neutrinos produced in these reactions, mainly the boron-8 neutrinos from the lower chain, that Davis can detect.**

the numbers of the different kinds of nuclei produced. They are able to reproduce—one at a time—the actual reactions that go on in the heart of the Sun, and to measure the efficiency of those reactions in terms of quantities that are known, for obvious reasons, as cross-sections.

Of course, the conditions in the colliding beams are very different from those inside the Sun. Willy Fowler of Kellogg likes to paraphrase

Eddington's famous remark by saying that "what is possible in the Sun is very difficult in the Kellogg Radiation Laboratory." But once the cross-sections are measured over a range of energies, it is possible to extrapolate the figures and to infer the appropriate reaction rates under the conditions of temperature and pressure that, the theorists say, exist inside the Sun.

When Fowler and his colleagues do this, they find that the main p-p reaction should be producing a flood of 60 billion neutrinos crossing each square centimeter of the Earth every second. Unfortunately, none of these has enough energy to be detected by the Davis experiment. The predictions for beryllium-7 and boron-8 neutrinos are very sensitive to the exact temperature fed into the calculations. The standard model of the Sun has a central temperature of 15 million K. For that temperature, there should be 4 billion beryllium-7 neutrinos crossing each square centimeter of the Earth each second, and these should produce five events per *month* in the tank at the Homestake Mine. The figures for the standard model also imply a flux of just 3 million boron-8 neutrinos per square centimeter per second at the tank, but these are so energetic that they should produce 20 events per month. Overall, the Davis experiment should be producing 25 events per month. In fact, over 20 years Davis has found an average of about 9 events per month that can be attributed to solar neutrinos (Figure 4.4).

There is another way of expressing this result, but it boils down to the same thing. Theorist John Bahcall, now of Princeton, has been closely involved in the search for solar neutrinos and has kept tabs on all the possible sources of error in the calculations. (From 1963 onward Bahcall has carried out successively more precise and sophisticated theoretical calculations of the rate at which solar neutrinos should be expected to be observed on Earth, and his work, in 1964, provided the theoretical basis for Davis's confidence that he could build a detector that would indeed "see" solar neutrinos.) For convenience, Bahcall has invented a unit called the "solar neutrino unit," or SNU, for measuring events like those detected by Davis. The standard model predicts that the Davis detector should be recording between about six and eight SNU, allowing for uncertainties in the calculations. The observed events correspond to between two and three SNU. Whichever way you look at it, in round terms the detector sees just one third of the expected number of neutrinos. Why?

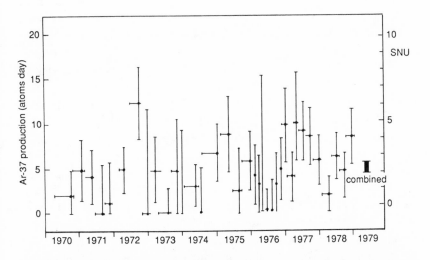

Fig. 4.4. **The first complete decade's worth of solar neutrino measurements, given both in numbers of argon-37 atoms produced and solar neutrino units. The standard solar model predicts a "flux" of 6 to 8 SNU; the measurements showed no more than a third of that. This is the "solar neutrino problem."**

○ DESPERATE REMEDIES

Either we don't understand how neutrinos are made in nuclear reactions or we don't understand how stars work—at least not as well as we thought we did. Any lingering hopes among theorists that there might, after all, be something wrong with the Davis experiment that would let them off the hook were well and truly squashed in 1988, when results from a Japanese detector (actually designed for another purpose, but capable of detecting boron-8 neutrinos from the Sun) confirmed the lack of solar neutrinos. Though by then nobody had really doubted Davis's results, the confirmation was reassuring to the Davis team, even if it left the theorists squirming to decide whether they had to revise their astrophysical theories or the particle physics. These two alternative implications of the results of the Davis experiment—revising either one theory or the other—are so alarming that they have led theorists into an almost desperate search for remedies to the solar neutrino problem. But before we look at some of those wild ideas, it is worth taking at least a crumb of comfort from the one piece of positive news to emerge from the Homestake Mine. I mentioned that the standard model of the Sun predicts that less than 2 percent of the solar energy is generated by the CNO cycle. If all of the Sun's energy were being produced by this cycle, then the predicted neutrino capture rate in the Davis detector would be 25 SNU. This is very definitely not observed, confirming that the theorists at least got that much of the energy generation process right.

Davis's results pose another fundamental question: How reliable have other theoretical calculations been? In the early and middle 1960s, estimates of the neutrino production rate in the Sun were amended as the theorists thought of extra factors that they should include in their calculations. Stimulated by the knowledge that Davis and his team were working on a neutrino detector, they made an intense effort to get their forecasts as accurate as possible, to include every relevant factor, and to use the best computer models of how the Sun was thought to work. Because nobody had made this intense effort before, it took a few years to develop the best possible models. By 1969, however, theorists ran out of "new" effects to include, leaving only the possibility of modest fine tuning of the standard model. The physics has stayed the same since then, and although computer power has improved enormously, the predictions are still around 6 SNU. The only way to shift the figure downward by the required amount is to make a drastic change in the standard model of the Sun.

"Drastic" is, in this case, a relative term. Because the Davis experiment only detects the kind of solar neutrinos whose own production rate is very sensitive to the temperature at the heart of the Sun, the simplest way to bring the theories in line with observations is to set the temperature at the heart of the Sun about 10 percent lower than in the standard models—a little below 14 million K instead of around 15 million K. Eddington would hardly have regarded that as a drastic step. When you recall that his first stab at calculating the temperature at the heart of the Sun gave a figure of 40 million K, only a human lifetime ago, and that this figure was later revised downward to 15 million K, a reduction by another million degrees or so might seem like nothing to worry about. But it is a measure of the sophistication and apparent accuracy of modern models of how stars work that an adjustment in the central temperature of the Sun of a mere 10 percent *cannot* be incorporated within the standard model.

As this realization sank in, astrophysicists tried every imaginable way to produce the necessary change in the structure of the Sun, rejecting each piece of the standard model in turn (sometimes all at once!). A few of these ideas were serious attempts to find out why the standard model does not work for the Sun and to consider how this might affect our understanding of stars in general. Most were what John Bahcall calls "cocktail party solutions," ideas dreamed up (probably over a few drinks) on a "one off" basis to account for the solar neutrino problem alone, without attempting to provide any serious insight into the structure of stars in general.

The more serious proposals included the idea that the Sun might be rotating much more rapidly in its deep interior than it is on the surface. This rapid rotation would help to hold the Sun up against the inward tug of its own gravity and reduce the pressure and temperature at its center. A similar argument proposes that there is a strong magnetic field inside the Sun, resisting compression by gravity. But either of these effects should distort the shape of the Sun, making it oblate (bigger across the equator than from pole to pole) instead of spherical; no such distortions are seen.

Wilder ideas—all of them published in the pages of serious scientific journals—include the possibility that there is a tiny black hole at the heart of the Sun, producing more than half its energy; a suggestion that the Sun formed in two stages and has a core rich in iron surrounded by an "atmosphere" of hydrogen that it gathered up from space at a later date; and (essentially the opposite of that proposal) the idea that the Sun's interior is totally devoid of heavy elements, so that radiation can escape more easily from the center than it can in the standard model.

One of the most intriguing of the desperate remedies to the solar neutrino problem is that the Sun might not be in a "normal" state today. The standard models of the theorists only tell us, after all, about the long-term, average conditions inside the Sun. As Kelvin and Helmholtz appreciated, the Sun need not be in a steady state today. Taking their idea forward, in modern terms, if we were to turn off all the nuclear reactions going on inside the Sun, it could maintain its present brightness for millions of years by shrinking slightly and converting gravitational energy into heat. The Kelvin-Helmholtz idea won't work as an explanation of how the Sun has stayed hot while life has evolved on Earth, but it is still, potentially, a useful buffer mechanism available to smooth out any temporary hiccups in the nuclear energy supply.

Alas, all the ideas put forward to "explain" how the Sun could have gone off the boil temporarily are in the category of cocktail party solutions.

I could go on, but to continue the catalogue of desperate remedies would be pointless. When one of the suggestions put forward is that the constant of gravity itself might be varying as the Universe ages, so that the standard calculations of how the Sun evolved are all wrong, it is surely time to call a halt. Not to all the speculations—when standard ideas fail, speculation becomes an integral part of science.* But constructive speculation has to be compared with observation and experiment to weed out the wilder flights of fancy, and none of the proposed changes in the standard solar model survive this test. In a review published in 1985,† Bahcall mentioned that between 1969 and 1977 he and Davis had kept track of all the new "explanations" of the solar neutrino puzzle as they were published and counted 19 independent ideas of what might be wrong with the standard model. They then gave up keeping detailed track, but "new ideas have been suggested at the rate of 2 or 3 per year since then." When speculation is so unfettered, a different approach to the problem is needed. In the past few years, this has come from the particle physicists, who have put forward several suggestions that, while still speculative, at least have the merit that they can be tested in the not too distant future.

○   **SPECULATIVE SOLUTIONS**

If we understand how stars work, and *if* we have the right numbers for the cross-sections involved in the boron-8 interactions, then there remains one possibility. Perhaps, a few physicists suggested in the 1970s, we don't understand the *neutrinos* as well as we thought we did. Could something be happening to neutrinos on their way to us from the Sun so that even though the "right" number start out, only a third of them are left for Davis to detect by the time they reach the Earth?

---

*Of course, a theory has to be in trouble before speculation is called for—which is why, for example, no scientist takes seriously the many attempts by amateurs to find fault with relativity theory. Any competent physicist at a cocktail party can dream up alternatives to Einstein, but such efforts are as contrived and speculative as the cocktail party solutions to the solar neutrino problem. The difference is that Einstein's theory passes every test, while the standard solar model does not.

†*Solar Physics,* vol. 100, p. 53.

The idea isn't completely crazy, because many particles are now known that do decay in this way, turning into something else after an appropriate interval of time, be it long or short. Even the neutron decays, within a few minutes (if it is not in an atomic nucleus), into a proton and an electron. But there is a slight problem in finding something else for neutrinos to turn into. According to the best modern understanding of the particle world, protons and neutrons are not truly "fundamental" particles, but are composed of another kind of particle, the quarks, which are themselves the most basic building blocks of matter. Electrons, on the other hand, *are* truly fundamental, and never decay; and neutrinos, always associated with electrons, are part of the same family, called leptons. There should be nothing more fundamental for a neutrino to decay into; but perhaps, just possibly, it might turn into another kind of neutrino.

This idea, called "neutrino oscillation," was first suggested in the early 1960s by Soviet and Japanese researchers working independently of one another. The motivation for their speculation goes back to the discovery of a particle called the muon, back in 1936. The muon is similar to the electron but has a mass 200 times greater than the mass of an electron; it is a member of the lepton family, but its place in the particle world remained a mystery until the 1970s. Left alone, a muon will decay into an electron, a neutrino, and an antineutrino within 2.2 microseconds (the remaining mass is converted into energy). The neutrinos, of course, could not be detected in the 1930s, and no significant advance in understanding the muon was made until 1959, when Bruno Pontecorvo, born in Italy but by then working at Dubna in the Soviet Union, and Melvin Schwartz, at Columbia University in the United States, suggested a technique for creating beams of muons, and their associated neutrinos, which was later carried out at CERN and Brookhaven. By 1962 Schwartz and his colleagues had proven that the neutrinos associated with muons are different from those associated with electrons. An electron neutrino, when it strikes a neutron, will always produce a proton plus an electron; a muon neutrino, when it strikes a neutron, will always produce a proton plus a muon.

This was the discovery that led to the suggestion that the electron neutrino might be able to metamorphose. Perhaps, the argument ran, a beam of neutrinos that initially contained only the electron variety might somehow metamorphose into a mixture of muon and electron neutrinos. The implications for the Davis experiment, which can only detect *electron* neutrinos, is clear. The fact that Davis has detected just one third of the expected number of electron neutrinos began to make some sense when in 1975, with the yet another member of the lepton family, the tau particle, was discovered. The "tauon" is just like the electron and muon except that its mass is twice as great as that of a proton. It is generally assumed that there must be a third type of neutrino associated with the tau particle, although this has not yet been confirmed by experiment.

This made for a striking coincidence. If a beam of electron neutrinos somehow became mixed into all three possible varieties, in equal numbers, then exactly one third of the original number of electron neutrinos would be left for detection. Of course, the coincidence would fail if yet more members of the lepton family were discovered; but, as it happens, there are just three principal types of pairs of quark, each associated with one of the three lepton pairs, and physicists now have sound reasons for believing that these are all the kinds of basic particle the Universe has room for.* But there is still the question of *how* a beam of electron neutrinos could metamorphose—a process Reines has likened, graphically, to a dog trotting along the road and transforming itself into a cat as it goes along.

This kind of transformation is, in fact, well known in the particle world, under the right circumstances. The "right circumstances," in fact the crucial factor, is that the particles involved have a little mass— it doesn't have to be very much mass, but it does have to be more than zero. Everyone had always *assumed* that the neutrino mass was precisely zero, but nobody had ever measured it. If you think a little about the difficulty of even detecting a neutrino, let alone weighing it, you'll see why. There are ways to estimate the masses of the neutrinos, however, by measuring the amount of energy they carry away during certain interactions; and in recent years Soviet researchers have consistently claimed that their experiments show that neutrinos do have mass, around 30 electron volts each, 0.006 percent of the mass of an electron. Other researchers disagree—their experiments only set limits on the maximum possible mass a neutrino might have, and these limits are typically around 20 eV. That doesn't mean neutrinos *do* have this mass; it means that there is no way, according to these experiments, that they can have *more* mass, and they might very well have a lot less—even zero mass. Obviously there is a conflict here, and the situation calls for more and better experiments. It is not

*See John Gribbin, *The Omega Point* (London: Heinemann, and New York: Bantam, 1986).

likely to be resolved to everyone's satisfaction in the immediate future, but at least it is possible that neutrinos do have a small mass, and therefore it is possible that they can metamorphose during the 8½ minutes or so it takes for them to travel from the Sun to the Earth. In this picture, each neutrino would be repeatedly changing millions of times every second, and the Davis experiment would only be picking out the ones that happened to be "electron neutrinos" at the moment they hit his tank of cleaning fluid.

Although Pontecorvo, and Masami Nakagawa in Japan, had suggested years before that electron and muon neutrinos (the only two kinds known in the 1960s) might change form in this manner, it took the impetus of the discovery of the tauon, and growing concern about the solar neutrino problem, to push experimenters into trying to measure the hypothetical effect in the early 1980s. The man who took up the challenge was an old hand at spotting neutrinos—Frederick Reines. Working now with Henry Sobel and Elaine Pasierb, he went back to the scene of his earlier triumph at the Savannah River reactor and tried to find out if the electron neutrinos produced in the reactor were changing into other varieties as they sped along. The test they used depended on the different way different neutrinos interact with nuclei of heavy water (deuterium oxide) placed in a tank 11.2 meters from the core of the reactor.

Some nuclear reactions involving electron neutrinos produce two neutrons in these interactions, but reactions involving other kinds of neutrinos produce only a single neutron each time. Some of the electron neutrinos also give rise to single neutrons, just to confuse the picture, but Reines and his colleagues were confident that by careful analysis they could deduce what proportion of electron neutrinos (if any) had changed into other varieties on the brief flight to their detector. They claimed to have found evidence of this effect in the spring of 1980. But these claims have not stood up to detailed scrutiny. Other experiments show no sign of the neutrino metamorphosing at work, and like the Soviet claims of measurements of neutrino mass, the suggestion that Reines and his team really have observed neutrino oscillations is at best controversial. But at least the idea can be tested in principle.

So things stood until the spring of 1986. Then an old hand at the solar physics game suddenly reappeared on center stage. Hans Bethe, back in 1938, had worked out, with Charles Critchfield, the details of the p-p chain that keeps the Sun hot. Now he took up and publicized a proposal to solve the solar neutrino problem developed by two Soviet researchers, S. P. Mikheyev and A. Yu. Smirnov, on the basis of a suggestion made by a U.S. physicist, Lincoln Wolfenstein. The human interest of a scientist coming back almost fifty years later to a field of research he had pioneered caught the imagination of scientists and popularizers alike and assured that this new version of the neutrino oscillation idea received a blast of publicity.

The key to the Mikheyev-Smirnov-Wolfenstein (MSW) variation on the neutrino theme is that the transformation of electron neutrinos into some other variety might occur *inside* the Sun, as a result of an interaction between the neutrinos and the material of which the Sun is made. Once again, some of the neutrinos involved have to have mass. But this time, it turns out, the mass must be tiny; and the electron neutrino itself need not necessarily have mass. According to the MSW model, electron neutrinos do experience a very weak interaction with solar particles on their way out of the Sun. The effect of this is to increase the energy being carried by the neutrinos, and since mass and energy are interconvertible this is equivalent to increasing their mass— but not by much. Provided that the mass of an electron neutrino is increased above that of a muon neutrino, the electron neutrino will decay into a muon neutrino. The muon neutrino, however, once formed, does not, in this picture, change back into an electron neutrino.

The amount of mass-energy that an electron neutrino can pick up in this way depends on the density of matter in the Sun, and that mass-energy is very small. This limits the possible range of masses of the neutrinos, if the effect is to work. Specifically, the mass of the electron neutrino must be essentially zero and the mass of the muon neutrino must be no more than about 0.01 electron volts. This might seem as implausible and contrived as any of the cocktail party "solutions" to the solar neutrino problem, except for the fact that there is a class of theories which predict that neutrinos ought to have masses in the range from about 0.00001 to 100 eV. They are called "seesaw" models and represent one of the many attacks by theorists on the problem of finding one mathematical framework in which to describe all of the material world—a grand unified theory. But there are other versions of grand unified theories, or GUTs, and the seesaw model is by no means the most favored these days, so this doesn't really mean a lot.

What really seems to have cast doubt on the MSW interpretation of the Davis experiment, however, is something that happened long ago in a galaxy far, far away.

○ COSMIC CONNECTIONS

Early in 1987, as we will see in Chapter 9, astronomers detected an outburst of light from a star in the Large Magellanic Cloud (LMC), a small galaxy that is a neighbor of the Milky Way. A star in the Large Magellanic Cloud had exploded as a supernova, which became known as Supernova 1987A. The distance to the Large Magellanic Cloud is 160,000 light-years, which means that as measured on Earth, the light of the explosion as we see it has been 160,000 years on its journey across space to us. This is the closest supernova to have been observed since telescopes were invented on Earth, and it has been the subject of intense scrutiny and debate. It was also the first supernova to have been detected not only by its visible light, but by the neutrinos that were produced during the explosion.

Two experiments in different parts of the world recorded neutrino bursts now interpreted as due to the supernova. At Kamiokande in central Japan, a research team is using a tank containing 2,140 tonnes of water as part of of a program attempting to determine whether protons decay. The detector is also very sensitive to neutrinos (indeed, this is the detector that has confirmed the accuracy of the Davis experiment), provided they have certain energies, and when news of the supernova came in, the Japanese team searched back through the records and found that it had "observed" a burst of 11 neutrino events, spread over a period of 13 seconds, with energies in the range from 7.5 to 36 mega electron volts (MeV). A similar detector near Cleveland, Ohio, is being operated by the University of California-Irvine, the University of Michigan, and by the Brookhaven National Laboratory. They, too, found a pulse of neutrinos at the right time—eight events spread over six seconds, with energies in the range from 30 MeV to 100 MeV (these energies far exceed those of solar neutrinos, which cannot be detected by these detectors). The similarity of the results from the United States and Japan, plus the fact that most of the neutrinos arrived in the first second of the pulse, has convinced scientists that these really were neutrinos from Supernova 1987A. And the tightness of the burst sets definite limits on neutrino mass.

If neutrinos have zero mass, then they all travel at the speed of light and would arrive together even after a journey as long as 160,000 years. But if neutrinos have mass—even if they all have the same mass—then the speed at which they travel will depend on their energy. Just as a baseball hit more powerfully will fly faster through the air, the neutrinos given the biggest boost in the supernova explosion will travel more quickly and arrive first. The effect is more pronounced if the neutrinos have more mass; the fact that several neutrinos with different energies arrived within a second of each other after a journey of 160,000 light-years shows that their mass must be less than 15 eV, the best limit yet set. This, of course, conflicts with the Soviet claims, but it is consistent with the neutrinos having zero mass, or having the tiny mass needed to make the MSW trick work. But at least one researcher, Ramanathan Cowsik from the Tata Institute in Bombay, thinks he can take things a step further.

At a meeting of astronomers in Hungary in June 1987, Cowsik suggested that instead of there being one pulse of neutrinos from the supernova, spread out over about 13 seconds, there were actually two pulses, separated by a few seconds. If that interpretation is correct, then a simple physical argument implies that one of the pulses represents the arrival of electron neutrinos, and these neutrinos have a mass of about 4 eV each; the other pulse would be either all muon or all tauon neutrinos, and each neutrino in that pulse would have a mass of 22 eV. And that would completely pull the rug from under the MSW hypothesis. According to Cowsik, there is only a one in five possibility that the pattern of neutrinos that was seen arose by chance and that neutrinos do not have these masses.

What this interpretation takes away from astronomy with one hand (a "solution" to the solar neutrino problem), it gives back with the other. If the mass of a set of the neutrinos, one of each type, adds up to more than 1.4 eV, then the total mass of all the neutrinos in the Universe would add up to more than the mass of all the bright stars in all the visible galaxies put together (because there are so many neutrinos). Some astronomers welcome this notion, since there is now an overwhelming weight of evidence that bright stars and galaxies make up less than 10 percent of all the matter in the Universe and that some form of "dark matter" is needed to hold things together gravitationally.*

At present, the Universe is expanding, with galaxies moving farther apart as time passes. One of the big questions in cosmology today is whether this expansion will go on forever or whether it will one day

*See *The Omega Point*.

reverse and become a contraction, as the gravitational pull of all the matter in the Universe overcomes the expansion. There is nowhere near enough bright matter visible to do the job, but a combined mass of 25 eV for all three neutrino types would suffice. There are simply so many neutrinos around that even such a tiny mass for each of them would add up to 100 times the mass of all the stars and galaxies put together.

So studies of relatively local events in our own cosmic backyard—the solar neutrino problem—have a major bearing on our understanding of such deep cosmic questions as the ultimate fate of the Universe. It is more important than was ever appreciated before that the solar neutrino problem be resolved, and at last there is the prospect, as we move into the 1990s, of a new generation of detectors to investigate the many neutrinos from the Sun that cannot be studied by the Davis detector, which has done such sterling work for two decades.

○ FUTURE PROJECTS

Solar neutrino astronomy today needs a new experiment—preferably several new experiments. There is just one substantial set of data, from just one experiment, and this tells us only that there are neutrinos arriving at the Earth. The Kamiokande detector confirms that the Davis experiment is working properly, but it adds no new information. Strictly speaking, since the Davis detector cannot tell which direction the neutrinos are coming from, we don't actually even know that it is detecting *solar* neutrinos, although this scarcely seems in doubt, since no other permanent cosmic source is within range. There are still ways in which more information might be gleaned by this experiment. For example, it already seems to show hints that the number of neutrinos recorded in the tank depends on the activity of the Sun and varies over the 11-year "sunspot cycle." This is a totally unpredicted result, which is very hard to explain, since neutrinos are thought to come from the secret heart of the Sun, while sunspots are a surface phenomenon.

We shall go into more detail about the nature of sunspots in Chapter 6. But to get ahead of my story a little, what matters here is that dark spots come and go over the surface of the Sun with a cycle roughly 11 years long. It is not *quite* a crazy idea that there might be more solar neutrinos detected on Earth when there are more sunspots, because the spots are associated with increased magnetic activity in the

Sun, and the changing magnetic activity might influence the kind of neutrino oscillations I have already mentioned. On the other hand, if that is the case, then occasional outbursts on the Sun, called flares, which are also associated with magnetic activity, would also increase the number of detectable neutrinos. But a search made by the Kamiokande team covering the period from July 1983 to July 1988 shows no significant neutrino signals at the time of solar flares. Another possibility is that solar cosmic rays, energetic particles produced by the Sun, might be producing neutrinos through interactions that take place in the atmosphere of the Earth. John Bahcall, however, believes that the apparent correlation between sunspots and solar neutrinos (Figure 4.5) is a fluke. Statistical tests, he says, show that a correlation as strong as this can occur purely by chance in 2 percent of the cases where random sets of data are placed alongside each other. And he points out that many important things in our lives, such as the sequence of events that leads to our first meeting with our spouses, have a probability of less than 2 percent. Such rare events certainly do happen! Ray Davis, on the other hand, believes that the correlation is real— and, echoing Pauli's famous bet but in a more modest way, Bahcall and Davis have a bottle of champagne wagered on the outcome of further tests of this coincidence.

Those tests are now being made. The Sun's activity was rising to a peak late in 1989, and it will be in decline again after about 1992, when you are reading these words. Observations up to about 1995 should provide the definitive test of this strange correlation. That alone would be sufficient reason to keep the Davis detector running. But it is hard to see any dramatic new breakthrough coming from the swimming pool of cleaning fluid.

Some researchers have suggested searching the records or making new observations, to try to find out if more neutrinos arrive when the Sun is overhead, in the daytime, than at night. Again, there shouldn't be any effect—neutrinos are *supposed* to pass through the solid Earth as if it were not there. But if solar neutrinos don't match up to predictions in some ways, it may be worth testing what ''everybody knows'' about their ability to pass through the Earth. Some variations on the MSW idea, in fact, would suggest that oscillations occur inside the Earth and might produce a measurable daily effect. But such tests are pushing beyond the limits of the Homestake neutrino ''telescope.''

There is, however, no shortage of proposals for new kinds of neutrino telescopes, detectors using technology that was either too ex-

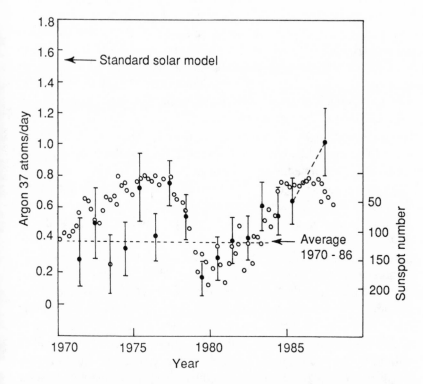

Fig. 4.5. **With nearly twenty years of solar neutrino data (dark spots), it looked as if there might be a correlation with sunspot number (open circles). Observations over the next few years should tell us whether this is a real effect or not.**

pensive or too difficult to contemplate in the 1960s. If Davis had found exactly the expected number of neutrinos, then most of these ideas would still be regarded as too expensive or too difficult to bother with. It is because of the puzzles raised by Davis's twenty years of observations that it now seems worthwhile—even urgent—to measure the energies of neutrinos, the directions they are coming from, and the types of the neutrinos themselves. I know of at least 12 different types of experiment now proposed to measure at least some of these properties of solar neutrinos. Each of the 12 techniques could be applied in several different ways. I will only mention the few possibilities that seem to have a realistic chance of becoming operational in the next few years.

The next logical step is to build a detector that will respond to the lower energy neutrinos produced in vast quantities by the p-p reaction. The front-runner for this kind of detection is likely to be some variation on the idea of an experiment using gallium to capture the neutrinos. The experiment is simple in principle and depends on the fact that when an electron neutrino interacts with a nucleus of gallium-71, the nucleus is transformed into one of germanium-71 and an electron is emitted. Without going into details here, chemists are happy that they can count the number of germanium atoms produced, using techniques that are conceptually similar to those used by Davis to count argon atoms. The great advantage of gallium-71 is that it interacts with p-p neutrinos. The immediate snag with a gallium detector is its cost; a secondary problem is that it might give an ambiguous answer to our questions about solar neutrinos.

Gallium itself is a metal with a very low melting temperature. If you hold a lump of it in your hand, it melts into a shiny puddle, like a little pool of mercury. It is also a very valuable metal, already used in the electronics industry to make light-emitting diodes (LEDs), the familiar little red lights on calculators and other pieces of electronic equipment. Moreover, by the time this book is in print, gallium arsenide may be a commonly used semiconductor, providing a generation of electronic equipment faster than the present one. All that makes gallium useful and desirable to modern industry. But it is also rare—less than 100 tons of gallium are produced each year, and a good solar neutrino detector would need at least 30 tons, perhaps as much as 60 tons, all to itself. The cost of the gallium for the detector alone would be between five and ten *million* dollars, at present prices—but, as the scientists have been quick to point out, you could always sell it to the electronics industry after you had finished with it!

Both Soviet researchers and a collaborative European team are planning such projects, and it had been hoped that by detecting p-p neutrinos a gallium experiment would solve the puzzle of why Davis detects only one third of the expected number of neutrinos. According to the standard model, such a detector should "see" about 120 SNU of neutrinos, with about 70 percent coming from the p-p process and most of the rest from the beryllium-7 interaction. If the new detector actually finds one third of the predicted number of neutrinos, that will certainly suggest that neutrinos are oscillating between the three types en route from the Sun to the Earth, since the p-p process is not very sensitive to the temperature at the heart of the Sun. But if the p-p neutrinos are present in about the predicted quantities, that could be explained in either of two ways. It might mean that there are problems with the astrophysics that influence only the Davis neutrinos (such as a central solar temperature 10 percent below that of the standard model). That would affect boron-8 neutrinos but not p-p neutrinos. Or it could still leave room for the MSW type of mixing of neutrino types *inside* the Sun, since that process may itself only work for high-energy neutrinos.

Another proposal involves using the metal indium instead of gallium to detect solar neutrinos. Norman Booth of Oxford University has plans for an experiment using a ton of indium-115, which should catch one solar neutrino every three or four days. When that happens, a nucleus of indium-115 is converted into tin-115 and an electron is released. Because the tin is created with excess energy—in an excited state—it immediately falls back into its most stable state by emitting two photons (gamma rays) that can be detected relatively easily. This technique has the advantage that the gamma-ray flashes signaling the arrival of neutrinos will be detected instantly, in "real time," as the neutrinos arrive, instead of experimenters having to wait for days or weeks before doing the equivalent of flushing out the tank and counting the number of neutrinos that arrived over a long period of time. It has the disadvantage that indium-115 is naturally radioactive, and a ton of the stuff will emit 200,000 electrons every second. But Booth thinks he can get around the problem of this huge "background" of electrons that threatens to swamp his detectors.

At the other extreme from Booth's approach, at least in terms of size, comes a series of proposals that depend on the fact that neutrinos can simply bounce off electrons—scattering, as it is called—and give up energy to the electrons. Such an event is rare, but if you have enough electrons in a detector, with enough neutrinos passing through, it is bound to happen occasionally. Build a big enough tank of almost anything, since all atoms contain electrons, and some of the solar neutrinos passing through will give energy to some of the electrons in the tank. "All" you have to do is capture the fast-moving electrons and work out where the scattering took place—feats that are far from easy but are routine for physicists who work with fundamental particles. The detectors that "found" neutrinos from Supernova 1987A work in this way, but have not yet been capable of detecting neutrinos at the lower energies typical of those coming from the Sun. The advantages of the technique are that it works in real time, recording the neutrinos as they arrive, and that in principle it is possible to work out both the energy and the direction of the incoming neutrinos. The disadvantage is the enormous amount of material you need. One proposal, involving 6,600 tons of liquid argon placed in a tank in the Gran Sasso Tunnel under the Alps, might be able to do the trick. The experiment is called ICARUS (a tortuous anagram for Imaging Cosmic and Rare Underground Signals), and it would be able to measure the energies of the electrons and thereby infer the energies of the incoming neutrinos.

This proposal is worth picking out for special mention because one of the physicists involved is John Bahcall, the world's authority on the theory of solar neutrino interactions. According to his calculations, the detector should "find" 4,700 solar neutrinos per year and would be able, he claims, to confirm (or refute) the accuracy of the standard solar model in just one day of operation.

The argument is disarmingly simple. According to standard theory, the electrons monitored in the ICARUS detector should have energies (gained from solar neutrinos) distributed evenly around a peak of 5 MeV; in other words, there would be the same number of neutrinos at 3 MeV, for example, as at 7 MeV. But any version of neutrino oscillations will shift the distribution of energies, either up or down, depending on which detailed theory you prefer. If ICARUS finds very few electrons on one side of the peak (which side doesn't matter), that will be a sure sign that oscillations are at work and would imply that the standard model of the Sun is correct and it is the neutrinos themselves that are playing tricks.

There are still other ways of detecting the arrival of solar neutrinos in the lab. Blas Cabrera of Stanford University is working on what is known as a bolometric detector. This relies on the simplest concept of all, the fact that when a neutrino interacts with the nucleus of an atom it produces an electron with a lot of energy. Instead of trying to detect the electron itself, however, Cabrera plans to measure the energy indirectly, from the rise in temperature of the detector that results. This is only possible if the detector is cold to start with and its atoms are arranged in a solid crystal. Then, when the emitted electron flies out of one nucleus, it collides with other nearby atoms, jostling them into a tiny vibration. This shaking of the atoms is equivalent to a rise in temperature—cold atoms move about only a little bit, hot atoms move about a lot. So if you start out with a very cold crystal of, say, silicon, and it is struck by a neutrino whose energy is absorbed, there ought to be a tiny rise in temperature of the silicon crystal. The trick is measuring this tiny rise in temperature—you certainly have to be operating the whole thing at temperatures close to absolute zero, a few K, where helium is a liquid.

Cabrera's step-by-step approach to the problem involves plans to build first a prototype detector using a kilogram of silicon, and study the way it responds to being bombarded with energetic particles and X rays. Then he hopes to build a larger detector, perhaps containing 100 kilograms of silicon, and to place it alongside a nuclear reactor to see how it responds to neutrinos. Only then will he be ready to proceed with a full-sized solar neutrino experiment involving 10 tons of silicon.

That timetable gives you some idea of how long it is likely to be before any definitive new data on solar neutrinos come in. A gallium detector, ICARUS, or the Cabrera bolometer could be operating in the early 1990s, if funds become available. More exotic ideas could really pin down the overall distribution of solar neutrinos at different energies (their spectrum) but are scarcely even on the drawing board yet. They are unlikely to be applied in practice until the twenty-first century. And, in spite of the optimistic claims made for ICARUS, somehow it seems unlikely that one day of operation will suffice to solve the puzzle. In 1966, many physicists (maybe including Bahcall) would have told you that only a month of observation with the Davis detector would suffice to confirm the accuracy of the standard solar model!

After two decades of puzzling over the results from the Homestake Mine, maybe the prospect of waiting another five or ten years for the next insight into solar neutrinos ought to be bearable. When such costly, long-term projects are planned, however, it is the duty of the theorists to try as best they can to predict what the experiments will find. Just as the advent of the Davis experiment itself concentrated the minds of astrophysicists, in the 1960s, on refining their calculations of the standard model, so the plans for a new generation of detectors cry out for the astrophysicists to make testable predictions of what those detectors might find. There is also the challenge, for theorists, of using their ingenuity to find a satisfactory solution to the solar neutrino problem that does not require spending years of effort and millions of dollars building detectors deep down holes in the ground, but which (unlike the cocktail party solutions) does relate what is going on inside the Sun to what is going on inside other stars and in the Universe at large.

Observational astronomy can also help. In the 1980s, while physicists have struggled with their designs for neutrino detectors and made technological progress toward a new generation of experiments, astrophysicists and astronomers have not been idle. They, too, have improved their instruments and their techniques, gaining new insight into the nature of the Sun and finding new ways to probe the secrets of its interior. Those new insights suggest that some of the cocktail party discussion of the solar neutrino puzzle may not have been so crazy after all. In order to see why, we have to go back to 1977, when the solar neutrino problem was less than ten years old and cocktail party solutions were a dime a dozen, to pick up the threads of what seemed at the time to be just another wild idea about what might be going on in the heart of the Sun.

5 ANOTHER WILD IDEA

John Faulkner is a british-born astrophysicist, now resident in California, where he works at the Santa Cruz campus of the University of California and at the Lick Observatory. An acknowledged expert on the physics of stellar interiors, he made his scientific name in the 1960s for research into the way stars evolve when they contain two sources of nuclear energy, with helium burning into carbon in their cores while a shell of hydrogen is still burning into helium outside the core. These calculations explained the appearance of what are known as "horizontal branch" stars,* fitting into place the last main piece of the puzzle of how stars evolve. When researchers began to be interested in the possibility that there might be "new" kinds of particles in the Universe and that the presence of these particles might affect the way stars evolve, it was natural for Faulkner to become involved in these speculations, in the latter half of the 1970s. But at first nobody thought that the speculations might be relevant to the story of solar neutrinos.

At that time, many astronomers were beginning to take seriously the idea that there might be a lot more matter in the Universe than we

---

*The name comes from the location of these stars in a diagram that relates the brightness of a star to its color. It is called the Hertzsprung-Russell, or H-R, diagram, after the two astronomers who developed this method of classification. Stars like the Sun, burning hydrogen in their hearts, lie in a band on the diagram known as the main sequence. Red giants and white dwarfs occupy their own regions of the diagram.

can see. Bright stars, and galaxies containing billions of bright stars, had to be the main focus of astronomical attention over the years, because only bright objects could be studied directly, by the light that reaches our telescopes. But ever since the 1930s there had been a suspicion among many astronomers, and a deeply felt belief among a few, that there is more to the Universe than meets the eye. Studies of the way in which stars move in a galaxy like our own, and studies of the way galaxies in groups (called clusters of galaxies) are moving suggest that they are being tugged by gravitational forces that are stronger than the combined gravity of all the visible bright stars added together. There must be dark matter in the Universe, as well as the bright stuff. But what was the dark matter, and where did it congregate?

The dark matter is sometimes referred to as "missing mass"—a name that has gone out of favor as astronomers have persuaded themselves, during the 1980s, that the matter really is there, and it is the light that is "missing." At first the natural assumption was that this dark matter might be in the form of very faint stars, or clouds of gas that had not condensed to form stars, or even planetlike objects, enormous numbers of "Jupiters" spread throughout the Galaxy. But in the 1970s new developments in particle physics led to the daring new suggestion that some, or all, of the "missing mass" might be found in the form of particles never detected in any laboratory on Earth and left over from the Big Bang in which the Universe was born.

○ **THE PARTICLE CONNECTION**

Particle physicists had no idea, at first, that their new theories might have cosmic repercussions. They were interested in developing a unified set of equations that would describe the behavior of all of the four forces of nature (gravity, electromagnetism, and the strong and weak nuclear interactions) in one package. A first, and major, step along the road to such a theory of everything (TOE) had been made by combining electromagnetism and the weak interaction into one package, the electroweak theory. But some versions of this theory required the existence of a new kind of particle in the Universe—a particle even more massive than the proton. The specific particle envisaged in calculations of this kind carried out in 1977 was a kind of heavy neutrino. That proposal has since fallen from favor as these theories have been improved, and has been replaced by other candidates for dark matter particles; but it provided the impetus to set some astrophysicists thinking along new lines. Such a particle could never be manufactured in accelerators on Earth, like those at CERN in Geneva or Fermilab in Chicago. The energy E required to manufacture particles with mass m several times bigger than the mass of a proton, in line with Einstein's equation $E = mc^2$, simply is not available. But astronomers have very good evidence that the Universe itself was born, about 15 billion years ago, out of a state of superdensity and superheat, the Big Bang.* The energy available in the Big Bang was ample to make vast numbers of these hypothetical particles—indeed, it is energy from the Big Bang, converted into mass in line with Einstein's equation, that is locked up in the form of protons, neutrons, and electrons in all stars, planets, and your own body today. If protons and neutrons could be left over from the Big Bang, then so could these other heavy particles. If there were enough of them around, their gravitational influence could add up to explain the way stars and galaxies move, and perhaps could even help to explain how galaxies had formed from collapsing clouds of gas in the first place. But what effect would the presence of such particles have on the behavior of stars themselves?

Faulkner's interest in the problem was hooked during a visit to the U.S. National Radio Astronomy Observatory in Green Bank, West Virginia, in 1977. There he met up with other astronomers interested in various aspects of the cosmic implications of the presence of a previously unrecognized form of heavy particles in the Universe. Three of those researchers, Gary Steigman, Craig Sarazin and H. Quintana, joined forces with Faulkner in a study of the way in which the presence of such particles would affect the evolution of the Universe at large, the formation of galaxies, the behavior of galaxies once they had formed, and the behavior of stars. They concluded that particles with masses between twice and twenty times the mass of the proton could represent "a dynamically significant component of the mass density of the Universe" and that they "would have all the required properties to form the 'missing mass' in clusters of galaxies, and galactic halos."†

The effect of these heavy particles on stars, though, seemed to be small, since it turned out that very few of the particles would collapse along with the hydrogen and helium in the clouds from which stars form—the dark matter particles stay spread out over a large spherical

*The evidence is summarized in my book *In Search of the Big Bang*.
†*Astronomical Journal*, vol. 83, p. 1050.

region surrounding a Galaxy like our own (the "halos" mentioned by the team). This is all to the good, since we know that the dark matter, whatever it is, is spread out and not concentrated inside the visible stars. But Faulkner had become intrigued by the possibility that even a few of these particles accumulating in the core of the Sun might change its structure just enough to account for the deficiency of neutrinos recorded by the Davis experiment. After all, it only needs an adjustment of 10 percent in the temperature given by the standard solar model to resolve the neutrino problem. Back at Santa Cruz, he enlisted the help of a research student, Ron Gilliland, to carry the calculations through. Sure enough, the trick worked. Adding heavy particles to the heart of the Sun *could* cool it enough to reduce the flow of neutrinos to match the measurements made by Davis. But Faulkner's colleagues were far from enthusiastic at the idea of including yet another cocktail party solution to the solar neutrino problem in their joint paper. Grudgingly, they allowed Faulkner to include a brief summary of his work with Gilliland at the end of subsection *c* of section five of the paper, just above the conclusions. The last sentence of the paper ended, "one could solve the solar neutrino problem without seriously affecting other aspects of stellar evolution." But nobody, not even Faulkner, thought at the time that this was the most important aspect of the joint paper. And although during 1978 Faulkner and Gilliland got as far as writing up a detailed account of their work, ready to present to the world in the form of an article published in a scientific journal, they received so much flak from their colleagues about the stupidity of the whole notion that they gave up the idea. The draft article was quickly buried under an accumulation of other paper in Faulkner's office at Santa Cruz and was soon forgotten. Steigman became convinced that new arguments ruled out the existence of heavy neutrinos (the whole basis of the original collaboration) anyway, and although Faulkner sometimes gave the idea an airing at scientific meetings the response was generally sufficiently unenthusiastic to discourage him from pressing the case—even though he now fondly recalls that one of the few people who actually liked the idea in the early 1980s was Nobel laureate Murray Gell-Mann.

But while Faulkner's enthusiasm for the idea was being quashed by his colleagues, in the world of particle physics theorists were, in the early 1980s, being forced ever more firmly to the conclusion that some form of "extra" particles must exist in the Universe, even if these particles are not heavy neutrinos. And at the same time astronomers

were finding more and more evidence of dark matter exerting its gravitational influence across the Universe. It was only a matter of time
before someone else combined the two sets of ideas. That someone
was William Press of the Harvard-Smithsonian Center for Astrophysics, who, with his colleague David Spergel, followed up the implications in the mid-1980s. Neither Spergel nor Press had read the 1978
paper in which the calculations made by Faulkner and Gilliland had
briefly been summarized, nor had they happened to be at any of the
meetings where Faulkner had tried to rouse interest in the idea since.
Quite independently, and starting from scratch, they developed their
own calculations of how such massive particles, which they called
cosmions, might affect the behavior of the Universe at large, galaxies,
and individual stars. And they, too, found that the presence of such
particles inside the Sun might solve the solar neutrino problem.

○ COSMIONS ARE WIMPS

Faulkner and Gilliland's work and Press and Spergel's are essentially
the same. The Harvard team avoided one mistake made by Faulkner
and his colleagues, however, by resisting the temptation to nail their
theory to the existence of one particular kind of "new" particle. A
theory based on the existence of massive neutrinos looks very silly,
as Steigman realized, if evidence comes in that massive neutrinos do
not exist; but by 1985 the particle theorists were invoking a plethora
of new particles to go along with various ideas about how the forces
of nature might be unified into a TOE. The underlying point is that
whichever theory turns out to be right, there will be room for *some*
form of extramassive particle. So don't specify which one you are
invoking in your astronomical calculations—just give it a catch-all
name, like cosmion.

Unfortunately, cosmion is not such a good catch-all name, since it
doesn't make the connection with developments in particle physics
theory clear. In fact, the astronomical observations *specify* what kind
of particle must be out there filling the role of missing mass, and that
tells the particle theorists what they should be looking for in their
calculations (the solar studies, as we shall see, even pin down the mass
of the particle). The term that most theorists prefer now is an acronym
based on a description of the important properties that any such hypothetical cosmion must have. It must be weakly interacting, in the

sense that it does not "feel" the strong nuclear force, otherwise such particles would be destroyed by nuclear interactions; and it must have mass, in order for it to produce a gravitational force and play the role of dark matter in galaxies. So it is known as a weakly interacting massive particle, or WIMP.

Where do WIMPs come from? There are still several detailed possibilities, and they cannot all be right. My own preference is for the idea that the existence of WIMPs in the Universe is intimately connected to the existence of everyday matter, the protons and neutrons (collectively known as baryons) of which we are made (we can leave electrons out of the discussion for now, since they have so little mass compared with protons, neutrons, or WIMPs). And this can best be understood in terms first expressed by the Soviet physicist Andrei Sakharov in the 1960s.

The puzzle Sakharov addressed was why, if the Big Bang theory is correct, should there be any matter in the Universe at all? In the Big Bang itself, energy was in the form of radiation at very high temperatures. At such high temperatures, the energy in electromagnetic radiation (photons) can convert directly into pairs of particles— an electron and a positron, a proton and an antiproton, a neutron and an antineutron. Almost all tests that can be carried out in terrestrial laboratories show that this kind of mass-energy interchange obeys a basic law of symmetry, that particles and antiparticles are created together. Because a baryon that meets its antibaryon counterpart annihilates in a puff of energy, leaving no particle behind, making particle-antiparticle pairs does not, in a very real sense, add to the number of baryons in the Universe. If each baryon counts for $+1$ and each antibaryon counts for -1, each particle-antiparticle pair adds precisely zero to the number of baryons in the Universe.

If this law of nature operated precisely in the Big Bang itself, then at a later stage, when the Universe had cooled down from its hot beginning, every baryon would, sooner or later, meet up with its antibaryon partner and be annihilated. After 15 billion years, we would be left with a Universe full of energy, but no matter at all.

Sakharov pointed out that there must have been processes at work very early in the history of the Universe that selectively produced a surplus of baryons over antibaryons when matter was created out of energy. Like many insights of pure genius, this seems obvious—

once somebody has spelled it out for you (and, of course, I have made it look even simpler by leaving out the mathematics that surrounds this neat insight and puts it on a secure scientific footing). Astronomers actually know how much radiation there is in the Universe today. They can monitor a weak hiss of radio noise, coming from all directions in space and known as the cosmic background radiation. This radiation is what is left of the fireball of the Big Bang after it has been cooling for 15 billion years; it fills the entire Universe and now has a temperature of just under 3 K (less than $-270°C$), which corresponds to the presence of just 488 photons in every cubic centimeter of space throughout the Universe. If all the matter in all the bright stars and galaxies (all the baryonic matter) were distributed uniformly across the Universe, there would be just one particle in every 10 million cubic centimeters. In other words, for every proton or neutron in the Universe there are, in round terms, a billion (10^9) photons.

That ratio, a billion to one, is a measure of the tiny size of the breakdown in the law that particles and antiparticles are always created in pairs—small wonder that it has never been measured directly under laboratory conditions! What it is telling us is that for every billion antibaryons that were produced in the Big Bang, there were a billion and one baryons. In each case, a billion pairs annihilated to produce a billion photons, and a single baryon was left over.

Physicists are still struggling to develop a version of a unified theory that will produce exactly the right balance between baryons and photons from the reactions that took place in the Big Bang. There are several contenders for such a theory, but as yet none of them gives exactly the ''right'' answer. But that is not what matters here. The important point is that measurements made by astronomers *tell* us what the right answer is—that there are a billion photons for every baryon. If there is dark matter in the Universe as well—as there must be, if observations of the movements of stars and galaxies are taken at face value—then the simplest and most natural assumption to make is that the dark stuff (the WIMPs) was made in much the same way; that is, until there is a good reason to abandon simplicity and go for some more complicated theory of how things got to be the way they are, we might guess that for every billion antiWIMPs created in the Big Bang there were a billion and one WIMPs, so that the surplus left over today is one WIMP for every billion photons, or one WIMP for every baryon.* If that is indeed the case, then WIMPs with a mass of about 5 to 10 times the mass of the proton would be exactly the right mass to provide all of the dark matter needed in our Galaxy. One implication would be that bright stars— baryonic matter—make up just 10 percent of the mass of the Universe, and that 90 percent of the mass of the Universe is actually in the form of WIMPs. For people made of baryons (and electrons), living on a baryonic planet circling a baryonic star, this is hard to accept. But that doesn't make it any less true. There is a wealth of evidence that what we see really is only one tenth of the Universe and that the rest is hidden from our gaze.

○ **COSMIC CONNECTIONS**

Apart from the fact that the way stars and galaxies move indicates that they are being tugged by the gravitational hand of a great deal of dark matter, cosmologists have puzzled for a generation over the problem of how galaxies ever came into existence at all. A typical galaxy has a mass equivalent to a hundred billion Suns, and galaxies like this are the basic features of our Universe on the large scale—sometimes re-ferred to as "islands in space." The Universe itself is expanding. We know this from measurements of light from distant galaxies, which shows a consistent displacement toward the red end of the spectrum. This "redshift" is explained if all galaxies are moving apart from each other—it is an effect on light equivalent to the effect on sound that makes the note of the siren on a police car deeper if the car is racing away from you. The redshift does not, however, mean that galaxies are moving through space, in the sense that the Earth moves through space as it orbits the Sun, or the Sun moves through space as it orbits the center of our own Milky Way Galaxy. Rather, it is interpreted as indicating that space itself is expanding—something that was actually predicted, before the redshift was observed, by Einstein's general the-ory of relativity.

Long ago, in the Big Bang, the Universe was a hot, dense fireball,

---

*To make both sets of particles, of course, we need two billion leftover photons. Don't worry— the calculation is sufficiently vague that the difference between one billion and two billion photons (a factor of two) is not important. What matters is that in each case the ratio is a billion to one, not a thousand to one, or fifty to one, or a hundred billion to one. Factors of ten *are* important; a factor of two is neither here nor there.

a maelstrom of violence. As it has expanded, it has thinned and cooled—all the way down to a temperature of 3 K and a baryon density of just one particle for every ten million cubic centimeters of space. But how could clouds of gas containing as much matter as a hundred billion Suns condense out of the expanding Universe, when the expansion of space was trying to spread the gas thinner, pulling clouds apart before they could collapse?

The answer, cosmologists had realized by the 1980s, is that they can't—unless they have help. The gravity of all the bright stars in a galaxy, or even a cluster of galaxies, is insufficient to explain how the original cloud of gas held itself together in the early phases of the expanding Universe. But computer simulations of the way clouds of gas collapse as the Universe expands show that the trick *can* be done, provided that there is ten times more dark matter spread out around each galaxy in an extended halo. WIMPs of the kind described in the previous section are exactly what are needed to make the equations balance and to provide the extra gravity needed to hold proto-galaxies together in the expanding Universe.*

But WIMPs don't form clouds that collapse down to form stars. Only baryonic matter does this. This is because they carry no electric charge and so cannot radiate energy away into space. When a cloud of particles shrinks under the tug of gravity, it gets hotter because gravitational energy is released—the particles move faster and the pressure inside the cloud increases, resisting any further collapse. The rule applies just as much to a cloud of WIMPs bigger than our Galaxy as it does to the Sun itself. If the cloud is made of baryons, the heat is converted into electromagnetic radiation by the charged particles and escapes. So the pressure is relieved, and the cloud carries on shrinking and getting hotter inside until nuclear burning starts up and provides the extra radiation pressure needed to halt the collapse (as John Faulkner is fond of remarking, in this sense nuclear reactions keep stars *cool*, by preventing them from collapsing even further and getting still hotter inside!). But if there is no way to release the energy from inside the cloud in the form of radiation, then the cloud stabilizes at an appropriate size. For WIMPs left over from the Big Bang, the appropriate size is quite large. The WIMPs are spread out through a roughly spherical halo around our Galaxy, reluctant to interact either

---

*Confusingly, the researchers who carry out these computer simulations of galaxy formation usually refer to the dark stuff as "cold dark matter," or CDM. Cosmions, CDM, and WIMPs are the same thing under three different names. In this book, I shall stick to the term WIMPs.

with baryons or each other except through gravity. But a star like our Sun, plowing through the WIMPy sea, must inevitably accumulate a relatively modest number of these particles in its interior, captured and held there by the Sun's own gravity. Which is how the Santa Cruz team and the Harvard researchers, independently of each other and working on opposite sides of the North American continent, explained why the Sun is colder in its heart than it ought to be.

○ **KEEPING THE SUN COOL**

It all depends on how many WIMPs the Sun has captured during its lifetime and where exactly they lurk inside the Sun. Fortunately, these properties are very easy to calculate. A single WIMP can pass right through the Sun without bouncing off more than one proton (or other nucleus)—they are nearly as reluctant to interact with everyday matter as are neutrinos. So gravity is, indeed, the only thing that matters as far as trapping WIMPs inside the Sun is concerned. At the surface of the Sun, a particle would have to be moving at 617 kilometers a second in order to escape from the Sun's gravity—this is the "escape velocity." Any particle that moves slower than this will be captured. Inside the Sun, at a distance where there is just half the solar mass between a particle and the center, the escape velocity is 2,100 kilometers a second. But this is much more than halfway from the surface to the center—remember that 40 percent of the Sun's mass is contained in a core filling just 25 percent of its radius. At the core itself, a particle would have to be moving at 3,000 kilometers a second and be lucky enough to avoid colliding with a proton or some other nucleus on its way out in order to escape entirely into space.

Each WIMP in the halo of particles around our Galaxy moves in its own orbit, held in place by gravity. The velocity needed to stay in any particular orbit is the same, whatever the mass of the particle is. At the Sun's distance from the galactic center, the appropriate orbital speed is about 300 kilometers a second, whether the orbiting object is a star, a WIMP, or a hypothetical dark planet. So it is easy to see that most of the WIMPs swept up by the Sun during its passage through space will indeed "stick." If the Sun is overtaking the WIMP, there is hardly any difference in speed at all, and even if the WIMP is moving the opposite direction of the Sun in a head-on collision its relative speed is only 600 kilometers a second, scarcely enough to escape even from the surface of the star. The accurate calculations take account of the way particles are gathered in by the Sun's gravitational field, allow for the distribution of WIMPs through the halo required to provide the ''missing mass,'' and give a total for the present WIMP population of the Sun allowing for the four and a half billion years it has spent plowing through the halo to date. The concentration of WIMPs required to provide the missing mass in our Galaxy, for example, is equivalent to one solar mass of material spread through every thousand cubic light-years of space. When this and the other relevant numbers are put into the calculation, it turns out that there should be just one WIMP inside the Sun for every hundred billion protons, provided that each WIMP has a mass (the same for each WIMP) in the range from five to ten times the mass of a proton.

This is a pretty small ratio. The proportion of WIMPs to protons inside the Sun is, in fact, one hundred times *less* than the proportion of baryons to photons in the Universe at large—and that seemed like a small number when we first encountered it. Can such a minute fraction of WIMPs really affect the way the Sun works? Astonishingly, the answer is yes.

WIMPs with masses in this particular range, about five to ten times the mass of a proton, will settle down into stable orbits inside the Sun that spread over no more than about 10 percent of the solar radius. They form a tenuous WIMPy core, moving through the densest part of the Sun almost as if the baryons were not there. But that almost holds the key to the way they cool the heart of the Sun. The neutrinos that Ray Davis and his colleagues can detect are produced only by the nuclear reactions that take place in the very hottest part of the Sun, the innermost 5 percent of its radius. Some nuclear reactions are still going on just outside this inner core, where the temperature is a little lower. Although the temperature is lower in this outer part of the core, so nuclear fusion proceeds less vigorously, the volume (which, of course, depends on the *cube* of the radius) is greater. So most of the energy being produced by nuclear reactions inside the Sun actually comes from the region outside the innermost 5 percent, out to about 12 percent of the radius of the Sun. This is exactly the region where WIMPs with masses in the interesting range congregate. Unlike particles in pure orbits affected only by gravity, WIMPs orbiting inside the Sun are also affected by the occasional collisions with protons and other nuclei, so the region where the WIMPs settle does depend on their mass. Lighter WIMPs would pick up energy from collisions with protons and escape from the Sun; more massive WIMPs would lose energy in collisions and sink down into the innermost core, so they could never affect what turns out to be the interesting region between 5 and 10 percent of the way out from the center. But if WIMPs have masses in the range required to provide the dark matter in the Universe, then their orbits take them across the inner 10 percent of the Sun's core.

In each orbit, each WIMP suffers one collision, on average, with a proton. If that collision takes place in the innermost core (the inner 5 percent), the WIMP will pick up energy and move faster as a result—it has gotten hotter. At the same time, the proton it collided with has lost energy and moves more slowly—it has got colder. But when a fast-moving WIMP collides with a slower-moving proton slightly farther out from the center, it gives up some of its energy. The WIMP slows down and gets colder, the proton speeds up and gets hotter. Moving rapidly about the inner 10 percent of the Sun and occasionally colliding with protons and other nuclei, the effect of the WIMPs is to average out the temperature conditions across the innermost 10 percent of the Sun, making the central peak of temperature less than it ought to be according to the standard model. The WIMPs make the innermost 5 percent of the Sun a little cooler, and the next 5 percent a little hotter, with the overall effect that exactly the same amount of nuclear energy is produced, but from a larger, more evenly hot core than in the standard model.

The WIMPs can do this, in spite of their scarcity, because of the speed with which they transport the energy. A photon, remember, colliding against billions of protons in its frantic pinball-machine random walk out of the heart of the Sun, will take hundreds of thousands of years to cross the innermost 10 percent of the Sun's radius. But a WIMP traverses that distance in about 17 minutes. Each WIMP makes the round trip across the innermost 10 percent of the Sun roughly twice every hour, 48 times a day, nearly 18,000 times a a year, year in and year out through all the billions of years that the Sun has been shining. And each time, it carries its quota of energy outward. The ratio of the time it takes for a WIMP to cross the inner 10 percent of the Sun to the time it takes a photon to negotiate the same journey is, in fact, about 100 billion to 1—the same as the ratio of the number of baryons to the number of WIMPs. The scarcity of WIMPs inside the Sun is almost exactly compensated for by their efficiency at moving energy outward over the critical region (Figure 5.1).

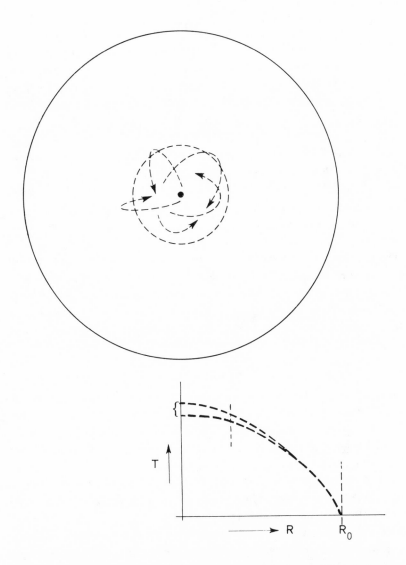

Fig. 5.1. WIMPs circulating in the innermost 10 percent of the Sun transport heat outward and make the temperature in the center drop by about 10 percent, indicated by the curly bracket on the temperature plot. This simplified schematic does not show how the redistributed heat actually *warms* the region just outside the solar core, so that overall just as much energy is produced. With or without WIMPs, conditions at the surface of the Sun (R_0) are the same. The key point is that the decreased central temperature exactly explains the scarcity of neutrinos detected by Ray Davis and his colleagues. (Based on figures supplied by John Faulkner.)

When the effects of WIMPs are added to the standard computer models of the Sun, they show that the temperature of the innermost core, where the Davis neutrinos are produced, is automatically reduced by the 10 percent required to match the neutrino measurements to date, provided that the WIMPs have masses between five and ten times the mass of the proton and that there are about 3 WIMPs for every 100 billion protons—the same, within the limits of accuracy of all these calculations, as the properties required for WIMPs to provide the dark matter in our Galaxy, and to help galaxies form in the first place. The effect of this cooling on nuclear reactions is to reduce the number of neutrinos that would be detectable by the Davis experiment by a factor of two or three, bringing theory and observations nicely in line with each other.

By cooling the very heart of the Sun, of course, the WIMPs also reduce the radiation pressure there, and that means that the density of matter must be a little higher than in the standard model in order for gas pressure to take on a bigger share of holding the Sun up against gravity. But this is no problem and may actually, as we shall see in Chapter 7, be an advantage.

○ CREDIT WHERE DUE

All of this actually emerged in a flurry of scientific papers published in 1985 and 1986, with credit eventually being shared equally between Faulkner, Gilliland, Press, and Spergel—but not without a little excitement along the way. It isn't hard to imagine the consternation felt by John Faulkner, early in 1985, when an advance copy (a ''preprint'') of the first paper on cosmions by Spergel and Press arrived at Santa Cruz. With a sinking feeling, he realized that the paper presented essentially the same solution to the solar neutrino problem that he and Gilliland had worked out seven years earlier but had never published. And the Spergel and Press paper was already set for publication in the most prestigious journal read by astronomers, the *Astrophysical Journal*. So much time had passed that Faulkner simply couldn't remember how much detail of his work with Gilliland had actually gotten into print (over Steigman's objection) in the 1978 collaboration with Steigman and the others. But he knew only too well that in science the credit for a new idea goes to the person who *publishes* the idea first, whether or not someone else thought of it first.

He searched his office for a copy of the 1978 article, only to find that he had long since given all his copies away. Then he went to the library on campus, only to find that the relevant volume of the *Astronomical Journal* was out on loan. He couldn't even find the unpublished draft of the paper he had worked on with Gilliland in 1978, and Gilliland himself, having completed his Ph.D. studies, had long since gone off to the High Altitude Observatory in Boulder, Colorado, where he was pursuing a quite different line of research into the behavior of the Sun (more of this in Chapter 6). Gloomily, Faulkner decided to call Press and compare notes. The reaction, he later recalled,* was understandable jubilation on the part of Press, who said, "Well, it's too bad, John," and laughingly went on, "You realize that all the credit goes to he who has the courage of his convictions and first puts [the idea] in the literature."

This did nothing to lift Faulkner's gloom. But the next day he found that the 1978 volume of the *Astronomical Journal* had been returned to the library. Hurriedly he flipped through the pages to the relevant article, scanning down to subsection *c* of section five. To his surprise and delight, he found that not only was the basic idea mentioned in there, but that he had squeezed in four out of the five main conclusions that had emerged from his work with Gilliland. There was enough there to establish scientific priority beyond a shadow of a doubt. With the boot now firmly on the other foot, he called Press back with the news. "He sort of cursed me out, in a genial fashion," says Faulkner, but once the chaffing was over the two teams quickly agreed that the sensible thing to do was to join forces to produce a definitive paper describing the WIMP scenario.

First, however, Faulkner had one enjoyable task to perform. A more thorough search of his office revealed the draft of the Faulkner and Gilliland paper, seven years old and literally covered in dust. It needed only a few changes to make it ready to send off for publication in the *Astrophysical Journal*—a revised introduction, acknowledging the independent work of Spergel and Press, and a new acknowledgments section, in which the authors thanked "many colleagues for discussions over the years, including especially Gary Steigman (without whose counsel this work would have been published prematurely)." With that off his chest and the paper duly published before the end of 1985, Faulkner was ready once more to start work on the implications of WIMPs for stellar evolution.

San Francisco Examiner, interview by Keay Davidson, 2 October 1986, page E–1.

The collaboration with Press and Spergel (which was also published in the *Astrophysical Journal,* in July 1986) was a natural progression from both teams' earlier work, not just a diplomatic exercise. Faulkner and Gilliland had used approximate techniques to estimate the way WIMPs would interact with other particles in the core of the Sun but had used detailed solar model calculations to determine the implications in terms of the output of detectable solar neutrinos. Spergel and Press, however, had worked out the WIMP properties in great detail, using the advances in particle physics theory and cosmology during the early 1980s, but had not worked out the details of the changes in solar structure, only that WIMPs could indeed lower the temperature at the heart of the Sun. Together, the two teams were able to tell the complete story, essentially as I have outlined it here.

Nobody has yet been able to *prove* that WIMPs exist—that would require catching one in the laboratory (which may not be impossible; see Chapter 8). But the circumstantial evidence in their favor is compelling. John Bahcall has commented that "WIMPs solve two fundamental and exasperating problems; this is such a beautiful idea that if it isn't right, God missed a great opportunity";* and Roger Tayler of the University of Sussex gave a keynote lecture to the Royal Astronomical Society in London late in 1988 in which he said that although "there have been many attempts" to solve the solar neutrino problem, "the only one which is at present under active study involves the presence of weakly interacting massive particles [WIMPs] in the solar interior."† In ten years, the WIMP theory had gone from being "just another wild idea" to being the *only* respectable theory currently being offered to explain the solar neutrino problem. And meanwhile Faulkner, in particular, had been applying it to resolve some other long-standing problems in stellar theory, as well.

○ **OTHER STARS**

The most useful tool astronomers have for studying the way stars change as they age is called the Hertzsprung-Russell diagram, after the two astronomers who pioneered its use. Stars live for so long

---

*Quoted by Gilliland, *Griffith Observer,* January 1987, p. 9.
†The George Darwin Lecture for 1988, published in *The Quarterly Journal of the Royal Astronomical Society* (1989), vol. 30, p. 125.

and change so slowly, by and large, that there is no hope of studying stellar evolution by watching an individual star or two age. But the H-R diagram enables astronomers to do the equivalent of a botanist who studies a forest of trees that includes seedlings, saplings, and mature specimens and uses those studies to work out the life cycle of a tree.

The H-R diagram is a kind of graph in which the overall brightness of a star (usually measured in units where the brightness of the Sun is 1) is compared with its surface temperature (which is equivalent to its color in a precisely quantifiable way, with blue stars being hotter than red, and so on). Most stars follow the fairly simple rule that brighter stars are hotter than fainter stars, and they lie on a band in the H-R diagram running from top left (hot and bright) to bottom right (cool and dim). The Sun is a main-sequence star (Figure 5.2). But there are exceptions to this rule. Some stars are both bright and cool, while others are both hot and faint. A star can be bright even though it has a cool surface (and therefore looks red) if it is very big. The amount of heat crossing each square meter of the surface is small, so it is cool; but the number of square meters involved is huge, so it is releasing a lot of energy altogether and is bright. Such stars are red giants, and lie in the upper right of the H-R diagram. Similarly, a faint star can be hot if it is very small, so that even though a great deal of energy flows through each square meter of the surface, making its light white, there are very few square meters for the energy to flow through. Such stars are called white dwarfs, and occupy the bottom left of the H-R diagram.

The main sequence corresponds to stars that are, like our Sun, burning hydrogen into helium in their hearts. The rate at which such a star is burning its nuclear fuel, and therefore its brightness, depends on its mass. The heavier a star is, the more energy it must produce in its heart each second in order to hold itself up against the inward pull of gravity. So the bright stars at the top of the main sequence are bright because they are more massive than stars at the bottom of the main sequence, and use up their fuel more quickly.

All this has been determined largely from studies of the H-R diagrams for different groups of stars. In particular, there are some groups, known as globular clusters, which each seem to have formed from a single collapsing cloud of gas when the Galaxy was younger. So every star in a globular cluster must have the same age. When astronomers look at the H-R diagram for such a cluster (Figure 5.3),

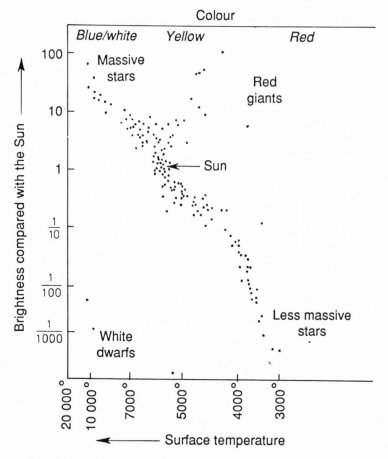

Fig. 5.2. The H-R diagram relates the brightness of a star to its surface temperature, or color. The Sun lies on the main sequence, a band running from top left to bottom right on the diagram.

they find that the stars at the bright end of the main sequence have gone and been replaced by cooler stars farther to the right in the diagram. There is also, usually, a trail of stars between the position where the upper main sequence "ought" to be and the new "red giant branch." This trail is the horizontal branch that I mentioned earlier.

Detailed studies of many stars in many globular clusters, compared with the computer models of how stars work based on standard physics, have produced a clear picture of how a star like our Sun evolves. (Very massive stars get involved in supernova explosions, of course, but that is a different story and I won't discuss it here.) When hydrogen burning

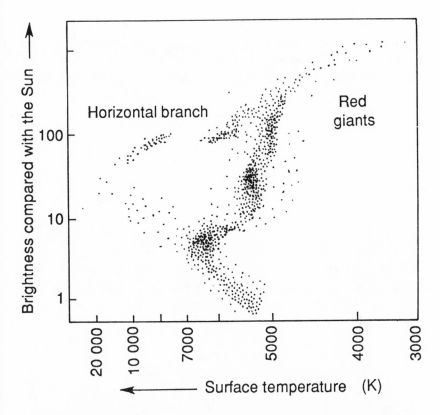

Fig. 5.3. In H-R diagrams of some clusters of stars the upper part of the main sequence is missing and has been replaced by red giant stars. The point at which the main sequence bends away to the right indicates the age of the cluster.

can no longer be sustained in its heart, the core of a main-sequence star shrinks and gets hotter, while its outer layers expand. The star becomes a red giant, with an inert core of helium surrounded by a shell in which hydrogen is still being "burnt." The star moves to the right and upward, off the main sequence in the H-R diagram and along the red giant branch. At the tip of the red giant branch, the core becomes so hot that nuclear burning can begin in the helium core. This makes the core itself expand, moving the hydrogen-burning shell out to a cooler region of the star and *reducing* the intensity of hydrogen burning. The combined effect is to shift the star, abruptly, on to the horizontal branch, where it stays while helium burning continues in its core and hydrogen burning continues in a shell outside the core. When all the helium in the core has been converted into carbon (and probably some oxygen as well), the inner part of the star again contracts, while its outer layers expand. Helium burning takes place in a shell around the inert carbon core, and hydrogen burning still goes on in a shell even farther out from the core. The star has once again become a red giant, at the top end of the red giant branch (the ''asymptotic giant branch''). After further evolutionary adventures, in which a great deal of its mass is lost, literally blown away into space during its life as a giant, what is left of the star shrinks in upon itself and moves down into the white dwarf part of the H-R diagram.

It took heroic efforts by generations of astronomers to work all this out. Just one key feature is particularly important to the story I have to tell here, however. More massive stars lie near the top of the main sequence, and more massive stars run through their life cycles faster. As a cluster of stars that were born together ages, the point at which the H-R diagram for that cluster bends away from the main sequence moves down the main sequence from top left to bottom right. So the point at which the main sequence bends away toward the red giant branch tells us how old the cluster is. The H-R diagrams of globular clusters, like Figure 5.3, provide the best measures we have of stellar ages. And, as a bonus, it turns out that globular clusters are the oldest stars in our Galaxy, formed when the Galaxy itself was just collapsing down from a huge cloud of hydrogen and helium gas, held in the gravitational grip of an even more massive cloud of WIMPs.* But there is a problem. The ages of the oldest stars in the Galaxy, inferred from these main-sequence turnoff points, are uncomfortably close to the age estimated by cosmologists for the whole Universe. There is scarcely any time available, after the Big Bang, for the WIMPs to do their work of pulling clouds of gas together to make proto-galaxies, and for some of the gas in at least one of those proto-galaxies, our own, to form the first stars. The effect of WIMPs *inside* those stars, however, goes some way toward alleviating the embarrassment caused to astronomers by this problem.

---

*Without wandering too far from the thread of my story, it is worth just mentioning that we know these are the oldest stars, formed when the Galaxy was young, because they contain almost all hydrogen and helium (revealed by spectroscopy) and very little in the way of heavier elements. Heavy elements are only made inside stars, so the *oldest* stars must contain the least, as they formed from virgin clouds of hydrogen and helium before any supernovas had been at work enriching the interstellar medium.

○ WIMPY CONNECTIONS

The ages of globular clusters, estimated from comparisons of actual main-sequence turnoff points with standard computer models of how stars work, may be anywhere from 13 billion to 19 billion years. This is not a spread of the ages of individual clusters, since all the globular clusters are thought to have formed together when the Galaxy was born. Instead, this time span is a measure of the uncertainty in the technique. In other words, clusters were formed at the same time, sometime between 13 billion and 19 billion years ago, with 16 billion years being the best bet for the age of the oldest of our Galaxy's stars. The age of the Universe (the time that has elapsed since the Big Bang) cannot be measured directly, and the inferred age depends on detailed theories of how the Universe has evolved.* As far as this can be pinned down, however, the best evidence is that the Universe is between 15 billion and 18 billion years old, and probably nearer to 15 billion than to 18 billion. Obviously, you cannot have stars 19 billion years old in a Universe just 15 billion years old (taking the worst possible disagreement between these two estimates), and even the middle value for each range, giving stars 16 billion years old in a Universe 16.5 billion years old, is embarrassing to astronomers, who cannot find any way in which galaxies could have formed just 500 million years after the Big Bang.

WIMPs change the picture, because they alter the rate at which stars like the Sun age. Interestingly, the effect is *only* important for stars with masses rather like that of our Sun. Much more massive stars capture more WIMPs each year than our Sun does, because their stronger gravity pulls in the particles from a wider range. But much more massive stars don't live long enough to gather in significant numbers of WIMPs, even allowing for their wider gravitational influence. Stars that are much less massive than our Sun, by contrast, have ample time to gather in WIMPs, but their more feeble gravitational range means that they gather them in more slowly. The accumulation of WIMPs in the hearts of low-mass stars will eventually have an important influence on their behavior—but the Galaxy is nowhere near old enough for them to have had a chance to accumulate sufficient WIMPs to do this yet.

*See *In Search of the Big Bang*.

The way the presence of WIMPs in its core affects the evolution of a star like the Sun is seen by adding the influence of WIMPs to those standard computer models of stellar evolution. The calculations show that the age of a star with WIMPs in its core when it leaves the main sequence is *less* than the age at which an otherwise identical star with no WIMPs in its core will leave the main sequence. In other words, if the globular cluster stars contain WIMPs, then all of the ages inferred from measurements of the main-sequence turnoff points in the H-R diagram should be revised downward. The effect is small, but as Roger Tayler commented in his George Darwin lecture, "Problems relating to the ages of the clusters would be eased if their stars contained WIMPs." Faulkner is cautiously (but only cautiously) pleased by his discovery of how this effect works. He told me that just about the biggest effect you can produce with realistic WIMP models is to reduce the turnoff ages by about 15 percent, bringing the "standard" age of 16 billion years down to about 13.6 billion years. "WIMPs," he says, "can turn modest embarrassment into modest agreement. Certainly they go in the right direction—thank goodness!"

This, of course, is the important point. If WIMPs had made the embarrassment worse, that would have been a major blow to the WIMP theory, hinting strongly that such particles might not exist at all and that astrophysicists might have to find some other solution to the solar neutrino problem. Just such a suggestion has, in fact, been made by some astronomers, who base their arguments on a study of horizontal branch stars. But Faulkner, who cut his teeth as a researcher by finding out how horizontal branch stars work, has responded with a counterblast that puts this criticism very much in question, at least for now.

These arguments about the influence of WIMPs on horizontal branch stars surfaced only in 1988, and there is sure to be more back-and-forth debate between the protagonists in the debate while this book is going through the presses, and in the years ahead. The issue is a subtle one and may never be resolved to everybody's satisfaction. But it is worth mentioning here because of the suggestion that WIMP masses might lie at the lower end of the range suggested by the original calculations. Although cosmologists would like WIMPs to have a mass of about 10 proton masses each in order to provide all of the dark matter in one form, there is, in fact, no reason why WIMPs could not have half this mass, leaving half of the dark matter in some other form. And the most beautiful prediction of the WIMP model, now borne out by observations of the Sun itself, also favors a mass in the lower end of the range, around five times the mass of the proton.

More of this in Chapter 7. But I wouldn't want you to run away with the idea that the only studies of the Sun that revealed anything new and interesting during the 1980s revolved around the idea of WIMPs. While the WIMP theory was languishing under a pile of paper in Faulkner's office at Santa Cruz, and even after it was given the kiss of life by Spergel and Press, there was a great deal of other work going on to probe the secrets of the Sun. The most exciting of this work, as we shall see in Chapter 7, turned out to be directly relevant to the WIMP story (although that is not why it was originally carried out) and points the way to a more detailed understanding of the deep interior of the Sun in the 1990s than ever before. Before we move on to this denouement of the story of solar studies, there is still something else to tell about the outer layers of our neighborhood star and the way changes in those outer layers may influence life on Earth. And there is still another connection with the WIMP saga—or, at least, with one of the participants in that saga. Just in case you were wondering what Ron Gilliland was up to in Boulder all the while the WIMP theory was languishing, here is your chance to find out.

6 THE BREATHING SUN

When he left Santa Cruz, Gilliland went on to other work concerning the Sun, but in the early 1980s he was more interested in what was going on in the outer layers of our nearest star, not in the secrets locked deep in the solar interior. After he completed his graduate studies in California, Gilliland went to Boulder, Colorado, where he became (and still is) a member of the High Altitude Observatory of the National Center for Atmospheric Research. This was in 1979, at a time when one of the senior scientists at the observatory, John A. ("Jack") Eddy, was making headline news with his claim that the Sun was shrinking measurably, at a rate of 0.1 percent per century. Such a dramatic change in the diameter of the Sun—far more rapid than anything envisaged by William Thomson or Helmholtz—could only, of course, be some sort of short-term phenomenon, a fluctuation that had been going on for, perhaps, a few hundred years. Shrinking at a rate of two meters *per hour*, as Eddy's claims implied, the Sun would vanish entirely in less than 100,000 years. Put another way, if the Sun had been shrinking at that rate for more than a few thousand years, then conditions on Earth would have been drastically different a few thousand years ago. All the old, familiar geological and evolutionary evidence shows that that simply was not the case.

So what *was* going on in the Sun? It was natural that Gilliland, joining the team in Boulder at this exciting time, should turn his attention to the problem. He was to be instrumental in showing that the solar variation is not as large as Eddy thought at first, but is real, and certainly large enough to have important repercussions for life on Earth. But in order to put these discoveries in perspective, we have to go back to the puzzle that started Eddy off on the trail of the shrinking Sun—the curious case of the missing sunspots.

○ A SPOT OR TWO OF BOTHER

Since the time of Galileo in the early seventeenth century, astronomers have known that the Sun is imperfect and that dark spots sometimes pass across its face. Chinese and Greek sky watchers knew about sunspots even before Galileo's time, but it was with his invention of the astronomical telescope that the era of modern observations began. By projecting an image of the Sun through a telescope and onto a white screen (never, of course, looking directly at the Sun through a telescope), Galileo and his successors were able to monitor the comings and goings of these strange dark spots. It wasn't until the nineteenth century that astronomers realized that these sunspots come and go with a more or less regular rhythm, some 11 years long. And it was only in the 1980s that the rhythms of sunspot variations were linked with rhythms of changes in the size of the Sun itself, which seems to "breathe" in and out on a time scale of decades and centuries.

Individual sunspots range in size from about 1,500 kilometers in diameter to irregularly sprawling dark features 150,000 kilometers across. They usually occur in groups of several spots which together spread over hundreds of millions of square kilometers on the surface of the Sun. They look dark against the bright background of the solar surface because they are relatively cool. But "relatively" is the watchword, for with the Sun's surface at a temperature of about 6,000 K, the darkest central region of a spot is still at about 4,000 K, and the lighter, outer region is at a temperature of around 5,500 K.

Astronomers believe that sunspots are regions where the convection currents that usually carry hot material up to the surface from deeper layers of the Sun are temporarily inhibited by strong local magnetic fields. Certainly, the magnetic fields—measured, like the temperature of the spots, by analysis of the spectral lines in light coming from a region of sunspot activity—are always associated with sunspot groups, and the spots themselves seem to be just the most obviously visible manifestation of a whole range of solar activities. These activities include great storms, and flares that send tongues of solar material licking far out into space. All of this activity varies over the roughly 11-year solar cycle of activity, from a quiet Sun to an active state and back again. The overall pattern of magnetic changes in the Sun takes two of these cycles to get back to where it started—in one 11-year cycle, the north and south magnetic poles of the Sun swap places, and in the next cycle they swap back again. So many astrophysicists argue that the basic cycle of activity is the "double sunspot" cycle, about 22 years long.

Each sunspot cycle follows the same overall pattern, although the details differ from cycle to cycle. Starting from the quiet point of the cycle, a few sunspots appear at latitudes about 40 degrees north and south of the solar equator. Each spot group builds up over about 10 days, then dies away slowly over a month or so. As the solar cycle develops, not only do more and more spot groups form, but they form closer and closer to the equator, so that during the time of maximum solar activity they are concentrated near latitudes 10 degrees north and 10 degrees south.

Although this pattern is regular and to some extent predictable, we still do not know exactly what processes inside the Sun drive the solar cycle. The most favored explanation involves a tightening of magnetic lines of force, wound up by the rotation of the Sun and pulling the spot groups toward the equator. But the life of a theorist trying to explain the exact behavior of sunspots and the solar cycle in general is not made any easier by the fact that individual cycles differ not only in length but in strength. Some cycles may be only 9 years long, measured from minimum to minimum; others stretch to about 14 years. Although both extremes are rare, it is only on average that we can talk of a sunspot cycle of 11 years. Sometimes there are few sunspots even in years of maximum activity; in other cycles, hundreds of sunspots are produced during the peak sunspot years.

Even without knowing details of how the cycle works, however, some researchers have drawn attention to apparent relationships between solar activity, as measured by sunspots, and the weather on Earth. Solar activity can be measured in terms of an index called "sunspot number," which is related to the area of the visible solar disk that is covered by dark spots and is usually averaged over a month or a year. A sunspot number of 100 on this scale does not mean that there are 100 individual spots on the disk, but tells us how much of the disk is covered by spots—on this scale, 100 corresponds to a good, strong maximum, while anything over 150 is a bit special, and in the quiet years of a solar cycle the sunspot number falls well into single figures, sometimes actually to zero.

One of the reasons it took astronomers so long to notice that there was an 11-year sunspot cycle is that in the decades following Galileo's observations of the Sun there were indeed very few spots at all to be seen. For the best part of a century it was as if, in modern terminology, the Sun was experiencing an extended minimum of activity. Of course, nobody at the time had any way of knowing that this was unusual. Sunspot activity picked up in general after about 1715, and by the middle of the nineteenth century astronomers had enough observations to notice the 11-year cycle, which was first reported (as a 10-year cycle) by Heinrich Schwabe, and then checked out in detail by Rudolf Wolff, who showed that it had persisted since the early eighteenth century. What, then, had happened in the seventeenth century? In the 1880s and 1890s both Gustav Spörer, a German researcher based in Potsdam, and Walter Maunder, who worked at the Royal Greenwich Observatory in London, published the results of their studies of old records, which showed that there had been very few sunspots at all between about 1645 and 1715. Maunder continued to try to persuade his colleagues of the importance of this discovery right up until his death in 1928. Astronomers paid little attention, preferring to believe that the seventeenth-century observers simply failed to notice or failed to record sunspots, rather than that the Sun failed to produce any sunspots. It was easier to assume that astronomers of past centuries (who were safely dead and couldn't argue back) were incompetent than it was, even in the twentieth century, to believe that the Sun was imperfect and variable. But some climatologists and popularizers took up the idea of a dearth of sunspots in the seventeenth century, and it was their claims that drew Eddy into the debate in the 1970s.

Until very recently, the idea that the climate of the Earth might change on a time scale of decades and centuries seemed as ludicrous to climatologists as the notion that the Sun might vary on the same time scale seemed to astronomers. Climate was regarded simply as a kind of "average weather," which might experience random fluctuations, so that one year or one decade might be colder or hotter than another, but which didn't really alter much from century to century. That idea began to lose its grip as the twentieth century progressed, and climatologists and historians realized that the weather in the 1930s and 1940s was distinctly warmer than that of the nineteenth century. A subsequent cooling of the Northern Hemisphere in the 1950s and 1960s encouraged more interest in climatic change and led to some scare stories about a new ice age being just around the corner. Largely through the pioneering efforts of Hubert Lamb, first with the Meteorological Office in London and later at the University of East Anglia, the study of climatic variations in historical times became respectable.

Those studies showed, among many other interesting features, that the seventeenth century contained the coldest decades of a period of climate so extreme that it is now known as the Little Ice Age.* Rivers and lakes across Europe froze on an unprecedented scale in winter, many crops could not be grown as far north as they are found today, and sea ice extended much farther south from the Arctic than anyone now living has seen. Some climatologists, confronted by the fact that the world was colder in the seventeenth century than it is today, but lacking any explanation for why this might be so, conjectured that the Sun's output of heat was weaker then and pointed to the evidence of the prolonged lack of sunspots, which happened at the same time as the Little Ice Age and is a phenomenon that is now known as the Maunder Minimum, in recognition of the astronomer who had most vigorously tried to draw attention to it.

But the climatologists, of course, knew nothing of the workings of the Sun, and the astrophysicists dismissed their claims of a link between sunspots and the weather as ludicrous. Still, the claims persisted, remaining unproven but also unrefuted, like a skeleton in the closet of solar physics. Nobody knew for sure if the Maunder Minimum was real. In the 1970s, this all became too much for Eddy, who later told reporter Sam Bleecker,† "I was annoyed by occasional references to it in connection with a coincident change in the world climate. As a solar astronomer, I felt certain that it never could have happened, and my interest in history made the prospect of cross-examining Maunder's assertions an appealing one." Eddy expected to find that Maunder (and Spörer) had been wrong and that a proper cross-examination of the historical records would show, not that there weren't sunspots in the late seventeenth century, but that nobody had kept proper records of solar activity then. He soon found out that he was wrong.

Eddy's research took him to the pages of long-unread journals in

---

*See Lamb's book *Climate, History and the Modern World* (London and New York: Methuen, 1982).
†*Star & Sky*, June 1979, p. 14.

the dusty corners of astronomical libraries, and to Europe and the Royal Greenwich Observatory in search of ancient manuscripts. What he found was a sobering reminder that modern scientists are no more intelligent or dedicated than their predecessors, but just better equipped in terms of instruments and technology. Astronomers of the seventeenth century were certainly motivated to study the Sun—Galileo's discovery of sunspots had caused enormous scientific interest. Records of observations of the planets and the rings of Saturn made at the time also showed how skillful the observers were and how meticulously they recorded their observations—they clearly had the skill to study sunspots. But did they have the inclination? Here, too, Eddy's expectations were shattered. He found that several observers had made regular observations of the Sun throughout the Maunder Minimum specifically searching for dark spots, and had kept records of their findings (or lack of findings) every bit as scrupulous as the records they kept of planetary observations. Precisely because sunspots were so rare in the seventeenth century, when one *was* discovered an observer would report it to his colleagues with a flourish and would achieve a modest measure of fame. Sunspots were eagerly sought during the decades of the Maunder Minimum, but they just weren't there to be seen—for 32 years, not one sunspot was seen in the northern hemisphere of the Sun, and for 70 years, from 1645 to 1715, no more than a single small group of spots was seen at any one time.

Setting out to lay to rest the myth that world climate was linked to sunspot activity, Eddy had, in fact, succeeded in establishing the link as much more than a myth. He went on to develop the work by looking further back in time, using other techniques, such as records of auroral activity in the sky of the Earth (known to be caused by solar activity) and the measurement of traces of radioactive carbon in old tree rings (known to be caused by cosmic ray particles from the Sun) to show that the link between climate and solar activity is not only real but extends back to well before the time of Christ. When the Sun is quiet—when there are few sunspots for decades at a time and even the peaks of the solar cycle of activity are low—the world cools.

The evidence was summarized at a meeting of the Royal Society in London during February 1989. Charles Sonett of the University of Arizona told the meeting that there is a cycle about 200 years long that dominates the tree ring record concerning solar activity. The same 200-year cycle shows up in the thickness of the rings themselves. Every two centuries, the rings tend to be narrower, indicating that the trees suffered some form of stress. The pattern suggests that there was not one Little Ice Age but many, with the Sun's activity declining, and the weather turning colder, every couple of centuries.

In fact, Sonett had been saying this for years, long before the February 1989 meeting of the Royal Society. It was one of the claims that Eddy set out to refute; but it was Eddy's work, in particular, that had now made such studies respectable enough to grace those hallowed halls. Why?

○ THE SHRINKING SUN

As a result of his interest in old sunspot records, Eddy learned of the existence of another series of intriguing solar observations, carried out at the Royal Observatory in Greenwich. Ever since 1750, astronomers at the observatory had been taking daily measurements (weather permitting) of the size of the Sun. The observations were made with an instrument called a transit telescope, which is mounted so that it can swing "up and down" along a north-south line, but cannot move from side to side. It happens that this particular instrument defines, by international agreement, the zero meridian, The north-south line through the telescope is the Greenwich Meridian, from which we measure longitude; and the passage of the Sun directly over this telescope defines noon, Greenwich Mean Time. Although the records of measurements of the Sun's diameter don't start until after the Maunder Minimum, Eddy was still curious about them. During a spell as a visitor at the Harvard-Smithsonian Center for Astrophysics, he examined the records with Aran Boornazian and saw immediately that there was a consistent downward trend in the measurements of solar diameter—taken at face value, the records implied that the Sun was shrinking dramatically.

At first the two astronomers didn't believe what they saw. They assumed that the astronomers of the past, working without the aid of modern clocks and measuring instruments, had simply been inaccurate in their measurements. But when Eddy and Boornazian studied copies of similar records from the U.S. Naval Observatory in Washington, they found a similar trend. Astronomers on both sides of the Atlantic, making the same kind of observations over the nineteenth and twentieth centuries, came up with similar figures, suggesting a rapid shrinking of the Sun. Clearly, something *was* going on, after all. So Eddy and

Boornazian went back to the records, pulled out the information on solar shrinking, and published it—to the consternation of many of their colleagues.

It is important to appreciate exactly how the measurements were made, since this has a crucial bearing on the arguments that followed about how reliable the observations were. The early observers determined the Sun's diameter by measuring how long it took for the image of the Sun to pass the cross-hairs of the telescope as the Sun moved from east to west across the sky because of the rotation of the Earth. They started counting when the edge of the Sun touched the cross-hair and stopped when the other side of the Sun left the cross-hair. But, of course, the early observers had no stopwatches or digital clocks to help them in this task. Instead, they had to count the number of ticks of a pendulum clock as the image passed the cross-hairs, and their measurements simply cannot have been as accurate as modern ones. So Eddy and Boornazian relied chiefly on the records since 1854, when a more accurate timing system (a chronograph) was installed at the observatory. The continuous records go up to 1954, when the observatory moved out of London to Herstmonceux, in Sussex, and the daily observations of solar diameter from Greenwich ceased, although the transit telescope defining the Greenwich Meridian is still in place at the old observatory.

It was this series of observations, together with the data from the U.S. Naval Observatory, that led to the claim that the Sun was shrinking at a rate of about 1,500 kilometers per century—a dramatically large fraction of its 1,392,000-kilometer diameter. In terms of the angle the Sun makes in the sky, which is just under 32 minutes of arc, the estimated shrinking amounted to 2 seconds of arc per century. It seemed astonishing, but Eddy had some other evidence to back up the claim.

When the Sun is eclipsed by the Moon, there is sometimes a complete blackout, and sometimes a ring of light still visible around the edge of the Moon. This latter type is called an annular eclipse and occurs when the Moon is slightly farther away from the Earth in its orbit, so that it covers slightly less than 32 minutes of arc on the sky (it is an astonishing coincidence that the Moon and Sun both appear the same size as viewed from the Earth). In 1567, the astronomer Christopher Clavius observed an annular eclipse from Rome. But modern calculations suggest that the Moon was too close to the Earth, on that occasion, for this to be possible—*unless* the Sun was a little bigger in 1567 than it is today!

There is some argument about what exactly Clavius saw. Was it really an annular eclipse, or did he just see flashes of light from the Sun (known today as "Bailey's Beads") passing through the valleys between the mountains at the edge of the Moon? Unfortunately, there are no photographs from 1567 to tell us. Even if Clavius did see an annular eclipse, that doesn't give very much guidance to exactly how big the Sun was then, but simply a hint that it was bigger than it is today. As circumstantial evidence in support of a case made by the transit telescope observations, however, it looked persuasive to Eddy and Boornazian.

Others were not convinced. In spite of this corroborative evidence, most astronomers dismissed the claims made by the Harvard-Smithsonian team. Critics pointed out that the observations from Greenwich (and, indeed, the ones made in Washington) had been made by a series of different astronomers, using different clocks and different techniques. At Greenwich, six different observers might be involved in the measurements in any one year, each one using his best judgment of exactly when the edge of the Sun touched the cross-hair of the telescope. When other researchers calculated the average diameter of the Sun determined by each of these observers, they found that even in the same year two different observers would produce figures that differed by well over a thousand kilometers.

Eddy was slightly chastened, but he still had another card to play. As well as counting the time it took for the Sun to pass across the hairline in the telescope, the old observers had also used another technique. While the noonday image of the Sun was in the field of view, an observer would quickly adjust a micrometer gauge to measure the vertical diameter of the Sun, the distance from the north pole to the south pole across the image. These measurements showed the same sort of effect as the horizontal measurements—a decline in solar diameter—but only half as much, at a rate of about one second of arc per century. At first Eddy had assumed that this technique would be less reliable than the timing technique because of the speed with which the observer had to work and the wear and tear, over the years, on the micrometer screws. But when he visited the old Royal Observatory at Greenwich and tried the technique out for himself, he found that he was wrong. In fact, the observer had *more* time to judge the position of the top and bottom of the Sun's image in the telescope's cross-hairs, and these measurements ought to be more reliable than the horizontal measurements.

Even so, there were questions about the reliability of some of the records, and the exact number that you got for the rate at which the Sun was shrinking depended on which observations you decided to trust most. Eddy and Boornazian interpreted the vertical measurements as implying a decline in solar angular diameter of 1 arc second per century; Sabatino Sofia and colleagues at the Nasa Goddard Space Flight Center interpreted the same observations as implying a shrinking of "only" about 0.2 arc seconds per century.

By 1979, Eddy had stirred up a hornet's nest with his claims, and many astronomers started to get in on the act, some claiming to have proof that the Sun's diameter was not changing, others equally convinced that there was a shrinkage, but much less than Eddy and Boornazian had claimed. Dusty old records of various kinds were dug out of the files and reinterpreted. Irwin Shapiro of MIT looked at old records of transits of the planet Mercury across the face of the Sun. This is a beautiful technique but can only be applied about 13 times every century, when Mercury passes across the solar disk, as viewed from Earth. Because we know the distance from Earth to the Sun, and from Mercury to the Sun, astronomers can calculate the size of the Sun by measuring how long it takes for the planet to pass across the Sun's disk. Shapiro showed, using this technique, that the Sun has not been shrinking by more than 0.3 arc seconds per century since 1700, and he suggested that it might not be shrinking at all.

Another gorgeous technique for measuring the diameter of the Sun involves eclipses. The exact position of the edge of the path of an eclipse (the shadow of the Moon on the Earth) depends on the positions of the Sun and Moon and their distances from Earth, which are all known very accurately and can be calculated even for eclipses that occurred centuries ago. It also depends on the size of the Moon (which nobody suggests is changing) and the size of the Sun. It happens that in 1715 there was a total eclipse of the Sun visible from England, and Sir Edmund Halley, later Astronomer Royal, collected data on the eclipse from many observers. These data can be used to work out where the edge of the shadow was, and therefore how big the Sun was in 1715. A reanalysis of these records carried out in 1980 led to one of the most delightfully ironic scientific juxtapositions of all time.

In the issue of the scientific journal *Nature* dated 11 December 1980, one of the featured articles was headlined THE CONSTANCY OF THE SOLAR DIAMETER OVER THE PAST 250 YEARS. It was authored by John Parkinson, Leslie Morrison, and Richard Stephenson, three British astronomers, and it drew on studies of the meridian circle evidence, the transits of Mercury, and eclipse observations (including the 1715 eclipse) to conclude "there has been no detectable secular change in the solar diameter."

That same week, in the issue of *Science, Nature*'s American counterpart, dated 12 December 1980, there was another featured contribution on the problem. This one was headlined OBSERVATIONS OF A PROBABLE CHANGE IN THE SOLAR RADIUS BETWEEN 1715 AND 1979. It came from an equally eminent team of astronomers, David Dunham, Sabatino Sofia, Alan Fiala, and David Herald in the United States, and Paul Muller in England. They used the records of the 1715 eclipse, compared with data from an eclipse seen in 1976 in Australia and one visible in 1979 in North America, to conclude that "between 1715 and 1979, a decrease in the solar radius of 0.34 ± 0.2 arc second was observed."

It looked as if one of the teams had to end up with egg on their face. In fact, though, in spite of their dogmatic statements, both teams could still be right. The clue lay in the "error bars" on the numbers they quoted, their own estimates of the reliability of the evidence they were working with. Dunham and his colleagues said that the Sun *was* shrinking, at a rate between 0.14 and 0.54 (that is, 0.34 ± 0.2) arc second per century; Parkinson's group said there was *no* evidence for shrinkage, and that their observations ruled out any change bigger than 0.15 arc second per century (the figure they quoted for the "constancy" of the solar diameter was a "change" of 0.08 ± 0.07 arc second per century, which they interpreted as zero within the limits of the error bars; 0.15 lies at the other limit of the error bars).

The time was clearly ripe for someone to take a long, hard, and careful look at *all* the available data and try to find out just what the Sun was really doing. It was a measure of the concern caused by Eddy and Boornazian's original claim that astronomers did not seem hugely bothered by a suggestion that the Sun might be shrinking at "only" a rate of 0.2 arc second per century. Such a shrinkage of the *whole* Sun would still release 20 times more energy each year than the Sun actually does put out and would pull the rug from under all the standard models of the Sun, let alone the solar neutrino puzzle. It was Ron Gilliland who put things in a (slightly) more comfortable perspective, by showing that the changes are part of a long-term cycle of gentle solar pulsations, with the implication that they do indeed have something to do with the outer layers of the Sun: its atmosphere—not its deep interior.

○ **THE BREATHING SUN**

Gilliland took all five of the available data sets that contained long-term records of measurements of the diameter of the Sun and subjected all of them to a searching statistical analysis using techniques developed by mathematicians to find long-term trends and periodic variations in such samples. Two of the sets of data used by Gilliland were the same as those used by Eddy and Boornazian, two additional sets of data involved records of transits of Mercury across the Sun's disk, and the fifth data set was a compilation of timings of various solar eclipses. Between them, these historical records provided Gilliland with information about changes in the size of the Sun over a period of 265 years, from the eclipse of 1715 up to 1980.

The results of Gilliland's analysis were published in the *Astrophysical Journal* in September 1981. That fact is almost as significant as the results themselves, since although the weekly journals *Nature* and *Science* are prestigious and usually reliable, they are, by their nature, places where scientists sometimes go for quick publication, and some of the work published quickly in their pages is later proven to be in error or incomplete. The *Astrophysical Journal,* on the other hand, has long had a reputation for the toughness of its refereeing system, whereby submitted papers are carefully checked by other experts before being published. Meaning no disrespect to the weekly journals, where I have published papers myself, their pages are the first place you would look for slightly offbeat research on sunspots and changes in solar diameter; when this work appears in the *Astrophysical Journal,* it has (like the various publications on solar WIMPs in 1985 and 1986) an added stamp of credibility.

After all the flurrying of sometimes contradictory papers here, there, and everywhere, Gilliland provided the definitive state-of-the-art analysis. And it is a mark of how respectable his work was that essentially no further progress has been made since it was published.

What did he find? By combining the five sets of data, the statistical analysis shows that there is a long-term decline in the size of the Sun, amounting to 0.01 percent per century, or 0.018 seconds of arc, and that this has been going on since at least the early 1700s. Of course, there are still problems with the uncertainties of many of the measurements—as Gilliland put it, "One is not inexorably led to the conclusion that a negative secular solar radius trend has existed since A.D. 1700, but the preponderance of current evidence indicates that such is likely to be the case."* Even more strikingly, though, the analysis revealed two cyclic patterns of changes in the size of the Sun.

One of these is a gentle pulsation, in which the Sun breathes in and out over a cycle 76 years long. Other researchers had found hints of this before, using very limited sets of data; Gilliland showed that the effect is real and covers a range of about 0.02 percent of the Sun's radius, some 140 kilometers. And the picture is further complicated by a hint (no more than a hint) that there is an even smaller-scale oscillation in the size of the Sun over the familiar 11-year solar cycle. Intriguingly, both the 11-year and 76-year oscillations follow the rule of thumb that when the Sun is bigger there are fewer sunspots.

That rule of thumb would also tie in with the decrease in solar radius and increase in sunspot activity since the seventeenth century. In addition, astronomers have long suspected that there might be a sunspot rhythm about 80 years long, and some climatologists have related this to an apparent 80-year cycle in average temperatures on Earth. Could they be linked with the 76-year rhythm of solar pulsations?

The long-term decline in solar radius is, perhaps, the most important piece of information to emerge from this analysis, since stellar evolution theory predicts that the Sun should actually be growing, although by an even smaller and undetectable amount. The best guess at present is that this, too, is part of a long, slow pulsation cycle—a guess reinforced by the evidence that there were sunspots hundreds, thousands, and (as we shall soon see) millions of years before the Maunder Minimum. The discovery of the shorter cycles, however, has implications that may be of practical value over the next few decades.

The Sun was at its smallest, on the 76-year cycle, in 1911, at a time

Astrophysical Journal, vol. 248, article beginning p. 1144; quote from p. 1150.

when it also showed strong activity throughout its sunspot cycle. The next minimum in radius should therefore have been in 1987. Nobody will be sure if the Sun did start expanding again in 1988, or thereabouts, until several years have passed and several series of measurements have been made. But recent events certainly fit the pattern of a smaller Sun being linked with more sunspot activity. The latest peak of the 11-year cycle was around 1979–1980, when the measured mean sunspot number rose rapidly from 28 in 1977 to 93 in 1978, 155 in 1979, and about the same in 1980. These are high peaks. At the time of this writing (1989), the Sun has passed through a quiet state, with sunspot numbers in single figures in 1986, and is rapidly building up to the next peak of the 11-year cycle, expected early in 1990. The observations so far show that this is going to be another high maximum, very much in line with Gilliland's calculations. But then we can expect a smaller peak of activity next time, roughly in 11 years from now, early in the twenty-first century.

Gilliland explored the practical implications of all this in a paper published in the journal *Climatic Change* in March 1982. He found that many features of the pattern of temperature changes of the Earth since 1850 can be explained in terms of a combination of the effects of dust from volcanoes (rising high in the atmosphere and blocking out heat from the sun), a buildup of carbon dioxide in the air (trapping heat by the so-called greenhouse effect), and a 76-year cycle linked with the breathing of the Sun. If he is correct, the solar influence has been acting to counteract the greenhouse effect for the past 30 years, acting to cool the Earth while the Sun expanded. But as we pass the minimum of the present 76-year cycle, the Sun will start to provide more heat, contributing an additional 0.28 percent over the next three decades and warming the globe by a quarter of a degree Celsius over and above anything that happens due to the greenhouse effect.

That effect is itself a result of human activities, including the burning of coal and oil and destruction of the tropical rain forests. Climate experts predict a continuing buildup of carbon dioxide in the air, warming the globe as we move into the twenty-first century. With solar and greenhouse effects combining, the rise in temperatures could be more rapid than any of the climate experts have calculated.

One of those experts, Tom Wigley from the University of East Anglia, discussed the implications at the Royal Society meeting in February 1989. He pointed out that because it takes the Earth a long time to respond to small changes in heat arriving from the Sun (mainly because the oceans take a long time to warm up or to cool down), climatologists would not expect tiny fluctuations over the 11-year cycle to show up in their records—the Earth doesn't have time to respond to a dip in solar output before the output increases again. But, as Wigley pointed out, a 200-year (or 76-year) cycle would be long enough for even small changes in the output of the Sun, over a range from of about 1 percent, to account for climatic fluctuations on the scale of Little Ice Ages.

This suggestion is still controversial (especially where astrophysicists are concerned) and unproven, but it points the way for future research on links between solar activity and climate that could have great practical value. This serves to emphasize the urgency of further efforts to measure the size of the Sun.

One such attempt came in 1983, when an eclipse of the Sun was visible from Java. An expedition jointly sponsored by *New Scientist* magazine and University College, London, duly set out to measure accurately the edge of the path of the eclipse, with the aid of 25 senior students from a local high school, who formed a human chain three kilometers long at right angles to the edge of the path of totality. Their observations show that the size of the Sun today is smaller by about 0.2 arc second, about 0.01 percent, than the standard value set by astronomical observations in the nineteenth century and used trustingly by astronomers ever since.

The ultimate test of the breathing Sun idea will only come, of course, when modern instruments far more accurate than those used in previous centuries have built up a reliable day-to-day record of measurements of the solar diameter. Following Eddy's work, a new meridian telescope has been installed at the High Altitude Observatory in Colorado, and this is automated to time the transits of the Sun at noon with greater accuracy than ever before. More than 500 light-sensitive diodes are used to measure both vertical and horizontal dimensions of the solar disk at noon each day—but it will take at least another five years before the measurements can reveal whether or not the size of the Sun is changing. If Gilliland is right, of course, we will not find a shrinking going on over the next decade or so, but rather an expansion of the Sun—an expansion that will, paradoxically, lend credence to the idea that the Sun has shrunk since the seventeenth century.

Even while solar astronomers wait for those genuinely new data to come in, a French team headed by Elizabeth Ribes, at the Observatoire de Paris, uncovered some "new" old data to add to Gilliland's five data sets. The study was actually carried out by Jean Picard in the second half of the seventeenth century. Picard was a pioneering astronomer who designed precision instruments and, among other things, made many measurements of the size of the Sun, even before regular daily measurements with the transit telescope began in Greenwich. In a careful reanalysis of his old records, the Paris team found in the mid-1980s that the Sun was indeed about 2,000 kilometers bigger during the Maunder Minimum than it is today. And, perhaps the most compelling evidence of all, they found that there was a clear decrease of three arc seconds in the measured size of the Sun, as recorded by the *same* skillful observer (Picard), using the *same* instruments and techniques, between 1683, in the depths of the Maunder Minimum, and 1718, when the sunspots returned in modest force. Records of the few sunspots that appeared during the Maunder Minimum can also be used to explore the Sun's behavior at the time.

Although the sunspots were few in number throughout the Maunder Minimum, they were slightly less rare in the years 1674, 1684, 1695, 1705, and 1716, suggesting that the familiar 11-year cycle was still operating, in a quieter way, at the time. In all these years except 1716, spots were only seen in the southern hemisphere of the Sun, and the observers of the day kept careful drawings of what they saw. Because there were so few spots, there is no ambiguity about these drawings, and the life history of each spot can be traced as it moves across the visible disk of the Sun, carried around by the Sun's rotation. Rotation measurements based on these old drawings show that the Sun was rotating more slowly at the time it was bigger. This is exactly what we would expect if the increase in size represents a genuine swelling of the material in the outer part of the Sun. Like a spinning skater whose arms are spread outward, the Sun slows as its outer layer expands. Ribes and her colleagues pointed out in 1987 that the observations fit the expected pattern of behavior for a real pulsation of the outer layers of the star, rather than hinting at any changes in the deep interior (where neutrinos are produced).

The key question that arises, as far as any understanding of the deeper secrets of the Sun is concerned, is whether this kind of behavior is "normal" in terms of the long history of the Sun, or whether the whole pattern of solar cycles and sunspot activity is something peculiar that has been going on only for a few hundred or a few thousand years. If we are living at a time of unusual solar activity, then perhaps those ideas which hold that there are few solar neutrinos detected today because the Sun is in an unusual state should be taken seriously, after all. But if there were some way of finding a trace of similar solar cycles of activity from a few million or a few hundred million years ago, then we really would be forced to conclude that it is normal for the Sun to produce fewer neutrinos than the standard model predicts. Almost incredibly, just the evidence we require turned up in sediments laid down hundreds of millions of years ago, in what is now Australia.

○ THE RECORD IN THE ROCKS

The sediments were deposited in late Precambrian times, somewhere between about 650 million and 700 million years ago. Although the exact dating depends on assumptions about the geological time scale, for convenience we can say that the ancient rocks studied by George Williams of the Broken Hill Proprietary Mining Company are roughly 680 million years old. At the time they were being laid down, the world was in the grip of a severe ice age, and part of the ground of what was to become south Australia was permanently frozen, like the permafrost regions of northern Canada today. On the edge of the permafrost region, a long, shallow lake or inland sea stretched roughly north-south, and fine sand and silt particles accumulated on the floor of this lake, gradually building up to form the rocks now known as the Elatina Formation. In summer, the temperature over the permafrost terrain to the west of the lake may have risen just above freezing; in winter, it dropped to −30°C or −40°C.

Today, the rocks laid down in that lake form part of the Flinders Ranges, west of Adelaide. During his geological work in the region, Williams noticed an unusual section of siltstones in the Elatina Formation. This section of sedimentary rock is roughly 10 meters thick and is formed in fine layers, or laminae, each between 0.2 and 3 millimeters thick. The pattern made by these narrow bands of clay and sand looks very much like the pattern of tree rings in a large piece of wood; in this case, the characteristic pattern of the bands in the Elatina Formation has dark red-brown layers, spaced between 2 and 16 millimeters apart, separated by several paler bands of material, the narrow laminae. The pattern persists over an area several hundred meters across.

The sediments were formed by fine particles of material settling on the bottom of an ancient lake, and the regular pattern of the stripes in the rocks shows that some more or less regular rhythm was bringing in water, laden with sediment, from outside. It might have been a monthly rhythm, associated with tides raised in the lake by the Moon; or it might have been an annual rhythm, associated with the seasonal melting of the nearby glaciers. Simply by counting the layers, Williams found that the pattern of thick and thin sediments repeated roughly every 11 layers with a ''double cycle'' of alternate thick and thin 11-layer cycles common in the sediments. The implication seemed obvious, and the discovery was reported in 1981 as evidence of a solar influence on climate in late Precambrian times. The laminae were identified as annual layers of sediment, which are produced in some lakes today and are known as varves.

Astronomers in general did not exactly fall upon this discovery of the same solar rhythms operating 680 million years ago as operate today with cries of delight. Many were suspicious about how any solar ''signal'' in the weather could appear so strongly, when there is only a very weak influence of the solar cycle on weather today; some wondered whether the claimed 11-layer cycle might really be linked with the lunar tides and not the Sun. Were they ''really'' 12-layer monthly cycles that Williams had miscounted? But one senior Australian solar astronomer, Ronald Giovanelli, enthusiastically supported Williams's work and helped him obtain funding for a drilling program to obtain a complete core through the 10-meter-thick varve layer. Armed with this core, Williams went to the Laboratory of Tree-Ring Research at the University of Arizona and analyzed the patterns in the layers exactly as if they were tree rings, using a battery of powerful statistical techniques developed by the tree-ring researchers.

First he analyzed 1,337 consecutive laminae (varves) from one continuous section of core; then he analyzed 1,580 consecutive ''sunspot cycles,'' flagged by the darker bands in the core. In 1985, he reported that as well as the basic cycle, which varies from 8 to 16 years in length, there are several other rhythms present. For example, the length of each basic cycle, in terms of the number of layers in a cycle, varies over a longer cycle that is 13 basic cycles long. And there is a sharp, distinctive pattern that recurs every 26 cycles in the Elatina record.

By now there was enough evidence to make more astronomers sit up and take notice. One who did so was Ronald Bracewell of Stanford University, who has made a lifetime study of sunspot variations. The reliable record of sunspot variations goes back less than 200 years, but what Williams seemed to have found was a record of sunspot variations spanning 1,337 years. Never mind how the solar activity was influencing the weather 680 million years ago; Bracewell dived in to analyze the record on the assumption that it was indeed a pattern of sunspot activity, and compared it with the modest historical record with which he was already familiar.

He found that he could explain the pattern of the varves in terms of basic 11-year and 22-year rhythms, modulated by two longer cycles, spanning 314 years and 350 years. The length of the "11-year" cycle varies regularly over the 350-year modulation, while the size of the "sunspot peak" reached in any 11-year cycle seems to depend on the position of the cycle within the 314-year modulation. Of course, there is no hope of finding cycles more than 300 years long, since the historical record of sunspots is less than 200 years long. But Bracewell found a neat way to test his discoveries.

Using all the rhythms found in the Elatina varves, Bracewell set his computer running at the sunspot minimum that actually occurred in the summer of 1986 and ran it *backward* in time to "predict" the pattern of sunspot activity back to 1800. He got an almost perfect match with the actual record of solar activity, with all the high and low peaks in the right years, and the variation in length of the cycles themselves correctly calculated. Using *only* the record in the rocks from 680 million years ago, Bracewell had obtained the best agreement ever between any theory of solar variations and the actual sunspot records from historical times.* There seemed little room for doubt that the clock inside the Sun keeps a steady time, and that the Sun today is in the same basic state that it was in 680 million years ago. We are *not* living at a time of unusual solar activity.

○ SOLAR CONNECTIONS

Why, then, is the solar signal so strong in the Elatina varves? This may have nothing to do with our present story, but perhaps it is worth

---

*Such room for doubt as there is was lessened in 1990–1991, when the Sun reached a peak level of activity, with sunspot numbers above 125, very much in line with Bracewell's calculations.

a slight detour to look at the possible explanations on offer. One possibly important point was noted by Williams in his original report on the discovery. Geological records show that in the late Precambrian the Earth's magnetic field was only 10 percent as strong as it is today. This was not particularly unusual; the Earth's magnetic field does vary over the eons, though nobody quite knows why. Whatever the reason, when the field was weak, charged particles from the Sun (protons and electrons of the solar wind) could then have penetrated deeper into the atmosphere of the Earth than they do today, thereby influencing the weather.

Another possible explanation for the link gives us a good feel for just how long ago the late Precambrian really was. At that time, life on Earth (we should say, life in the *sea*, since even plants did not begin to colonize the land until about 420 million years ago) had not yet released much oxygen into the atmosphere. Today, oxygen in the atmosphere absorbs ultraviolet radiation from the Sun. This happens chiefly in the stratosphere, about 20 to 30 kilometers above our heads. The stratosphere gains energy as a result and is warmer than the upper layers of the troposphere, the layer of the atmosphere from the ground up to the stratosphere. Because the stratosphere is warmer than the troposphere, convection stops at the top of the troposphere,* and weather (which is driven by convection) is confined to the troposphere. In Precambrian times, there was little or no stratosphere, because there was little or no oxygen to absorb incoming ultraviolet radiation.

This would have had at least two potentially important effects. First, weather would not be confined so close to the ground, and convection columns could rise higher into the atmosphere than they do today. Second, the utraviolet radiation from the Sun could penetrate virtually to the ground, so any changes in solar ultraviolet associated with the sunspot cycle could have a big effect on temperature at the surface of the Earth. And anything that affects temperature and convection, of course, is also going to affect rainfall patterns.

Perhaps *that* explains why the Sun had a bigger influence on climate 680 million years ago than it does today. Even so, the effect would only have shown up in regions very sensitive to seasonal changes in rainfall, and we are extraordinarily lucky that the preserved remains of just such a sensitive set of sediments are exposed to view today. The important point to grasp, however, is not which possible expla-

---

*Hot air rises, but only if the air above it is colder than the rising air.

nation might be right, but the fact that conditions were so very different on Earth in the Precambrian that we cannot really make comparisons with the climatic patterns of the present day. Or can we? Just at the time this chapter was being prepared, another variation on the theme was produced by Kevin Zahnle, of NASA's Ames Research Center, and James Walker, of the University of Michigan. I can't resist including it here, even though it adds very little to our attempts to unravel the secrets of the Sun.

○ A LUNAR CONNECTION

Zahnle and Walker have linked the Elatina cycles with the cycles of lunar tides raised in the atmosphere of the Earth 680 million years ago. The details of their argument are rather subtle, but the key point is that there seem to have been *two* cycles interacting with one another to produce a strong "beat" effect. One of the cycles required is 10.8 years long, and the other is 20.3 years long. According to Zahnle and Walker, these are, respectively, the standard cycles astronomers expect to be associated with the Sun and the Moon in the Precambrian.

It is well known that the Moon raises tides in the atmosphere, as well as in the oceans, of the Earth, and there is some evidence that the changing lunar influence affects rainfall in some parts of the world. Today this influence repeats with a rhythm 18.6 years long—but astronomers calculate that things were different in the past, when the Moon's orbit was slightly different. Indeed, at the time the Elatina varves were laid down the equivalent lunar rhythms would have been 20.3 years long.

The Sun itself should also have been behaving slightly differently when it was younger. Robert Noyes and colleagues at Harvard University have studied other stars for evidence of "starspot" cycles like the cycle of our Sun and conclude that the length of such a cycle is related to the speed with which the star rotates. Since the Sun rotated faster (according to standard theory) when it was younger, the sunspot cycle should have been just 10.6 years long 680 million years ago. And, as a final ingredient to their theory, Zahnle and Walker allow for the fact that the Earth itself was rotating faster then, so that the day was only 21 hours long.

Putting all of the ingredients together, they suggest that the lunar and solar rhythms may have set up a resonance in the Earth's atmosphere at that time, rather like the way in which a wineglass may resonate in sympathy with a pure musical note. The influence of this on rainfall fluctuations could explain all of the patterns of thick and thin bands seen in the Elatina formation.

What is particularly nice about the work by Zahnle and Walker is that it shows how changes in the Earth, rather than changes in the Sun, can explain the record in the rocks of climatic events 680 million years ago. The Sun seems, on this picture, to have been behaving very steadily over the past 700 million years or so, and the very small adjustments in the length of the sunspot cycle that are needed to fit the varve record are themselves exactly in line with the standard model of a Sun rotating a little more rapidly then, and exactly in line with observations of other stars. The Sun is not in an unusual state today. It is a normal star, doing normal things. So we can confidently expect that any tricks astronomers can use to probe the secrets of the solar interior will be telling us things that are relevant to the whole life history of the Sun, not just to some special conditions that happen to be operating just at the time intelligent life has arisen on Earth to look into those mysteries. This is good news indeed—for astronomers *do* now have a means to probe the solar interior, using techniques reminiscent of the way seismologists study the interior of our planet by monitoring earthquakes, Vibrations in the atmosphere of the Earth may explain links between Sun and weather 680 million years ago. But now, it seems, vibrations in the outer part of the Sun reveal what is going on in its deep interior today. The new technique is called "helioseismology"—and it has a direct bearing on the solar neutrino problem.

7 THE SHAKING SUN

It wasn't until the 1980s that our shivering Sun opened its heart and revealed its innermost secrets to astronomers. But the discovery that made it possible to probe the solar interior had actually been made in 1960, years before the first solar neutrino was halted in Ray Davis's underground tank. Nobody realized just what those observations were telling us for ten years, and then it took a further ten years (and more) to design and bring into operation equipment to monitor the Sun's shivers with sufficient precision to probe the interior. The 1990s will probably prove to be the great decade of helioseismology; but already the first detailed observations are telling us more than we ever knew about the structure of the Sun and its internal temperature variations. Those revelations do not match up perfectly to the theorists' standard model of the Sun; but they do match up, very well indeed, to the modifications of the standard model calculated to be caused by the presence of WIMPs.

The story began with the discovery, by researchers from the California Institute of Technology, that all over the surface of the Sun there are little patches that move in and out in periods of about five minutes long. The discovery was made by accident, using instruments designed to study what the observers expected to see—random, or chaotic, movements of gas at the Sun's surface, being turned over by convection. In order to measure such motions, Robert Leighton and his colleagues used a sensitive refinement of the Doppler technique, measuring the varying positions of spectral lines in the light from the Sun with great precision.

All hot gases produce characteristic patterns of lines, as uniquely identifiable as a fingerprint, in the spectrum of light—this was the way the various elements were identified in the atmosphere of the Sun and their proportions calculated back in the 1920s. If the gas is moving bodily toward you or away, those lines are shifted to slightly different wavelengths from the ones associated with the same elements when they are at rest. When these lines are shifted toward the red end of the spectrum (stretched to longer wavelengths), it means that the gas emitting the light is moving away; when they are shifted toward the blue end of the spectrum (squeezed to shorter wavelengths), it means that the gas is coming toward you. You can get some ideas of the precision of the instruments used by the CalTech team from the nature of their discovery—they found that patches of the Sun oscillate intermittently, bouncing in and out five or six times in the space of roughly half an hour, with velocities of about 500 meters a second and an overall displacement of about 50 kilometers. The oscillations move a patch of the Sun's surface roughly in step over a distance equivalent to no more than 2 percent of the Sun's diameter, and at first they seemed to be some sort of localized phenomenon, nothing to do with the behavior of the Sun as a whole. But this was wrong.

○ **RINGING LIKE A BELL**

It wasn't until the beginning of the 1970s that several astronomers independently came up with the insight that enabled these solar oscillations first to be understood and then to be used to probe into the heart of the Sun. The key realization was that each of these short-lived bouncing movements of a patch of the solar surface was not due to some purely local effect. They could be better explained as an effect caused by literally millions of much smaller vibrations, sound waves trapped inside the Sun and making the surface ring like a bell. What seemed to be a series of five-minute oscillations was actually the superposition of hundreds of different frequencies of oscillation, with periods ranging from about three minutes to about an hour. Whereas a gong might be struck once with a hammer to produce a pure tone, the Sun was behaving like a gong in a sandstorm, being repeatedly struck by tiny particles of sand, with new vibrations starting up and old vibrations dying away all the time. The trigger for all this activity might very well be the random "blows" struck by the chaotic motions that Leighton and his colleagues set out to investigate in the first place—but the Sun was responding to those blows like a many-stringed instrument. Mixing the metaphor slightly, the mixture of tones is the sort of thing you might expect if the lid of a grand piano is being repeatedly thumped at random. Along with the random banging there would be the sound of all the strings vibrating gently, each with its own pure note.

There are no strings inside the Sun, but there are many pure notes that can resonate between the surface of the Sun and the bottom of the convective region. These are sound waves, akin to the waves that sound in an organ pipe when it is blown. And they combine to shake the surface of the Sun in a regular way because of the way the speed of sound varies at different depths inside the Sun.*

It works like this: From the surface of the Sun down to the bottom of the convective layer, the speed of sound increases as you go deeper. There is no mystery about this—deeper layers are hotter, and the speed of sound is greater in a hotter gas. So however and wherever it starts in the convective zone, as a sound wave angles down below the surface of the Sun, the bottom of the wave moves faster than the top. This bends the moving sound wave away from the bottom of the convective zone and back up to the surface of the Sun.† At the surface, however, the wave cannot escape—there is only empty space outside the Sun, and sound cannot travel through a vacuum. So it bounces from the surface, reflecting back into the depths like light reflecting from a

---

*Because it is so hot, the speed of sound in the interesting region of the Sun is about 150 times the speed of sound in the Earth's atmosphere. But the distance from the center of the Sun to the surface is about 5 million times greater than the length of a wind instrument such as a clarinet. The solar equivalent of the vibration of air inside a clarinet would be a wave oscillating with a period roughly 30 minutes long, five million times the vibration frequency of sound in a clarinet. Douglas Gough, who made this neat analogy, stresses that although such a low "note" is far outside the range of sound to which our ears are sensitive, it is still correct to call these solar vibrations sound waves, because they are sustained by exactly the same physical processes that sustain sound waves inside a clarinet on Earth.

†The same sort of thing happens to sound waves in the atmosphere of the Earth. On a hot, still day, the air just above the surface of a lake may be significantly cooler than the air a little higher up. Sound waves that start moving up from one shore of the lake are bent back down toward the surface and may carry the sound of voices, for example, clearly for a great distance across the surface of the water—a kind of acoustical mirage.

mirror. The whole process repeats, and the sound wave loops its way around the Sun, diving repeatedly into the convective zone and repeatedly being bent back and reflecting off the surface (Figure 7.1).

The depth the wave penetrates to and how far the wave travels around the Sun in each hop between reflections off the surface depend on the wavelength. Many waves bounce around inside the Sun and eventually fade away without contributing much, if anything, to the regular oscillations discovered in the early 1960s. But for some waves the length between bounces is just right to make an exact number of hops fit into a complete circuit around the Sun. The wave may bounce three, or six, or some other number of times on its travels, but as it goes around and around the Sun it always touches the surface in exactly the same three, or six, or whatever number it is, places. So those particular patches of the Sun's surface are pushed in and out by the wave not once but every time it passes right around the Sun. The pattern it makes is called a ''standing wave'' (Figure 7.2), and it is exactly equivalent to the standing waves that make a plucked guitar string or a blown organ pipe vibrate to produce a pure note. By analyzing the notes produced by an organ pipe, a physicist could tell you what the di-

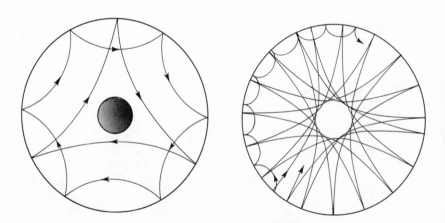

Fig. 7.1. Sound waves moving inside the Sun are bent as they pass through the hot interior, and reflect when they strike the surface from below. So patterns of standing waves can build up inside the Sun, as indicated in these two diagrams. Where such standing waves touch the surface of the Sun, they cause a regular oscillation which can be measured from Earth.

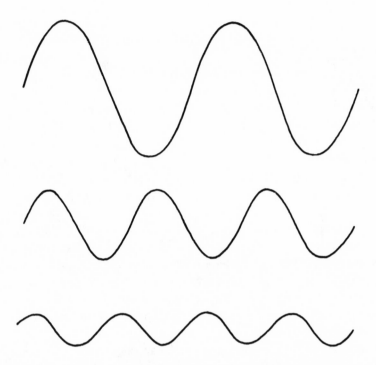

Fig. 7.2. **A standing wave is like the waves on a plucked guitar string or in air vibrating in an open-ended organ pipe, shown schematically here. These three waves are part of the same family of overtones, and each fits the same space—one with two peaks and two troughs, one with three peaks and three troughs, one with four peaks and four troughs. A physicist could tell how big the organ pipe that made these notes was by analyzing the notes. The same technique tells astrophysicists about conditions inside the sun.**

mensions of the pipe were, without ever seeing it.* Similarly, by analyzing the "notes" produced by sound waves traveling around the Sun, an astrophysicist can tell you about conditions inside the Sun without ever seeing below the surface. The situation is more compli-

*Indeed, the eminent geophysicist Sir Edward Bullard once told me that trying to work out the detailed structure of the Earth by analyzing earthquakes (geoseismology) was like trying to work out the detailed structure of a grand piano by analyzing the noise it made when pushed down a steep flight of stairs. Happily for astrophysicists, the structure of the Sun is simpler than either a grand piano or the interior of the planet we live on. Once solar sound waves were identified, helioseismology became practicable.

cated, because the "cavity" inside the Sun is three-dimensional, not a straight, one-dimensional tube. But the principles are exactly the same.

○ FINE TUNING

Until the 1970s, these ideas, as neatly explanatory as they were, were nevertheless just theory. During that decade, however, improved observations confirmed that the Sun really was "ringing" in this way. First, astronomers found that the five-minute vibrations can even be seen in the overall brightness of the Sun, as a tiny variation in what they call the "integrated" light. This, in effect, treats the Sun as if it were a distant star, looking at its total brightness, not at the variations from place to place over the surface. Then, by refining their spectroscopic studies, they were able to show that each patch of the Sun that we see moving in and out within a five-minute period is actually being pushed by an enormous number of much smaller standing waves.

Measuring the way such a small region of the solar surface moves up and down over a distance of a few tens of kilometers five or six times in half an hour is impressive enough. But by using a technique known as Fourier analysis this movement can be broken down into its constituent parts. Once again, there are appropriate musical analogies. The deepest note that can be produced by an organ pipe, for example, corresponds to sound with a wavelength just the right size for one wave to fit into the length of the pipe. This is called the fundamental note of that particular pipe, and organs are made with pipes of various lengths in order to be able to play different fundamental notes. There is another way to get different notes out of the same length of pipe, however. The fundamental note has a wavelength that fits once inside the pipe. This is the "natural" note produced by the pipe, the one you get just by blowing across the end and making the air inside resonate (blowing across the top of an empty bottle does the same trick). But you can also fit a wave with half that length into the pipe twice, a wave with one quarter that wavelength will fit in four times, and so on. These shorter waves that also fit the pipe are known as harmonics, or overtones, and correspond to appropriately higher notes, related to the fundamental. Even if the organist is trying to play a pure note— the fundamental—some of the vibration of the air in the pipe will be producing the overtones, and this helps to give different kinds of wind instruments different sound textures, even when they are playing the same note.

Using Fourier analysis, a physicist could unravel this complexity of overlapping notes and tell you exactly which pure notes, harmonics, and overtones have been combined in the pipe to produce the rich sound that we hear. Exactly the same technique makes it possible to break down the pattern of vibrations actually observed at the solar surface into the individual standing waves that have combined to produce the observed variation. Although the number of individual standing waves cannot be counted precisely, the statistical evidence shows that there are actually tens of millions of separate vibrations—separate "notes"—interfering with each other (adding in some places and canceling in others) to produce the observed effects. Each individual vibration moves the surface of the Sun in and out by only a few tens of meters (compare this with the diameter of the Sun, which is about a *million* kilometers) at speeds of only a few tens of centimeters a second. But any one standing wave may persist for several days, always moving the same patches of the Sun's surface in and out, and this longevity helps the observers to gather enough information for the Fourier analysis to be effective. It is the combined effect of millions of these tiny vibrations that produces the larger, short-lived pulses of vibration that were first noticed in the early 1960s.

There is another way in which you can get a grasp of just how subtle this fine tuning of the spectroscopic technique really is. It all depends, remember, on the way in which lines in the spectrum of light from the Sun are shifted to and fro over a small range of wavelengths as the region of gas that is being observed moves toward or away from the spectroscopic instrument. This is equivalent to a change in the color of the light. A particular wavelength (color) of light that is emitted from the surface of the Sun becomes shorter (bluer) when the patch of the solar surface we are studying is moving toward us, and longer (redder) when that patch of the surface is moving away. As the Earth rotates, the observing instrument itself is carried, during the course of the day, first toward the Sun and then away from it, with velocities that cover a range of about 800 meters a second, comparing dawn with dusk—far bigger than the effect being studied on the Sun, but a regular, well-known cycle that can easily be allowed for in the calculations. But even this effect on the measured wavelengths (colors) of the light is small. The speed of light itself is 300 *million* meters a second. In principle, if you drive fast enough down the road toward a red stoplight you could change the color you see to green, by the Doppler ''blue-shifting'' of the light (green is a bit more than halfway through the visible part of the spectrum from red to blue). But in order to do the trick, you would have to move at about one third of the speed of light, some 100 million meters every second. The effects being measured on the surface of the Sun correspond to motions with speeds of around 10 *centimeters* every second, about a gentle walking pace, an effect one billion times more subtle. Perhaps it is not so surprising, after all, that even though the solar oscillations were first observed in the early 1960s, it was not until the 1970s that they began to be understood and analyzed in detail, and it was only in the 1980s that the subtleties of the information they contained began to provide new insights into the inner workings of the Sun. Still, those insights were worth waiting for.

○ FIRST RESULTS

The depth at which a traveling sound wave is turned around and bent back toward the surface of the Sun depends on how quickly the speed of sound increases as the wave goes deeper into the Sun. That, in turn, depends on the way the temperature increases. By analyzing different standing waves (different vibration modes) which probe the Sun to different depths (Figure 7.1), helioseismologists can construct a temperature profile for the outer layers of the Sun—a picture of exactly how temperature increases as you move deeper below the surface. The speed of sound also depends on the exact composition of the Sun—whether it contains 25 percent helium or, for example, 30 percent or even 20 percent.

Before helioseismology was developed, there was no way to measure temperatures inside the Sun directly. They were inferred from computer models using standard physics. With helioseismology those models could be tested. The standard model of the Sun that astrophysicists had developed before the advent of helioseismology could be used to make predictions about the frequencies of the acoustic vibrations that now were being discovered and analyzed (indeed, this could have been done *before* the vibrations were discovered, but nobody imagined that such subtleties would actually become part of observational studies of the Sun). The frequencies predicted by the standard model were a little higher than the ones actually observed. But the predictions of the model can be made to fit the observed pattern if the convective zone in the outer part of the Sun extends a little deeper than the astrophysicists had thought, down to about 200,000 kilometers, roughly 30 percent of the way from the surface of the Sun to the center. Once that adjustment is made, the standard model and the observations are in broad agreement, provided that the outer convective region of the Sun does indeed contain about 25 percent helium, exactly the proportion required by another standard model of astrophysics, the one that describes the Big Bang in which the Universe was born. Yet, while solar seismology immediately made it possible for astrophysicists to fine-tune their standard model of the Sun, these subtle adjustments did not change calculation of the temperature at the heart of the Sun, so the solar neutrino problem was still present in full force.

In fact, the study of solar vibrations initially made the solar neutrino problem look worse. It did so because the insight into solar structure the vibrations provide pulls the rug from under some of the ideas put forward over the years to "explain" the scarcity of solar neutrinos. It is easy to dream up cocktail party solutions to the neutrino problem, unhindered by actual observations of the solar interior, as long as the inside of the Sun is uncharted territory (like the regions labeled "Here Be Dragons" on old maps); but it is much harder for those wild ideas to survive once we begin to find out how the inside of the Sun actually does work. For example, one particular "explanation" of the solar neutrino problem depended on the possibility that some of the material in the heart of the Sun, processed by nuclear fusion reactions, could have gotten mixed outward, contaminating the outer layers with processed material (a kind of nuclear ash) and changing the composition of the core by dragging in unprocessed material (extra fuel) from above. Such mixing can be arranged to produce a computer model that forecasts a lower output of solar neutrinos—but it also affects the way in which the speed of sound changes with depth inside the Sun. And the kind of change that this mixing would produce can now be ruled out with helioseismology; astrophysicists have looked for it, but it is not there.

The first results from helioseismology rule out not only this particular astrophysical "solution" to the neutrino problem, but also virtually all the other attempts to get around the problem by interfering solely with the astrophysics of the standard model. The way the Sun shakes shows that the solution to the problem must not lie simply in adjusting the astrophysics, but must involve "new" particle physics as well.

Indeed, it's almost time to bring WIMPs back into the story. First, let's take a quick look at the power of the new discipline of helio-seismology by the way in which it has settled a dispute that has run for decades, concerning the way in which the Sun rotates.

Galileo knew that the Sun rotates, because he discovered the dark spots on its surface and watched some of them move as they were carried around by the rotation of the Sun. Modern astronomers study solar rotation in the same way. Because the Sun is not a solid object like the Earth, but is a fluid body, it doesn't all rotate at the same speed—the gas at the equator takes about 25 days to spin once, while the polar regions rotate once in 30 days. Obviously, in each case this is only the speed of rotation at the surface—things might rotate faster (or slower) on the inside. This possibility has especially intrigued astronomers who have studied the way in which the planet Mercury (the closest planet to the Sun) moves in its orbit.

The orbits planets follow around the Sun are not circles, but ellipses, with the Sun at one focus of the ellipse. This has been known since the pioneering work of Johannes Kepler early in the seventeenth century. But in the nineteenth century astronomers realized that even after taking into account all known factors, such as the gravitational tug of each of the other planets, the orbit of Mercury is a little more complicated still. Instead of always tracing out the same ellipse, the orbit shifts sideways slightly, pivoting around the focus that is locked to the Sun, each time the planet goes around the Sun. If you could trace out the looping complexity of the orbit on paper, it would form a series of overlapping ellipses like a child's drawing of the petals of a daisy. The effect is tiny (it amounts to a shift of only 43 seconds of arc per century), but it is real, and nobody could explain it until the second decade of the twentieth century, when Albert Einstein formulated the general theory of relativity. Among its many other triumphs, general relativity (which is a theory of gravity subtly different from Newton's gravitational theory, on which all previous orbital calculations had been based) *exactly* explained the change in the orbit of Mercury over the centuries.

More recently, partly out of singlemindedness and partly through a laudable wish to test general relativity to the limits, some astrophysicists have pointed out that there is another way to make the orbit of Mercury shift in the observed way (the nineteenth-century astronomers *could* have thought of the trick, but didn't). If the inner core of the Sun is rotating very fast, and bulging outward as a result, the gravitational influence of the bulge will also make the orbit of Mercury shift around the Sun. And if that really is happening, then general relativity is not needed to explain the phenomenon!

The debate didn't exactly rage through the halls of science—there is plenty of other evidence that general relativity works okay. But the idea of a rapidly rotating solar core remained an irritating possibility until the end of the 1970s. Then astrophysicists realized that the fast-spinning, bulging core of such a solar model would also affect the pattern of vibrations in the Sun. When the observations were compared with appropriate model calculations, they showed no sign of the effect. If anything, they suggest that the Sun may actually be rotating slightly slower in its interior than outside (which nobody seems to have predicted). General relativity *is* needed to explain what is happening to the orbit of Mercury, as well as all the other things it explains so well. And since general relativity is rather well established as a "good" theory, the argument can be turned around—the accuracy of using the solar vibrations as a probe of the Sun's interior is confirmed by the fact that the internal structure the vibrations describe matches the internal structure we expect if the shift in the orbit of Mercury is indeed produced by relativistic effects. So what *can* this new technique of helioseismology tell us about surviving attempts to solve the neutrino problem?

○ **SPLITTING THE DIFFERENCE**

The answer emerged as a result of a visit by John Faulkner to the Tata Institute in Bombay in November and December 1985. There he met an Indian graduate student, Mayank Vahia, who was interested in the solar neutrino problem and asked Faulkner how the presence of WIMPs in the models would affect the expected vibrations of the Sun. Faulkner did not, at that stage, know; but both he and Vahia were already planning to attend a meeting of the International Astronomical Union in New Delhi at the end of November. There, Faulkner knew, Douglas Gough, from Cambridge, would be giving a talk on solar variations. It would be the perfect opportunity to find out.

Gough's talk opened the eyes of Faulkner and Vahia to the fact that as well as there being a solar neutrino problem, there was also a solar pulsation problem. It concerns measurements one stage more subtle than the ones I have discussed so far, dealing not with the periods of

the vibration inside the Sun, but with the *difference between* the vibration periods of closely related acoustic waves. The waves I have
described so far are technically known as p-modes, or pressure waves.
They are exactly equivalent to the pulse of sound waves that would
ripple through the bulk of the water in your bathtub if you slapped the
palm of your hand down on the surface of the water. Some of the
pressure waves that disturb the surface of the Sun pass right through
the solar core, so you might guess that they would be useful for studying
conditions in the heart of the Sun. But because the temperature of the
core is so high, the speed of sound there is very high, they pass through
the core very quickly, and they only have time to be affected in subtle
ways. One of those subtleties involves the difference in vibration
frequency between various sound waves that have very nearly the
same period—in the jargon, "the frequency separation of adjacent
p-modes." This was the feature of Gough's talk that caught Faulkner's attention.

Gough mentioned that the standard solar model (even after the fine
tuning mentioned earlier) not only "predicts" too many solar neutrinos, but it also predicts a separation of these p-modes that is about 10
percent bigger than the value revealed by helioseismology. That doesn't
seem too bad on its own. But, as Gough also pointed out to his audience
in New Delhi, all the existing solar models which "solved" the neutrino problem by making the center of the Sun 10 percent cooler (the
models with internal mixing, that I have already mentioned) made the
situation worse—for those models, the frequency separation is too big
by as much as 50 percent.

Faulkner immediately asked what happened with the WIMP models.
Gough replied that he had not carried out the calculation for those
models and didn't know; but since WIMPs also made the center of
the Sun cooler he guessed that they would also make the vibration
problem worse. Faulkner chewed over the problem in his mind and
became convinced that the WIMP model differed from all other models
with a cooler core in one critical respect: Whether or not the shift in
frequency separation was the right *size* it would certainly go in the
right *direction,* reducing the discrepancy that Gough had highlighted.
After all, the mixed models have a *higher* sound speed in their centers,
in spite of the lower temperature, because of the difference in composition compared with the standard models; but the WIMP model has
a *lower* sound speed, because the temperature is lower and the com-

position is basically the same as the standard model. Would the effect be big enough to do the job?

When Faulkner tracked Gough down during the evening following his talk, his colleague was intrigued by the idea and agreed that it was worth looking into properly. But when? And where? It turned out that Gough was, in fact, heading for the Tata Institute for a couple of weeks—quite unaware that Faulkner would also be there. It was too good an opportunity to miss.

Working intensively for five days at the Tata Institute, the two friends from Cambridge and their new Indian colleague were able to show that the change in the internal structure of the Sun (caused by the presence of just enough WIMPs to solve the solar neutrino problem WIMPs) shifts the vibration periods by just the right amount—the p-mode separation predicted by the model exactly matched the separation measured by helioseismologists. Figure 7.3 shows just how beautifully the WIMP model fits the observational constraints—and how all other astrophysical ''solutions'' to the neutrino problem make the vibration problem worse. In these days of computers, Faulkner takes great delight in telling how the calculations were carried through in the old-fashioned way, using pencil and paper—and how, because all his data had been left back in Santa Cruz, they had to read off the numbers they needed for their calculations from the graphs published in the printed version of the earlier WIMP papers he had coauthored (the Tata Institute library, of course, stocks the *Astrophysical Journal*). The collaboration between Faulkner, Gough, and Vahia was completed early in December 1985 and reached the offices of the journal *Nature* in London on the last day of the month. Faulkner also sent a copy to his former student, Gilliland, in Boulder—and then learned, on his return to California, that Gilliland had already been thinking (and working) along the same lines.

For once, pencil and paper had beaten the computerized approach. Gilliland and his colleagues in Boulder had been ''number crunching'' in the now standard way, using a large computer to work out many different vibration modes and the physical conditions needed to make the modeled oscillations match the observations of the Sun. They came up with the same answer—that the presence of the right amount of WIMPs brings theory and observation in line with each other. But it turned out that the two approaches were complementary. One group (Boulder) had started with oscillations, picking the ones that match

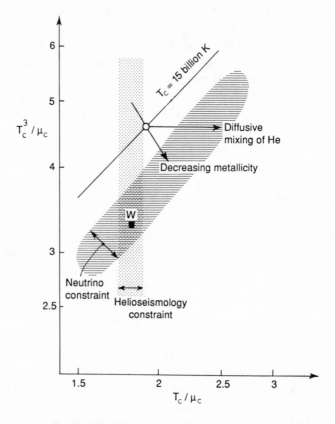

Fig. 7.3. John Faulkner's *pièce de résistance*. He invented this plot to show just how good the WIMP theory is. In this diagram, the standard model of the Sun is represented by an open circle, on the diagonal line corresponding to a central temperature of 15 billion K. This is barely within the region allowed by helioseismology studies and well outside the region allowed by solar neutrino studies. Standard tricks to "solve" the solar neutrino problem by changing the assumed composition of the Sun ("decreasing metallicity") or mixing helium more thoroughly take the models *away* from the region allowed by helioseismology. Only the WIMP model (W) sits smack in the heart of the region allowed by *both* helioseismology *and* neutrino studies. Don't worry too much about the strange coordinates, which Faulkner chose in order to make everything interesting in the diagram happen along straight lines. T_c is the calculated temperature at the center of the Sun, and μ_c is the molecular weight there. The abscissa (X coordinate, along the bottom) is proportional to the square of the speed of sound in the Sun's heart, and the ordinate (Y coordinate, up the page) is proportional to the square of the sound speed multiplied by the square of the temperature.

observations and working back to find out what that told them about conditions in the heart of the Sun. The other group (Tata) started out with the temperature profile that matched the WIMP model, calculated what kind of vibration modes that ought to produce, and found that these match the observations.

The key, in each case, is that the presence of WIMPs in the model lowers the temperature at the heart of the Sun without mixing the interior, and therefore without changing its structure, so the sound speed is also lowered. And because the two approaches were different, the Boulder team hurriedly prepared their version of the story for publication in *Nature* as well, while Faulkner and his colleagues agreed to wait, so that the two papers appeared alongside each other in the issue dated 15 May 1986. And this was far from being the end of the burst of excitement about WIMPs.

○ **THE TRIUMPH OF THE WIMP**

Using a new theory to explain a puzzle you already knew about—the shortage of solar neutrinos, the splitting of p-mode frequencies, or whatever it might be—is all very well, but never entirely satisfactory. The best test of a scientific theory is when it predicts something that has never been measured before, but can be. Then, if the new measurement is carried out and matches the prediction, the theory gains hugely in terms of credibility. In the late spring of 1986, WIMP theory would make that just such a prediction and take that giant step toward full respectability. It all came out of the collaboration in Bombay, although it involves another kind of solar vibration.

Waves on the surface of the sea, or the waves you can make in your bathtub by sloshing the water from one end to the other, are not p-modes. They are known instead as gravity waves (or g-modes), because it is the force of gravity that determines how quickly they rise and fall.* Gravity waves occur where there is a difference in density between two layers of fluid, such as the difference between air and water, or the difference between layers inside the Sun. Such waves should be produced deep inside the Sun and should be very sensitive to conditions in the core. But there is a big snag for helioseismologists who want to use g-modes to probe the heart of the Sun. Gravity waves

*Not to be confused with gravitational radiation, which is ripples in the fabric of space-time that are predicted by general relativity and that are also sometimes referred to as gravity waves.

have periods of hours or days, quite different from the five-minute oscillations of p-modes; thus, they can only be studied from space, since instruments on the ground cannot view the Sun at night. And even from space it is no easy job to pick them out; their influence is strong in the core but extends only weakly out to the surface, where any effect they produce on the motion of patches of the solar surface is very small in comparison.

In spite of the difficulty of identifying such vibrations, several groups of researchers had been looking for them before the Tata team's paper was published. After all, the observers knew that *if* they could find traces of g-modes they would have a direct clue to the structure of the deep interior of the Sun. Standard models predicted that there should be an identifiable g-mode feature in the spectrum of solar vibrations with a ⟨period⟩ of about 36 minutes.* Solar models using the fuel-mixing concept to resolve the neutrino problem shift this ⟨period⟩ by 40 percent or more, out to about 56 minutes. Trustingly, the observers who had been looking for such a feature in the spectrum of solar vibrations had searched for anything from a little below the value appropriate for the standard model, around 32 minutes, up to the values appropriate for the mixed models, 56 minutes and even longer. In their *Nature* paper, however, Faulkner, Gough, and Vahia pointed out that, just as in the case of the p-modes, the WIMP model produces the opposite effect. For the WIMP model, the g-mode feature should appear at around 29 minutes—where, as far as they knew, nobody had looked or even gathered data.

Within three weeks of the publication in *Nature*, Faulkner heard that a researcher based in Switzerland, Claus Fröhlich, had found a trace of just the effect Faulkner and his colleagues had predicted. The evidence actually came from old data, observations of the Sun carried out from space by the Solar Maximum Mission satellite and dating back to 1980. Nobody had found the 29-minute feature before because the researchers (with the aid of their computers) had only looked for longer ⟨periods⟩, having put too much faith in the theory that the neutrino problem could be solved by mixing! Fröhlich had read the *Nature* paper and immediately run the data through the computer to search for shorter ⟨periods⟩; the only one he found was the one that

---

*The feature is actually not a true "period" but, as in the case of the p-modes, a difference between periods. Technically, "the asymptotic normalized period spacing of high-order g-modes of low-degree." With apologies to my astrophysical friends, I will use the (strictly speaking incorrect) term ⟨period⟩, with angle brackets, as shorthand.

had been predicted by Faulkner and his colleagues on the basis of the WIMP model.

There is, to be fair, no more than a hint that the ⟨period⟩ can actually be picked out from the data—but there isn't even a hint of any other ⟨period⟩, and the feature is exactly where it was predicted to be. Assuming the feature is real, more detailed analysis shows that the g-modes are being affected by rotation deep in the heart of the Sun in exactly the same way as the p-modes (that is, the two sets of observations both tell us that the Sun's core is rotating at the same rate). The two sets of data are completely independent—they are obtained from different instruments (one set on the ground, one in space) using different techniques to study two different kinds of oscillations (p-modes and g-modes) which have completely different period ranges (about five minutes as against many hours). And yet the "answers" they give are the same! The WIMP model is the *only* model of the Sun that simultaneously explains these details of the spectrum of solar vibrations *and* resolves the neutrino problem.

There are astronomers—many astronomers—who are still not persuaded by the WIMP model and prefer at least to stay sitting on the fence until the next phase of solar observations has been completed. But the weight of evidence that the heart of the Sun is kept cool by the presence of previously unknown particles, one for every hundred billion protons inside the Sun and each with a mass somewhere around four to six times the mass of the proton, has surely now become something more than merely circumstantial. This is no longer "just another wild idea." Those who still want to wait and see, however, will not have to wait long, since the next generation of instruments, designed to monitor solar vibrations for 24 hours a day over a time span of several years, is even now coming into operation.

○ **THE GONG TEST**

The major problem for astronomers attempting to improve their observations of solar oscillations is the rotation of the Earth. Observations made from a single site on Earth are affected by the cycle of day and night. Because solar oscillations are so small, long runs of observational data must be added together and analyzed to reveal the tiny periodic fluctuations. The only way to do this, if you are restricted to observing the Sun from a single site on the ground at one of the great observatories, is to add the data from different days together, taking care to join the records up so that the oscillations you are studying stay in step and do not cancel each other out. But such "artificial" long runs of data, from different days added together, contain spurious "signals" caused by the nighttime gaps—signals not only with a rhythm 24 hours long but at many harmonic frequencies associated with this 24-hour fundamental. These signals show up in the Fourier analysis and confuse the picture, making it hard for the researchers to be sure which periods are real solar variations and which ones are artifacts.

There are three ways to get around this problem, all of which are being tackled by different research groups as we move into the 1990s. A joint team from France and the United States has tried making observations from the South Pole in summer, when the Sun never sets. It worked—they obtained a stretch of observations spanning five days back in 1980. But working conditions at the pole are hardly ideal, even in summer—and the weather conditions are so poor that five days without cloud cover is about the best continuous observing run you can hope for.

The second approach is to make the observations from space, from a satellite placed in an orbit where it can monitor the Sun continuously. Just such an approach was used for the Solar Maximum Mission, whose data seem to bear out the Tata team's prediction. A joint mission of the European Space Agency and NASA, called the Solar Heliospheric Observatory (or SOHO) is scheduled to fly in 1995 and will carry an instrument to monitor solar oscillations. It should send back data for several years.

But even before SOHO is launched, the third technique for eliminating the night should be coming into its own. This involves making observations of the Sun from different sites around the world and combining the measurements to provide a continuous record spanning many years. There are three such projects now under way, and I'll mention just one of them in a little more detail. This is known as the Global Oscillation Network Group, or GONG. In principle, you need a minimum of three observing sites, evenly spaced around the world 120 degrees of longitude apart, cloudless skies, and instruments that never break down. In practice, GONG is going for six sites, spaced as evenly as possible around the globe.

As of 1990, ten sites were being tested: at Mauna Kea and Haleakala in Hawaii; Mount Wilson and Big Bear in California; Yuma in Arizona;

Cerro Tololo and Las Campanas in Chile; Izana in the Canary Islands; Udaipur in India; and Learmouth in Western Australia. In addition, there is a "reference instrument" at the U.S. National Solar Observatory in Tucson, Arizona—the parent institute for the project. During site testing, there have already been several runs of a few days when the Sun never set on the functioning prototype GONG network, and the longest such run spanned more than two weeks.

At each site, an automated instrument with a 50-millimeter aperture (the size is so modest that astronomers are reluctant to call them "telescopes"—they are more like camera lenses) will take a snapshot of the Sun every minute. The design philosophy of the package resembles that of a space mission—the team chose a rugged, low-technological-risk instrument that works without any help from a human operator. Two instruments should be looking at the Sun at any one time, to cover the inevitable occurrence of cloud cover or breakdowns. And each measures velocities as patches of the Sun move in and out, using an instrument known as a Fourier tachometer, which can measure redshifts and blueshifts as small as one part in a billion.

The GONG instruments take these measurements at 65,000 points across the surface of the Sun simultaneously, generating an enormous amount of data to be stored (initially on tape, later on optical disks) and processed. The details of the computer power required for all this aren't important, but there certainly wouldn't have been much point in making observations of this kind in the 1970s, since the computers of that time would not have been up to the job of analyzing it. (One reason for saving the data on optical disks is the hope that twenty-first–century scientists may have even better techniques for analyzing it than we have today.) The whole network should become fully operational during 1991 and is funded to run initially for three years, generating a gigabyte of data every day.* The project involves more than 150 individual scientists from 61 different research centers in 15 different countries.

That should be enough to settle the question of whether the vibrations really do match the predictions of the WIMP theory. But that will surely not be the only important result to come out of the GONG project; most astronomers will be highly surprised if the new observations do not throw up new and unexpected problems to puzzle over

---

*For comparison, this book contains somewhere between a half and one kilobyte of information, less than one millionth of the amount of data gathered by GONG in a day.

in the 1990s, just as every new observing technique, from Galileo's telescope to radio astronomy and X-ray satellites, has thrown up new and unexpected surprises about the Universe. Most astronomers will also be disappointed if the funds are not found to keep the GONG project running for at least the length of a full solar cycle, 11 years, so that we can see how the solar vibrations change, if at all, as the Sun runs through its overall cycle of activity.

And *I* will be disappointed if half this book isn't completely out of date by the year 2000: The chances are that over the next ten years, GONG, SOHO, and other observations will provide us with a completely new picture of the workings of our neighborhood star, a picture painted with unprecedented attention to detail. What matters is not so much whose pet theory is correct, but that we are about to find out more of the inner secrets of the Sun than have been revealed throughout all of history to date. The most exciting thing about the WIMP theory and the evidence so far that it is on the right track is that it links these anticipated new discoveries both to the Universe at large and to the submicroscopic world of elementary particles—while raising the possibility of building new kinds of detectors, much cheaper than GONG or SOHO, which can be constructed in individual laboratories here on Earth and which may reveal not only the innermost secrets of the Sun but also the ultimate fate of the Universe itself.

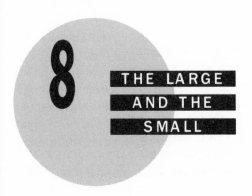

8

THE LARGE AND THE SMALL

The most dramatic development in theoretical physics in the 1980s has been the way in which particle physicists and cosmologists have been forced to combine their talents in order to improve their descriptions of the world around us. Particle theorists, trying to develop the elusive unified theory that will explain the behavior of all the particles and forces of nature in one mathematical package, have been forced to contemplate the implications of processes that go on at energies far greater than anything that can be achieved artificially in their accelerators here on Earth, or even in the heart of a star like the Sun. The only place where the interactions that the theorists describe actually took place was in the Big Bang in which the Universe was born, some 15 billion years ago. So the latest theories of particle physics are "tested" by finding out whether the kind of reactions they describe could have produced the kind of Universe we live in. Improved particle physics helps the cosmologists develop a better understanding of how the Universe began; improved cosmological observations of the Universe at large help set limits on what could possibly have happened in the Big Bang and thereby constrain some of the wilder speculations of the particle theorists.

At the same time, cosmologists themselves have found a need, as I have mentioned, for more matter than meets the eye in the Universe. From studies of the way galaxies and clusters of galaxies move, and measurements of the rate at which the Universe itself is expanding, it is clear that as well as all the bright stars and galaxies there is at least ten times and possibly one hundred times more "dark matter" in the Universe, exerting its gravitational influence on the bright stuff.

The calculations of conditions in the Big Bang, in which particle physics and cosmology combine so fruitfully, establish beyond reasonable doubt that this dark matter cannot all be in the form of atoms like those of which the Sun, stars, and planets are made. The bright stuff of the Universe is predominantly composed of protons and neutrons (which make up most of the mass of atoms), and the laws of physics tell us how much (or rather, how little) of this kind of stuff (known as baryonic matter) can have been made in the Big Bang. The limit roughly matches the amount of matter in all the bright stars and galaxies—a coincidence that fooled astronomers for decades into thinking that stars and galaxies were, indeed, the only stuff in the Universe. Now that there is compelling evidence for the influence of additional dark matter, the inescapable conclusion is that most of this dark matter—the *bulk* of the stuff of the Universe—is not in the form of homely baryons, but must consist of exotic particles never yet detected here on Earth.

This was the rationale behind the first attempts to resolve the solar neutrino problem by considering the effects of WIMPs on the structure of the Sun. There is little point in inventing a "new" particle just to explain the paucity of solar neutrinos. But if cosmology *requires* the existence of extra particles anyway, it is natural to consider how they might affect the behavior of stars. In fact, the unified theories being developed by particle theorists all require the existence of extra kinds of particle in the Universe. These requirements are a result of theories developed independently of cosmological studies of how galaxies move. Cosmology needs extra matter that is not in the form of baryons to explain how things move in the Universe; particle physics needs extra particles that are not in the form of baryons to make the unified theories work. Theorists studying the largest observable objects (galaxies) and theorists studying the smallest known entities (sub-atomic particles) independently find that they need the same sort of new stuff to make everything fit together. The natural explanation is that this is a powerful indication that both groups of theorists are working along the right lines. Otherwise, it is an impressive coincidence, if that is all it is, that one type of particle that meets the needs of theorists working with the very large *and* the very small also solves the major outstanding puzzle concerning a middle-sized object, our Sun.

But not all of the particles postulated to make the unified theories work would affect the solar interior in the right way to resolve the neutrino puzzle; nor, indeed, do the particles required by cosmologists to hold the Universe together have to fit the description of WIMPs outlined in this book. Instead of particles that each have a mass of around five times the proton mass, there could be a correspondingly larger number of correspondingly lighter particles, or even a relatively small number of *very* massive particles. The variety of possible candidates for dark matter that are now being actively considered is enormous.* But these candidates cannot all be present in the actual Universe, so I shall focus only on the small proportion of them that also solve the solar neutrino problem.

If both particle physics and cosmology tell us that there must be "extra" varieties of particles in the Universe, and solar studies show that some of the candidates to meet *both* these needs can also solve the neutrino puzzle, then the simplest and most parsimonious assumption is that this kind of WIMP really might be the most important constituent of dark matter. If unified theories are on the right track, there may be other dark matter particles as well—one very light particle, the axion, almost certainly exists, and some of the dark matter (equal to the amount we see in bright stars and galaxies, but no more) could even be in the form of baryons. But 80 percent of the mass of the Universe (at least) is definitely not in the form of baryons, and a sizable fraction of that 80 percent may well be in the form of WIMPs with masses around five times that of the proton. How could we ever hope to detect them, except by their influence on the Sun and by the invisible tug of their gravitational fingers?

○ **THE CANDIDATES**

Neutrinos themselves were once considered to be candidates for the missing dark matter, and in their early work on the effects of massive solar particles on the neutrino flux, Faulkner and Gilliland, back in the 1970s, were thinking in terms of a heavy variety of neutrino. But

*See John Gribbin and Martin Rees, *Cosmic Coincidences* (New York: Bantam, 1989).

this was mainly because at the time scientists had not yet gotten used to the idea that there might be completely different varieties of particles around—they knew neutrinos existed, so it was natural to try to make neutrinos fit the astrophysical requirements. But it was a frame-up, and it didn't stand up to further investigation.

In 1987 astrophysicists received a veritable gift in the form of a pulse of neutrinos from a supernova in a nearby galaxy, the Large Magellanic Cloud. According to astrophysical theory, the supernova produced 10^{58} electron neutrinos—ten times more than the total number of electrons, protons, and neutrons inside the Sun! About three thousand trillion (3×10^{15}) of these are calculated to have passed through a 7,000-cubic-meter detector on Earth (it is run by a joint team from the University of California-Irvine, the University of Michigan, and Brookhaven, and is therefore known as IMB). Out of this flood, the IMB detector actually recorded just eight neutrinos, arriving over a six-second interval. As explained in Chapter 4, if neutrinos had mass the ones with more energy would travel faster and arrive at the detector sooner. If they have no mass, then, like photons, they would travel at precisely the speed of light, always, and would arrive together (assuming they set off together). Other researchers, as I described earlier, have tried to estimate neutrino masses by considering the implications of the arrival times of neutrinos from the supernova in various different detectors on Earth. But what happens if you look at the IMB data alone, assume that all of the events it detected were caused by the arrival of electron neutrinos, and ignore the rest? Measurements of the spread in arrival times of this pulse of neutrinos from the supernova show that they cannot possibly have a mass bigger than 10 eV, and probably have masses close to 3 eV, while they may not have any mass at all. These units (electron volts) are tiny, and so the estimated masses are very small—it would take the combined mass of 150,000 such neutrinos to equal the mass of one electron. These estimates have a direct bearing on the solar neutrino problem in two ways.

First, if the 3 eV estimate (or even the 10 eV limit) is correct, then the masses are *too big* to permit the kind of neutrino oscillations (the MSW effect) that some theorists have proposed to resolve the puzzle. Second, neutrinos with so little mass could not provide anywhere near all of the dark matter required by cosmologists, leaving ample scope for unknown particles to fill the gap. On both counts, the supernova neutrino studies make the case for WIMPs more compelling.

That doesn't *quite* rule out the possibility that another kind of neutrino might masquerade as such a WIMP. There are, remember, three kinds of neutrinos already known to exist, associated with, respectively, the electron, the tau particle, and the muon. None of them has enough mass to be the WIMP we are looking for. This tripling is, however, a very tidy arrangement that fits neatly within the framework of the most highly regarded of the present crop of unified theories* and seems to relate the three neutrino "families" to the varieties of fundamental particles known as quarks. It also happens that the combination of particle physics and cosmology to describe what happened in the Big Bang suggests that there should be just three such families. But there is just enough leeway in these calculations to allow for the possibility of a fourth type of neutrino— and ample uncertainty in any predictions about the nature of such a particle to allow for the possibility that it might have a mass of about five times the proton mass. Suggesting such fourth-generation neutrinos as WIMP candidates is stretching credulity, but is not absolutely forbidden by the current crop of particle theories or by our understanding of the Big Bang.† More plausible candidates, however, are not hard to find.

I mentioned one way to make WIMPs—my favorite—in Chapter 5. We know that an asymmetry in the laws of physics allowed the production of just one baryon (proton or neutron) for every billion photons that emerged from the Big Bang. If there happens to be another kind of particle that has a mass in the range from 5 to 10 times the mass of a proton and that is also produced in the same way, obeying the same asymmetry with the same billion-to-one ratio, then there would be one WIMP in the Universe for every baryon, and in a galaxy like our own the mass of all the WIMPs put together would be just right to account for the way stars move, perhaps leaving some leeway for more dark matter in the Universe in the form of light neutrinos or the axions that particle physicists are so fond of.

The second plausible way to make WIMPs concerns not *asymmetry*

---

*For a better understanding, see *In Search of the Big Bang*.

†Just after I had written these words, late in 1989, physicists at CERN reported new measurements that definitely restrict the number of possible neutrino types to three. If these new results stand up to closer scrutiny, as seems likely, that will close this particular loophole for good.

but *symmetry*. In a manner reminiscent of the way the laws of physics indicate a symmetry between matter (electrons, protons, and the like) and antimatter (positrons, antiprotons, and so on), modern ideas about the relationship between particles and forces suggest that there should be another counterpart for every type of particle that we know. Some particles, like photons, are actually the carriers of forces in our world. Photons carry electromagnetic forces, gravitons carry gravity, and so on. Other particles, like neutrons and protons, are lumps of matter that are affected by forces, but which do not in themselves carry a force. As part of their search for a unified theory to explain forces and particles in one package, physicists see a need for symmetry between the two, and this can best be achieved by allowing every type of particle to be accompanied by a ''new'' force-carrier, and every type of force-carrier to be accompanied by a ''new'' particle.*

This is not as bad as it sounds, since out of all this menagerie of new particles only one variety should be stable. All the new heavy particles, in this scheme of things, decay into successively lighter particles, except for the lightest one of all, which has nothing to turn into. For obvious reasons, this kind of theory is known as supersymmetry. It predicts that there should be just one previously unknown variety of particle at large in our Universe, the ''lightest supersymmetric partner,'' or LSP. And the most likely candidate for the LSP is the counterpart to the photon, which is dubbed the photino. *Completely independent* of any of the cosmological considerations about dark matter, or the speculation that WIMPs in the heart of the Sun may resolve the solar neutrino problem, supersymmetry theory predicts that the photino will have a mass a few times bigger than the mass of the proton and that it will interact only weakly with everyday matter. The photino, if it exists, is *exactly* the kind of WIMP I have been talking about.

Even if cosmologists were not eager to find dark matter to explain how stars and galaxies move, and even if there were no solar neutrino problem to be resolved, particle physicists would be eager to carry out experiments aimed at detecting WIMPs in the laboratory. With three compelling reasons to search for WIMPs (and bearing in mind the Bellman's comment, in Lewis Carroll's *The Hunting of the Snark*,

---

*This is explained in more detail in *Cosmic Coincidences*, where Martin Rees and I also explain why the axion is so highly favored by particle theorists.

that "what I tell you three times is true"!) it is hardly surprising that such experiments are now moving out of the planning stage.

○ HOW TO CATCH YOUR WIMP

If WIMPs do provide the solution to these separate problems of cosmology, astronomy, and physics, there ought to be plenty of them around to find. The averaged-out density of such dark matter required in our part of the Galaxy must be equivalent to about one proton mass in every three cubic centimeters of space. If WIMPs each have a mass of about five times the mass of a proton, there should be one WIMP in every 15 cubic centimeters—and that doesn't just mean in "empty space" out above the Earth's atmosphere, but passing through the room I am sitting in as I write, your body as you read these words, and every physics laboratory on Earth. Each liter of air around you actually contains between 60 and 70 WIMPs, according to this line of thought.

Each WIMP is moving with its own independent velocity through the Galaxy—but it is only independent up to a point. Like the planets orbiting around the Sun, the stars orbiting around the Galaxy, or indeed the molecules of air in the atmosphere of the Earth, the motion of a WIMP is constrained by gravity. The appropriate average velocity for objects held by the gravity of the whole Milky Way system and orbiting at about the distance of our Solar System from the center of the Milky Way is the same whatever the mass of the object is, for a proton or a star—no more than roughly one thousandth of the speed of light, which works out to just 300 kilometers a second. The speed of the Sun and Solar System in orbit around the Galaxy is about 220 kilometers a second, for a circular orbit; this is roughly the same as the speed of a WIMP in our neighborhood, because the Solar System has to obey the same law of gravity—but the WIMPs may be moving in any direction, not in circular orbits, so the range of speeds relative to the Earth covers the span from zero (for WIMPs moving the same way around the Galaxy as we do and thus keeping up with us) to about 500 kilometers a second (for WIMPs moving the opposite way, colliding with us head-on).

To get some perspective on what this all means, let's compare these numbers with those for molecules of air itself. The all-important oxygen, for example, is in the form of molecules made of two atoms of oxygen and has a mass roughly 32 times that of the proton—several times more massive than a WIMP. And a mass of 32 grams of oxygen would contain more than 600,000 billion billion molecules. And those molecules are moving pretty fast—about 500 meters a second for the oxygen in the air that you breathe—though not as fast as many of the WIMPs. But unlike molecules of air, the WIMPs do not take part in everyday interactions involving electromagnetism; they interact only weakly with everyday matter, which is almost as transparent to WIMPs as it is to neutrinos.

Among other things, electromagnetic forces are what make a solid object solid. Atomic nuclei are surrounded by clouds of electrons, and it is the electrons that interact with the electrons from other atoms in a solid to lock the atoms rigidly in place. Rigidly, that is, as far as other atoms and molecules are concerned. When I hit the keys on my computer with my fingers as I type these words, my fingers don't go through the keyboard because the electrons surrounding the atoms in my fingertips meet resistance from the electrons surrounding the atoms in the keys. The nuclei buried deep within those atoms take no direct part in this process at all—compared with the electron cloud, the size of the nucleus is roughly equivalent to a pea in the center of a concert hall. A molecule of oxygen will bounce off a lump of lead, say, because its own electron cloud interacts with the electrons in the atoms at the surface of the lead. But a WIMP doesn't notice the existence of electrons. Any WIMP that arrives at the surface of a lump of lead will plow on happily through the clouds of electrons, brushing them aside like a cannonball moving through fog. It will only "notice" the lead if it runs head-on into a *nucleus*—a rare, but not impossible, occurrence. Therefore WIMP detectors being designed and built today are intended to take advantage of such rare events by measuring changes in a solid crystal caused by the impacts of WIMPs with nuclei.

The task is just feasible, but requires some sophisticated measuring techniques. What makes it feasible is that atomic nuclei happen to have masses in the range of possible masses for WIMPs. The lightest element, hydrogen, has a nucleus (a single proton) with just one proton mass; carbon nuclei have 12 times the proton mass; and so on. Energy is transferred from one particle to another most efficiently in a collision when the two particles have roughly the same mass—so ordinary materials are just right for "noticing" the impact of WIMPs.

There should be somewhere between 1 and 100 WIMP collisions

per day in each kilogram of a lump of matter—the exact numbers depend on details of the properties of WIMPs, details which we can only find out about by detecting some and measuring their influence on lumps of matter. Happily, you don't need an impossibly large lump of, say, germanium to act as a WIMP detector (you certainly don't need as much as the mass of cleaning fluid in Ray Davis's neutrino detector, for example). But you do need sensitive means to detect the changes in your lump of germanium (or whatever) caused by the arrival of WIMPs.

Researchers are now pursuing several different ways of attacking this problem. Some of them are rather subtle and have to do with changes in the properties of the "target" that can only be properly understood if you have a thorough grounding in quantum physics. But others are easier to understand in principle and more straightforward to interpret in practice. I'll cover three of the less esoteric examples here.

One possibility is that the impact of WIMPs with the nuclei of a semiconductor, such as germanium, will alter the electrical properties of the material in a measurable way. Semiconductors are rather curious materials in which some of the electrons that are attached to the nuclei in a crystal lattice are only loosely held in place. Under the right conditions, an electron can be encouraged to jump out of its place in the crystal, leaving a hole behind. Because electrons carry negative charge, the hole, in a sea of electrons, behaves exactly like a positively charged electron. And the impact of a few WIMPs on the nuclei in such a crystal ought to shake things up sufficiently to produce a few electron-hole pairs, which could be detected.

Another possibility is to listen, literally, for the sound made by a WIMP striking a nucleus in a crystal. As the nucleus recoils from the blow, it will jostle its neighbors slightly, sending a ripple of disturbance—a sound wave—through the crystal. Blas Cabrera and his colleagues at Stanford University propose mounting an array of small sensors on each surface of a suitable crystal, sensitive enough to measure the tiny vibrations, like miniature earthquakes, produced when the shock wave from the impact of a WIMP sends ripples out to the surface. This is my favorite technique, since it raises the possibility of using "crystal seismology" to detect WIMPs in the lab, tying in nicely with the use of helioseismology to measure the effects of WIMPs on the Sun. If they can do this, it will be a very neat trick indeed.

But perhaps the simplest approach to the problem of monitoring

WIMP impacts with everyday matter (and the one most likely to succeed first if WIMPS do have the properties suggested by solar studies) is simply to measure the heat released by the impact. Heat is simply a measure of the amount of movement of the molecules and atoms that make up a solid, liquid, or gas—a hotter object is one in which the atoms and molecules are moving faster (vibrating to and fro in a solid, wandering about more freely in a liquid or gas) and jostling each other more vigorously. When a WIMP slams into a nucleus and causes it to jostle its neighbors, the temperature of the crystal increases as the kinetic energy of the incoming WIMP is converted into heat. Unfortunately, the amount of heat released is tiny—for a detector made of pure silicon, weighing one kilogram, under ideal conditions, the impact of a single WIMP will raise the temperature by less than five thousandths of a degree (less than 5 millikelvin). Nevertheless, if the crystal is very cold to start with (cooled by liquid helium down to a temperature of only a few K, around *minus* 270°C), there is a real possibility of measuring such modest temperature changes.

The effort involved in trying to detect WIMPs certainly seems worthwhile, given that it may reveal the whereabouts of the ''missing'' nine tenths of the Universe. Nobody has yet done the trick—indeed, nobody has yet measured any of these effects that could be unambiguously attributed to WIMPs. But all of these possibilities and more will be tested by operational experiments during the 1990s. So far, like experiments to measure the masses of neutrinos, the results only set limits on the range of possibilities for WIMP masses. The limits will get tighter as new experiments come into operation over the next few years—unless, or until, an actual WIMP detection is made. As of now, the limits are far from embarrassing to those theorists who so eagerly anticipate the eventual detection of WIMPs.

○ RESULTS SO FAR

The best limits on WIMP masses so far come from experiments that were designed and built to study other particle interactions, but which happen to be sensitive to certain kinds of WIMPs as well. No dedicated WIMP detector searching in the ''right'' mass range is actually running yet. But one of the existing experiments gives you a good feel for the kind of effort involved.

This particular experiment was actually built to investigate another phenomenon, known as double beta decay, which, like "new" particles, is required by the best unified theories of physics.* It works by monitoring the behavior of electron-hole pairs in a germanium crystal. The goal is to detect the pulse of energy released by an electron when it falls back into the hole, shortly after the original impact from an outside particle disturbs the semiconductor and creates a hole. Such equipment is now fairly standard and, in the case of the detector developed by Ronald Brodzinski of Battelle Pacific Northwest Laboratories and Frank Avignone of the University of South Carolina, uses a germanium crystal weighing about three fourths of a kilo. The problem is that almost anything that collides with the nuclei in the crystal lattice will trigger the electron-hole response. So it has to be shielded from cosmic rays and from any background radioactivity. Where better to site the apparatus than alongside the Davis neutrino detector, 1,600 meters underground in the Homestake Gold Mine?

Even there, the team ran into problems. The surrounding rocks are themselves radioactive enough to trigger the detector, which has to be shielded by some inert material that contains no radioactive nuclei at all. Such material is, in fact, very hard to find on the surface of the Earth today. As well as by short-lived radioactivity induced by the impacts of cosmic rays themselves, most modern materials are contaminated by traces of radioactivity from all the nuclear bombs that have been exploded in the atmosphere since World War II. One source of nonradioactive steel, still being "mined" for use in some scientific work, lies in the remaining hulks of German battleships of World War I vintage, scuttled in Scapa Flow on the north of Scotland after the German fleet surrendered at the end of that war. But lead provides an even better shield against radiation, and the apparatus in the Homestake Mine is actually shielded by lead obtained from the ballast in the wreck of a Spanish galleon that sank early in the sixteenth century.

After all this and other efforts to reduce background "noise" affecting the apparatus, the team could still "only" set an upper limit on WIMP masses. They found no evidence of any particles with masses more than 20 times that of a proton, and they are confident that such particles would have been found if they were present. As far as it goes,

---

*In fact, double beta decay *has* now been observed, confirming that those unified theories are on the right track—circumstantial evidence that WIMPs also exist.

this is good news; the discovery of WIMPs with such high masses would have been a severe embarrassment for astrophysicists trying to resolve the solar neutrino problem.

Yet another detector in the Homestake Mine, actually intended to search for neutrinos, sets a limit at the low-mass end of the range. Edward Fireman, from the Smithsonian Astrophysical Observatory in Cambridge, Massachusetts, headed a team that reported this new limit in 1988. Their apparatus consists of six tons of potassium hydroxide, in which argon-37 might be produced by the interaction of either neutrinos or (as it happens) certain kinds of WIMPs with nuclei of potassium-39. After three years of operation, the experiment produced no evidence for either neutrino or WIMP interactions. The way this detector works actually makes it more sensitive to *lighter* particles (it was, after all, designed to detect neutrinos)—so the absence of any observed interactions tells us that if there are any WIMPs around, they must have masses *above* one proton mass, and probably greater than three proton masses.

This is beginning to get interesting, since the solar physicists need WIMPs with masses in the range from about five to ten proton masses, with a preference for the low end of that range. It is even more interesting since another germanium detector, run by a team from three research centers (the University of California—Santa Barbara, the Lawrence Berkeley Laboratory in California, and the University of California-Berkeley) came up with a tighter *upper* limit, also in 1988. That experiment says that the mass of the WIMP must be *less* than nine times the mass of a proton. Tantalizingly, the range of possibilities still allowed by the observations is *exactly* the range required by the astrophysics; but until that crucial experiment that actually measures the mass of a WIMP, we won't know for sure that the astrophysicists were right. The answer should be in before the year 2000.

○ **INTO THE FUTURE**

It is a sign of how astronomy has changed in recent years that the detectors involved in this search are not telescopes mounted in observatories high on mountaintops on the surface of the Earth, but contain tons of potassium hydroxide (or whatever) buried deep below ground at the bottom of mine shafts. By any standards, the Homestake

Mine, where several astronomical particle detectors may be found running simultaneously, surely now deserves the description "Homestake Observatory."

The contrast between the old and the new ways of astronomy is even more marked than it appears at first sight. John Faulkner makes the point with striking force when he talks about the solar neutrino problem. The important piece of a telescope like the 120-inch reflector at the Lick Observatory, where Faulkner works, is *not,* he stresses, the 50 tons or so of girders in the supports and the mirror (120 inches across) itself. The important part of the telescope, the bit that actually interacts with photons of light and focuses them onto the detectors, is a thin film of aluminum spread over the surface of the mirror. That film amounts to just one cubic centimeter of aluminum—which is all you need if you want to study photons.

But while the mirror surface of the 120-inch telescope is coated with just one cubic centimeter of aluminum, the interior "surface" of the impressive steel box that holds the Davis detector is "coated" with a hundred thousand gallons of perchloroethylene. And you need all that "working surface" if you want to study neutrinos. This contrast in volume provides a genuine measure of the intrinsic differences between photon and neutrino telescopes—and WIMP detectors closely resemble neutrino detectors, to such an extent that, as we have seen, some detectors can double up in both roles.

New kinds of detectors always open up new horizons in astronomy. Telescopes like the 120-inch at Lick were themselves instrumental in transforming our understanding of the Universe, and we are on the threshold of a new revolution, which will once more transform our understanding of the Universe, when positive results begin to emerge from the new generation of detectors. In light of all the circumstantial evidence, the indications are strong that we stand at the threshold of a wonderful new discovery, the identification of the kind of particles that make up more than 90 percent of the mass of the Universe. *Everything* studied by previous generations of astronomers represents only the tip of the cosmic iceberg. Alternatively, all of the assumptions and observations on which those experiments are based may be wrong. Disconcerting though that would be, especially to astrophysicists seduced (like myself) by the beauty of the WIMP solution to the solar neutrino puzzle, in some ways it would be an even more exciting discovery. It would force theorists to start afresh in trying to work out how stars operate, what holds galaxies together, and how it might be possible to unify the description of particles and forces in one mathematical package.

We—or rather, our recent ancestors—have been in this situation before—not once, but twice, in little more than a hundred years. And then, as now, it was studies of the Sun that held the key to developments with implications that would reverberate through the world of science. William Thomson (later Lord Kelvin), convinced that the power of the Sun must come from gravitational collapse, was as sure of his assumptions in the 1860s as any proponent of WIMP theory was sure of his own assumptions in the 1980s. But Thomson lived to hear Rutherford describe the discovery of a new source of energy, from the breakdown of radium. And almost exactly halfway in time between Thomson's definitive expression of the gravitational contraction theory and the work by Faulkner and others that makes the case for WIMPs with equal eloquence, the puzzle of how nuclei could be stuck together in stars was a factor in the development and establishment of a new quantum physics describing nuclear fusion and the tunnel effect.

Are we, like Thomson in the 1860s, deluding ourselves in thinking that the laws of physics as we understand them today are adequate to solve the mystery of how the Sun works? Or should we, like Arthur Eddington in the 1920s, be looking for a revolution in physics to enable us to explain the observed fact that the solar furnace does indeed operate at a temperature that is not the one that standard theory tells us it "ought" to be operating at? Either way, solar astronomy seems certain to be one of the most exciting areas of science in the 1990s, after decades in which more remote and superficially more exotic objects, such as pulsars, quasars, and black holes, have held the center of the astronomical stage. Strictly speaking, our story ends here, although the revelation of the innermost secrets of the sun is just beginning. Before I bring this book to a close, however, I shouldn't miss the opportunity to describe one of those exotic objects, a supernova. The most recent, SN 1987 A, was perhaps the greatest observational event not just of the twentieth century but of several centuries, and has helped to confirm our understanding of the Sun as it has been outlined in this book.

9 THE SUPERNOVA CONNECTION

Our Sun is not fated to become a supernova. But it was born out of the debris of supernova explosions of the distant past, when our Milky Way Galaxy was young. Apart from hydrogen, every atom in your body, and every atom on Earth except for hydrogen and helium,* was manufactured inside stars and then expelled into space by supernova explosions to spread the clouds of hydrogen and helium from which the Sun and its family of planets formed. Without an understanding of supernovas, we would have no understanding of the origin of the Sun (let alone of our own origins), and the story I have told in this book would be incomplete.

Over the previous three decades, theorists had developed what seemed to be a satisfactory understanding of supernova explosions, based on their understanding of the laws of physics, on observations of such explosions in distant galaxies and of the debris from old supernova explosions in our own Galaxy, and on computer models of how stars work, like those I have described earlier. But until 1987 they had no means of checking this understanding directly. The explosion of a star known as Sanduleak $-69°$ 202 into a supernova first visible from Earth on the night of 23–24 February 1987 was, therefore, possibly the single most important event in astronomy since the in-

*There is no helium in your body.

vention of the telescope. The event, dubbed SN 1987A (denoting the first supernova observed in 1987) took place in the Large Magellanic Cloud, a galaxy so close to our own Milky Way that it is part of the same system of galaxies, held together by gravity and known as the Local Group. At a distance of 160,000 light-years (just next door, by cosmological standards), SN 1987A was by far the closest supernova to have occurred since 1604, when the last known supernova exploded in our own Galaxy, just before the development of the astronomical telescope. SN 1987A was close enough to be studied in detail by a battery of instruments—including conventional telescopes on mountaintops, X-ray detectors onboard satellites in space, and neutrino detectors buried deep beneath the ground. Both in broad outline and most of the details, those observations showed, over the two years following the outburst, that the astronomers did have a good understanding of how supernovas work. Although some details did not match up to expectations, there were no major surprises. It seems that we do indeed understand where the material that made the Sun and ourselves came from, and it also seems appropriate to celebrate this landmark in astronomy by looking at SN 1987A in a little more detail.

○ **DISCOVERING A SUPERNOVA**

In one sense, the story of Supernova 1987A begins about 160,000 years ago, when planet Earth was experiencing the ice age before last. Since the star that exploded is about 160,000 light-years away, it took that long for the light to reach Earth. But as far as residents of this planet are concerned, the story begins on the night of 23–24 February 1987, when a young Canadian astronomer, Ian Shelton, was making observations from the Las Campanas Observatory, high on a mountaintop in northern Chile. Shelton was using a modest telescope, by professional standards—one with an aperture of just 10 inches. He had just gotten permission to use this instrument in a survey of the Large Magellanic Cloud, a search aimed at finding variable stars, ones that change in brightness from one day to the next, one week to the next, one month to the next, or on even longer time scales. Professional astronomers scarcely ever ''look through'' their telescopes these days; apart from the battery of electronic technology that can be used to obtain information from starlight, even the humble photograph reveals more than the human eye can see, because it can be exposed for a long time (hours, in many cases), building up an image all the time. The human eye will see no more after staring at a star for hours than it will at first glimpse.

Shelton took his first photographic plate of the Large Magellanic Cloud on the night of 21–22 February—and because he hadn't yet gotten used to the system, it was a pretty poor snapshot. On the night of 22–23 February, he did rather better, obtaining a reasonable plate of the Large Magellanic Cloud using a one-hour exposure. This photograph was to assume great importance as the last one of the region taken by that instrument before the supernova became visible.

On the night of 23–24 February, Shelton had everything working properly and obtained a good, long exposure, three hours ending at 2:40 A.M. Satisfied with a job well done, he was ready for bed—but decided to develop the photographic plate first. As soon as he did so, he noticed a bright spot, looking like a star, which hadn't been there when he photographed the same region the night before. At first he thought it might be a flaw on the plate. Any star that bright, he realized, would be easily visible to the naked eye. Just in case, he stepped outside the telescope building to take a look. The new star really was there.

Earlier that same night, around midnight, one of the people working on the nearby 40-inch telescope had gone out to take a look around. Oscar Duhalde, the night assistant on the 40-inch, knew the southern skies, where the Large Magellanic Cloud is a prominent feature. He noticed that there was a new star in the Large Magellanic Cloud, but didn't draw the attention of the two observers using the telescope to the phenomenon. One of them later commented wryly, "We must have been working Oscar too hard."* Shelton, however, was quick to share his discovery with his colleagues. He went over to the control room of the 40-inch and asked them how bright a nova would look at the distance of the Large Magellanic Cloud. A nova (from the Latin for "new" star), though by no means common, is a fairly routine astronomical event, when a star passes through an unstable phase and flares up brightly for a short time. It isn't really a new star, but an old star that has suddenly brightened enough to be noticed. The more experienced astronomers working with the 40-inch told Shelton that such a nova would reach a magnitude of about 8, on the standard astronomical brightness scale (on which a *lower* number indicates a

*Ronald Schorn, *Sky & Telescope*, May 1987, p. 470.

brighter object). That was interesting, commented Shelton, because he'd just photographed a star in the LMC that had a magnitude of 5. Barry Madore immediately said that it must be a supernova*—at which point Oscar Duhalde mentioned that he, too, had seen a bright new star in the Large Magellanic Cloud earlier that night. Everybody went outside to take a look—but, ironically, they could do nothing to study the phenomenon immediately. The supernova lay too low in the sky to be investigated by the 100-inch telescope at the site, while the 40-inch was rigged up for that night's observing with an instrument called a charge-coupled-device, used for studying faint objects and so sensitive that pointing it at the supernova would have burnt it out in less than a second.

All they could do was alert the rest of the astronomical community— which is easier said than done from the top of a mountain in Chile. After fruitless attempts to telephone the clearinghouse for astronomical discoveries, the International Astronomical Union's Central Bureau in Cambridge, Massachusetts, a messenger was sent down the mountain to send the news by telex from the nearest town. The report eventually arrived in Cambridge just half an hour ahead of the second report of the discovery. By that margin, Shelton and Duhalde were officially recognized as the discoverers of the supernova.

The discovery caused huge excitement among astronomers, spilling over into the general press and making the cover of *Time* magazine on 23 March. The reason for all the excitement was partly the importance of supernovas themselves—the biggest explosions that have taken place since the Big Bang in which the Universe was born, and the source of all the heavy elements—and partly their rarity. Only four definite supernova explosions have been observed in our Galaxy over the past thousand years, and the last one visible to the naked eye (and that only just) blew up in the Andromeda Galaxy two million light-years away (ten times farther than SN 1987A) and was visible as long as 1885.

○ **BLASTS FROM THE PAST**

The study of supernovas begins, after a fashion, in the mists of antiquity, with records of what Chinese astronomers called "guest stars"

---

*The origin of the term is obvious, but a supernova, in fact, has nothing in common with a nova except that it is a star that suddenly increases in brightness.

in the centuries before Christ. Of course, those astronomers (or astrologers, as they really were) did not know what it was they were seeing. But they regarded the appearance of "new" stars in the sky as highly significant, and kept records of their occurrence. Unfortunately, those records are not always simple to decipher. Some of the objects recorded as guest stars may have been the less spectacular novas, not supernovas; some may even have been a different kind of phenomenon altogether (perhaps comets). But what might be the earliest known mention of a supernova is an inscription on a bit of bone that dates from 1300 B.C. and records a bright star appearing out of nowhere near the star we call Antares.

The first unambiguous identification of a supernova dates from A.D. 185 and describes the brightness of the star and its slow fade back into obscurity in terms that leave no doubt about the identification. Over the next thousand years, Chinese skywatchers recorded five more supernovas in our Milky Way Galaxy, some of which were also noted by observers in other parts of the world, including Japan, Egypt, and, possibly, the Americas. The last of these was the one that has made the biggest impact on modern astronomy—a bigger impact, indeed, than any other object outside our own Solar System.

That supernova blazed in the sky above Earth on 4 July 1054. It shone in the constellation Taurus and marked the death throes of a star just 6,000 light-years away from us. Chinese and Japanese observers recorded the event, but no records of the supernova of 1054 have come down to us from their European contemporaries, although the star must have been visible from Europe. Curiously, this may be the supernova recorded in images left by native Americans on rock walls in Arizona (little did they know the significance the fourth of July would have in that part of the world a few centuries later).

Because this supernova was so close, astronomically speaking, and so recent, it has left behind a glowing mass of gas that can be studied in great detail by modern telescopes, and a rapidly spinning, dense neutron star in its heart, detectable as a pulsar at radio frequencies, in optical light, and even using X-ray equipment. This Crab Nebula (so called because its outline in some astronomical photographs resembles a crab—if you have a vivid imagination) is virtually an astrophysics laboratory, a site where many phenomena can be observed and many theories tested, almost on our astronomical doorstep. The study of this object is so important that astronomers have been known to quip that the observational side of their craft can be divided neatly into two roughly equal portions—the study of the Crab Nebula, and the study of everything else.

Since 1054, less than a handful of other supernovas have been observed, and Europeans only got in on the act in 1572. The last supernova seen in the Milky Way occurred as long ago as 1604.* Although this was studied in detail by Johannes Kepler, frustratingly for astronomers today his records were entirely based on observations with the naked eye. The supernova was visible from Earth just five years before Galileo first applied the telescope to the study of the heavens. Before the astronomical telescope was invented, supernovas visible from Earth had been popping up in our Galaxy at a rate of about four every thousand years. By blind chance, *two* had been visible in the span of a single human lifetime, in 1572 and 1604. But in all the time from 1604 to 1987, as telescopes lay waiting for their prey, the only supernova that could (just) have been seen by the unaided eye was the one that occurred in the Andromeda Galaxy just over 2 million light-years away, visible from Earth at the end of the nineteenth century. All this explains why SN 1987A caused so much excitement among astronomers. It wasn't quite in the Milky Way, but in the galaxy next door; it was, however, certainly visible to the naked eye, and it could be studied in unprecedented detail by all of the instruments that now exist to supplement Galileo's simple telescope.

○ **BACK TO THE PRESENT**

The news that came in to the International Astronomical Union's Bureau in Cambridge just half an hour after the telex from Chile was from an astronomer in New Zealand, Albert Jones, who spotted SN 1987A that same night. And from the same part of the world came key observations made even before the supernova was noticed, by astronomers taking routine photographs of the Large Magellanic Cloud. Robert McNaught, in Australia, photographed the brightening star about 16 hours before it was identified as a supernova, using a large astronomical camera known as a Schmidt telescope—but the photographs were only developed and studied after the news from Chile reached Australia. And about three and a half hours later, two

*Curiously, though, modern astronomers have found the remains of a supernova that ought to have been visible from Earth in the middle of the seventeenth century, but which nobody seems to have noticed at the time. It is called Cassiopeia A.

astronomers testing a new piece of guiding equipment on a telescope in New Zealand just happened to pick the Large Magellanic Cloud as the target for their test photographs. Together with the observations from Chile the night before the supernova burst into view, these photographs help to establish the timing of the event and the speed with which the progenitor star, Sanduleak − 69° 202, flared up. Even better for astronomers, this is the first time in which the star that became a supernova has been identified on old photographic plates, so that they know in some detail what it was and what it was doing before it flared.*

All of this helped astronomers test their theories of how supernovas work. The key theoretical insight actually dates back more than half a century, to 1934. At that time, less than two years after the discovery of the neutron, Walter Baade and Fritz Zwicky made the dramatic suggestion that ''a supernova represents the transition of an ordinary star into a neutron star.'' But although half a century of observations of distant supernovas and theorizing had filled in the details of how that might happen, the theories could only be tested fully by studying a nearby supernova at work.

By the late 1980s, astronomers were satisfied, from their studies of supernovas in other galaxies, that there are two different basic types of supernova. In each case, an ordinary star is indeed converted into a neutron star, releasing energy along the way—just as William Thomson would have appreciated—from its store of gravitational energy. Nineteenth-century physics is enough to explain the energy released in a supernova—once you know that neutron stars exist. The difference between a supernova and the mechanism Thomson proposed to keep the Sun hot is primarily one of scale—the formation of a neutron star from an ordinary star involves a collapse so dramatic that the energy released makes the biggest bang since *the* big one—the one in which the Universe was born. The mass of a neutron star contains roughly the mass of our Sun packed into a volume comparable to that of a mountain on Earth. Such a star will form from any lump of matter that is no longer kept hot by nuclear fusion in its heart (a dead star) when the inward tug of gravity overwhelms the forces that give atoms their structure. The only proviso is that its mass is a little more than

---

*Strictly speaking, the *second* known progenitor. Supernova 1961V, in a disc (spiral) galaxy known as NGC 1058, was probably the explosion of a star that had been recorded in a photograph taken 37 years previously. But in that case there was not enough information to study the progenitor star in detail.

a critical amount (actually slightly bigger than the mass of our Sun which is why we know it won't become a neutron star). If the mass is *much* bigger than this, even neutrons are crushed out of existence by gravity, turning the dead star into a black hole. The range of masses for stable neutron stars is, therefore, only from a little over the mass of our Sun to about twice the solar mass.

The first way to make a supernova (Type I) is if a cold, dead star that has *less* than the critical amount of mass gains matter from a companion. Such a star starts out as a white dwarf, a dead star with about the mass of our Sun, maybe a little less, contained in a volume the size of the Earth. It is the fate of our own Sun to end its life as a white dwarf, because it does not have enough mass to become a neutron star and it has no companion to steal mass from. But a star like our Sun which has become a white dwarf and orbits around another star can gain mass, tugging streamers of gas off its companion through tidal forces and swallowing them. When its mass reaches the critical value, the atoms of which the star is made will collapse, with electrons being forced to merge with protons to become neutrons. The star, more massive than our Sun, will shrink from the size of the Earth to the size of a mountain, releasing the appropriate amount of gravitational energy in the process.

But that is not what happened in SN 1987A. SN 1987A was formed by the second method of creating a supernova, known as Type II. This happens, according to theory, when a very massive star, near the end of its life, runs out of nuclear fuel to keep its heart hot. The inner part of such a star, already with more than the critical mass needed to make a neutron star, collapses all the way to the neutron star state, without stopping off as a white dwarf. In a few seconds, comparably huger amounts of energy are liberated— at least a hundred times as much energy, as our Sun has radiated in its entire lifetime—blasting the outer layers of the star outward at speeds of around 20,000 kilometers a second (actually 17,000 kilometers a second in the case of SN 1987A) and triggering a wave of nuclear reactions, creating heavy elements that can be formed naturally in no other way.

Like most simple definitions, this broad description of supernovas as Type I and Type II can be refined and subdivided. The experts split each main category into at least two subcategories. But that is not important for now. What matters is that SN 1987A was a Type II supernova, a representative of the most energetic kind of stellar event that can ever take place. And, because the progenitor star has been identified, astronomers can reconstruct the history of the supernova, from the time that star was born right up to the dramatic events observed in 1987.

That story is reconstructed, of course, with the aid of the computer models of how stars work that I mentioned earlier. Different researchers have developed slightly different models which tell a slightly different set of stories, although the broad outlines are always the same; the outline I give here is based on the models used by Stan Woosley and his colleagues. Woosley, a supernova expert, works at the University of California–Santa Cruz (the same campus where John Faulkner is based), and he has told his version of the supernova story in some detail in an article with Tom Weaver in the August 1989 issue of *Scientific American*. According to this model, the star we are interested in was born only about 11 million years ago, in a region of the Large Magellanic Cloud particularly rich in gas and dust. Because the star contained about 18 times as much matter as our Sun, it had to burn its nuclear fuel more quickly in order to provide enough heat to hold itself up against the inward tug of gravity. So its fuel was exhausted more quickly than the fuel of a star with the mass of our Sun, and it shone about 40,000 times brighter than the Sun. In just 10 million years, it had burned all the hydrogen in its core into helium. As a result, the core slowly shrank and got hotter until helium burning could begin.

It is during this phase of its life that such a massive star becomes a supergiant, with the outer layers swelling up to stretch across a distance roughly the same size as the diameter of the Earth's orbit around the Sun. One of the surprises that astronomers found when they examined old photographs of SN 1987A's progenitor, Sanduleak − 69° 202, was that the star was actually not a red supergiant but a blue supergiant, a smaller and hotter type of star. The outer parts of the star had contracted again slightly, perhaps as recently as 40,000 years before the explosion. This does not affect the basic understanding of Type II supernovas, but it gives the theorists plenty of interesting detail to sink their teeth into. A favored explanation at present is that this late shrinking of the outer part of the star has to do with the fact that the Large Magellanic Cloud, unlike our own Milky Way Galaxy, contains only relatively modest amounts of heavier elements than helium. One of those elements deficient in stars of the Large Magellanic Cloud, oxygen, helps to make a red supergiant swell up, because a little oxygen in the outer part of the star absorbs radiation that is trying to escape, holding it in and making the star swell like an inflating balloon. With less oxygen present, once such a star reaches the stage of its evolution where the outward flow of radiation drops slightly, the "balloon" might deflate again. While helium burning was going on, the star probably was a red supergiant; but helium burning could only sustain the star for about a further million years after hydrogen burning in the core ended.

In the last few thousand years of its life, Sanduleak −69° 202 must have gone through its remaining possibilities for energy production with increasing speed. Carbon, itself a product of helium burning, was converted into a mixture of neon, magnesium, and sodium; neon and oxygen (another product of helium burning) "burned" in their turn; and at the end nuclear fusion reactions were consuming silicon and sulphur in the heart of the star, while all the other nuclear fuels were being burned in successively cooler layers working outward from the center (Figure 9.1). All the while, the pace of change quickened. According to the calculations made by Woosley and his colleagues, helium burning lasted nearly a million years, carbon burning only 12,000 years, neon kept the star hot for 12 years, oxygen provided the necessary energy for a mere four years, and silicon was burnt out in a week. And then things began to get really interesting.

○ DEATH AND GLORY

Silicon burning is the end of the line even for a massive star, because it produces a mixture of nuclei—including cobalt, iron, and nickel—that are among the most stable arrangements it is possible for protons and neutrons to form. Sticking lighter nuclei together to make iron nuclei releases energy (once you overcome the electric barrier between the lighter nuclei). But sticking iron nuclei and other nuclei together to make heavier elements uses up energy, *over and above* the energy needed to overcome the electric barrier. Indeed, through fission heavier elements may split to form nuclei more like those of iron and giving up energy in the process. There is a kind of natural energy valley for nuclei, with iron at the bottom and light elements up one side of the valley while heavier elements lie up the other slope of the valley. All nuclei would "like" to roll down the valley

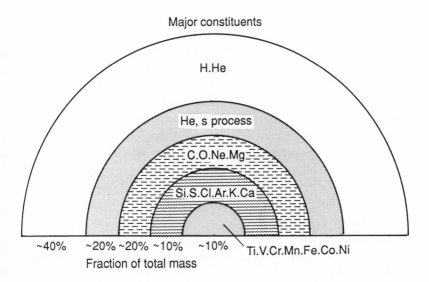

Major constituents

H.He

He, s process

C.O.Ne.Mg

Si.S.Cl.Ar.K.Ca

Ti.V.Cr.Mn.Fe.Co.Ni

~40%   ~20% ~20% ~10%   ~10%

Fraction of total mass

Fig. 9.1. **The structure of a heavy star like the precursor to SN 1987A, just before it explodes. The iron-rich core is ready to collapse; the various fusion processes described in the text are all taking place in different layers throughout the star, at lower temperatures in each successive shell from the center.**

and become iron, light ones through the fusion route and heavy ones through the fission route. In this sense, iron and nickel are the most stable nuclei. So where do elements heavier than iron (lead, uranium, and all the rest) come from? From supernovas, like SN 1987A. And although that statement was well founded in scientific calculation before February 1987, it has only been proven correct by studies of SN 1987A.

In fact, there are two kinds of elements that cannot be produced inside stable stars. The lightest elements (deuterium, helium-3, lithium, beryllium, and boron) must have come from somewhere else, before the first stars formed. That "somewhere else" can only have been the Big Bang, in which the Universe was born.

The standard model of the early Universe is derived by winding back (in our imagination, and with the aid of computer models) the observed expansion of the Universe today. If we do this, like Gamow did, we arrive at a "moment of creation," some 15 billion years ago, when density was infinite. Leaving aside exactly what this infinity means,* cosmologists can use information from their understanding of particle physics and the description of the Universe provided by general relativity to describe how the Universe evolved from a few seconds after this moment of creation.

At an "age" of about 25 seconds, the temperature is about 4 billion degrees and the *energy* density is roughly 2 ton per liter! The fireball that is the Universe consists essentially of neutrinos and photons, with just a trace of protons, neutrons, and electron-positron pairs. The density of *matter* is only 10 grams per liter—just 10 times the density of the air we breathe. At this stage, protons cannot link up electro-magnetically with electrons to form stable atoms of hydrogen, because atoms would be broken apart by the intensely energetic radiation. For the same reason, protons and neutrons cannot yet combine to form deuterium nuclei.

But when the Universe is about a minute old, it has expanded and cooled sufficiently for deuterium nuclei to hold together. This triggers a chain of nuclear reactions, lasting a couple of minutes, that converts almost all of the deuterium into helium and produces very small quantities of a few other very light elements. But with all the deuterium used up, as the Universe cools further, fusion reactions stop. After a further hundred thousand years or so the Universe is so cold (about at the temperature of the surface of our Sun) that naked protons and helium nuclei link up with electrons to form atoms.

The proportion of primordial material that is converted into helium depends on how rapidly the Universe expands in its early stages. This in turn depends on the number of varieties of elementary particles present, and the way they interact. Taking all of these factors into account (including the latest evidence that there are just three types of neutrinos), the standard model tells us that about 23 percent of the matter in the early Universe was processed into helium. The fact that we see 25 percent helium, by mass, in old stars today is a striking vindication of the standard model of the Big Bang—a model that also

*I discuss it in some detail in my book *In Search of the Big Bang*.

accounts for the existence of small amounts of lithium and the other light elements in our Universe.

So the lightest elements come from the Big Bang, and everything else up to iron can be made inside massive stars. Particle theorists, drawing on the studies of their experimental colleagues, can also explain how elements heavier than iron can be produced, provided that nuclei are bathed in a sea of neutrons. And neutrons are one thing that a supernova produces in abundance—although there are, in fact, more gentle processes also at work transforming lighter elements into heavier elements in the Universe.

Most of the elements more massive than iron, as well as some of the isotopes of less massive elements, are produced when nuclei built up by nuclear fusion processes capture neutrons from their surroundings inside a star. Any free neutron is itself unstable and emits an electron by beta decay, turning into a proton, if left to its own devices for a few minutes. So the neutrons involved in these capture processes have to be freshly released by other nuclear interactions. This is no problem inside a star where nuclear burning is going on. For example, every time one nucleus of deuterium and one of tritium fuse to produce helium-4, one neutron is released; this and similar reactions inside stars provide a profusion of neutrons—as many as a hundred million in every cubic centimeter of the interesting region of a star—which may interact with other nuclei.

Adding a single neutron to a nucleus increases its mass by one unit but does not change its electric charge or its chemical properties—it becomes a different isotope of the same element. In many cases, however, the newly formed isotope is unstable, and given time (in some cases, a few seconds; in others, a few years) it will eject an electron by beta decay, converting one of its neutrons into a proton and becoming a different element. Then the whole process may repeat, when the same nucleus captures another neutron. This step-by-step buildup of heavy elements, in which a nucleus has time to convert into a stable form in between interactions with neutrons, is known as the slow, or **s,** process of neutron capture.

But when large numbers of neutrons are available, which certainly happens as a result of explosive interactions occurring during the early stages of a supernova, there may be so many neutrons around that a nucleus can capture several of them before it has time to spit out an electron or decay in some other way. A density of a mere 100 million neutrons per cubic centimeter is nowhere near enough to make this happen; it requires a density of about 300 billion billion (3×10^{20}) neutrons in every cubic centimeter of star stuff. The result, when these enormous neutron densities are briefly achieved as a supernova explodes, is a rapid buildup of elements and isotopes which have a surplus of neutrons and which are almost all unstable. This is the rapid, or **r**, process of neutron capture. Once the wave of neutrons has been absorbed, the unstable, neutron-rich nuclei that are left behind will decay into stable nuclei, losing neutrons (converting them into protons) and becoming more like the isotopes produced by the **s** process. Many isotopes are produced by both processes. A handful of stable, slightly neutron-rich nuclei are produced only by the **r** process and subsequent beta decays. And just 28 isotopes, astrophysicists calculate, can be produced only by the **s** process.

In a diagram of the elements that plots the number of neutrons in a nucleus against the number of protons, stable isotopes lie on a roughly diagonal band along which the number of neutrons is slightly greater than the number of protons. Elements formed by the **s** process (and by the ultimate beta decay of **r** process elements) lie on a zigzag track through this ''valley of stability''; unstable isotopes produced by the **r** process lie far off to the right, in the neutron-rich half of the diagram, and as they decay they shift toward the bottom of the valley of stability, ''raining down'' on the **s** process elements (Figure 9.2). Both processes end for very massive elements where nuclei are split apart either by alpha decay (emitting a helium nucleus) or by fission (producing two roughly equal nuclei, each with about half the mass of the one that splits).

Both these processes are very well understood. Studies of the way nuclei and neutrons interact in experiments here on Earth, combined with computer models of conditions inside stars, satisfactorily explain how almost all of the known elements are built up. The main exceptions are some isotopes rich in protons, which are thought to be formed by a proton capture process, but this is not fully understood; there are also some rare isotopes that are produced in space by interactions involving cosmic rays. But these are minor effects and the studies on SN 1987A showed just how well astrophysicists really do understand the way elements are built up in supernovas. Without getting too bogged down in the details, the key thing to remember is that making elements heavier than iron requires an *input* of energy, which comes from the gravitational collapse of the supernova's core to become a neutron star.

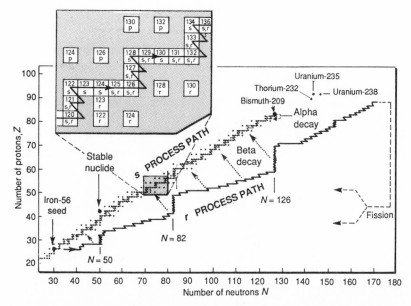

Fig. 9.2. The *r* and *s* processes at work. Stable heavy elements are built up from iron-56 by the *s* process, described in the text. They lie on a diagonal line (the valley of stability) in this plot. The inset shows in detail the *s* process at work, building up new nuclei by absorbing a neutron (moving one space to the right) and emitting an electron (moving up and to the left) as required. The number in each box indicates the total number of particles (protons plus neutrons) in a particular nucleus. *s* indicates that a particular element can be made by the *s* process, *r* by the *r* process. *p* indicates elements formed by the still poorly understood *p* process.

When many neutrons are availiable in a supernova explosion, neutron-rich nuclei build up rapidly through the *r* process (lower line). These then decay by emitting electrons (beta decay), raining down into the valley of stability. Very heavy nuclei split apart by fission or alpha decay.

○ THE SUPERNOVA INSIDE OUT

Except in the case of our Sun, where neutrino studies may be providing a direct clue to conditions in the deep interior, we cannot study any of the nuclear processes at work inside stars directly. The observations that provide both the input to theories of stellar astrophysics and the tests of those theories are indirect studies of material expelled from inside stars. First, the material has to be processed inside a star, carried to the surface, and ejected into space; then it can be studied from Earth by the way in which the elements produced either radiate or absorb light. Everything has to fit together—and it does.

One simple example shows what is involved. The carbon-nitrogen-oxygen (CNO) cycle should, according to particle physics theory, convert carbon into the most common isotope of nitrogen, nitrogen-14. At the same time, the set of interactions reduces the amount of the isotope carbon-13 relative to carbon-12. All of the products of these interactions should, according to astrophysics theory, get mixed up to the surface of red giant stars. And when stellar spectroscopists analyze the light from red giants, they find just the mix of nitrogen and carbon isotopes predicted by theory.

Clouds of gas ("planetary nebulas") produced by relatively small stellar explosions (mere novas) also show the "right" mix of elements and isotopes in line with the kind of stellar cooking of the elements described earlier in this book. But as well as providing the biggest input of energy to make heavy elements, supernovas also provide the biggest blast to blow material out into space, giving astronomers their best opportunities to study star stuff. Many old supernova remnants have indeed been identified and studied by spectroscopy. But there's a snag. A cloud of gas blown out into space by a supernova explosion sweeps up gas and dust from between the stars as it moves through space. So when astronomers study the glowing cloud of material today, hundreds or thousands of years after the supernova explosion lit up the night sky for our ancestors, they cannot untangle the information they want about the elements produced in the supernova itself. SN 1987A, caught on photographic plates before, during, and after its explosion, was different.

According to astrophysical theory, just before the supernova exploded, all of the standard nuclear reactions leading up to the production of iron-group elements were going on in shells around the core, and in addition the s process should, theorists were confident, have been at work in the region of the star rich in carbon and oxygen (Figure 9.1). Silicon burning, remember, had held the star up against the inward tug of gravity for just about one week (as it happens, barely long enough for Ian Shelton to get his photographic survey of the Large Magellanic Cloud under way), and had left a core composed of the most stable nuclei—iron, nickel, and the rest—incapable of releasing energy *either* by fusion *or* by fission (although, as we shall see, some of those iron group nuclei can decay to iron itself). After 11 million years, the heart of the star was left with no means of support, and it collapsed, in a few tenths of a second, into a lump no more than a hundred kilometers across. During this initial collapse, very energetic photons ripped iron nuclei apart, undoing the work of 11 million years of nuclear fusion processes, and electrons were squeezed into nuclei under such enormous pressures that beta decay went into reverse, converting protons into neutrons. Gravity provided the energy for all this. All that was left was a ball of neutron material, essentially a giant "atomic nucleus" two hundred kilometers across and containing nearly one and a half times the mass of our Sun.

The squeeze of the in-falling material was so great that at this point the center of the neutron ball was compressed to densities even greater than those of the nucleus of an atom. Then, like a golf ball being squeezed in an iron grip and then released, it rebounded, sending a shock wave out through the ball of neutron stuff and into the star beyond. Material from farther out in the core of the star, plunging inward at a speed roughly one quarter of the speed of light, met the rebounding shock from the core of neutron stuff and was literally turned inside out, becoming a shock wave racing *outward* through the star. It was this shock wave that blew the star apart—but not before a flood of neutrons emitted by all this activity had caused a sizable production of heavy elements through the **r** process.*

The neutrinos easily outpaced the shock. They traveled at nearly the speed of light (exactly the speed of light if they have zero mass), but the shock moved at about 2 percent of the speed of light, even after getting a boost from the neutrinos, taking a couple of hours to push the outer layers of the star into space and light up the star visibly— which is why the neutrinos were captured by detectors on Earth shortly before the star brightened visibly.

While all this was going on, even though the iron core of the star had been converted into a ball of neutrons, according to theory there should have been a massive burst of nuclear reactions farther out in the star in the hot, high-pressure shock wave, producing iron-group

---

*The shock wave was actually helped on its way by a blast of neutrinos from the core as it collapsed all the way down to become a neutron star just 20 kilometers across—a relatively leisurely process that took several tens of seconds (not tenths of a second) to complete. And by the time it was completed, the neutrinos were long gone. The outgoing shock wave, trying to push more than 15 solar masses of material along in front of itself, became so dense that it could absorb a significant fraction (a few percent) of this neutrino outburst (as I describe in more detail in my book with Martin Rees, *Cosmic Coincidences*), gaining enough energy to finish the job of blowing the star apart. The rest of the neutrinos—carrying a couple of hundred times as much energy as the supernova radiated in visible light—went on through the star and out into the Universe at large, where just a few ended up in detectors on Earth.

elements. Most of the elements produced inside the star by such fusion reactions were made, in effect, from successive additions of alpha particles (helium-4 nuclei, each made of two protons and two neutrons combined together) and had equal numbers of protons and neutrons in their nuclei. Carbon-12 (six protons, six neutrons) and oxygen-16 (eight protons, eight neutrons) are typical examples. When these nuclei were processed by explosive interactions, then according to theory most of the material was converted into nickel-56, which has 28 neutrons and 28 protons in each nucleus. But nickel-56 is unstable; it decays, emitting positrons to convert protons into neutrons (just the inverse beta decay). The first step in this decay has a half-life of just over six days and produces cobalt-56; the cobalt-56 then decays into iron-56 (26 protons, 30 neutrons) with a half-life of 77 days.

The unstable nickel-56 had been built up by the input of gravitational energy from the collapse of the core of the supernova. When it decayed, it gave up some of that borrowed energy. The standard theory of supernovas, developed before SN 1987A was seen to explode, predicted that almost all of the energy radiated by the star during the first hundred days of its life as a supernova would come from the decay from cobalt-56 to iron-56. This decay follows a characteristic pattern, a decreasing exponential curve; and the fading of the supernova itself followed exactly the predicted curve. During that first hundred days, this evidence showed, 93 percent of the output of the supernova was indeed provided by the decay of cobalt-56; and the slow fade of the supernova was still following the appropriate curve at the end of 1989, when I was finishing this book, almost three years after Shelton first noticed the brightening of the supernova. Astrophysicist Roger Tayler of the University of Sussex says these observations of cobalt decay "are probably the most important and exciting ones concerned with the origin of the elements, confirming that the theoretical model is broadly correct."

It wasn't just the "light curve," as it is called, that he was referring to. As the material expelled by the supernova moved out into space, successive layers of its interior were revealed to the telescopes of the patiently watching observers, in a kind of cosmic striptease. Eventually, the observers could see material coming out from the regions where the explosive nuclear interactions should have taken place— and what their spectroscopic studies revealed was characteristic lines associated with nickel-56, just as expected, indicating that as much nickel-56 as the equivalent of 8 percent of the mass of our Sun had been manufactured in the supernova—closely in line with theoretical calculations. The spectroscopic studies also revealed the presence of barium, strontium, and scandium—all s process elements produced before the star became a supernova. And studies of helium and nitrogen in the outermost layers of the expanding cloud of material around the supernova are helping astrophysicists improve their understanding of how material produced by the CNO cycle gets mixed up to the surface of a star.

Of course, there were also surprises. Details of the behavior of SN 1987A do not in every case match precisely with the details of the theories, and there is ample scope yet for astronomers to refine their understanding of how stars like this explode. But the mention of new insights into the way carbon and associated elements are produced and mixed into the Universe provides a cue to bring my present discussion to an end. These, after all, are the elements of which we are, in large part, made—carbon, oxygen, and nitrogen have a key importance for life as we know it. And observations of the spectra of these elements in the expanding cloud of material around SN 1987A provide a re-minder that while such an explosion marks the death of a star, it is quite literally the beginning of the story of life-forms like ourselves. We would not be here, wondering about the secret life of the Sun, if it were not for those previous generations of supernova explosions that scattered their share of carbon, nitrogen, oxygen, and other elements through interstellar space billions of years ago. As far as life forms like us are concerned, in fact, my story ends—in the beginning.

POSTSCRIPT: SEESAW SCIENCE

Studies of the secrets of the Sun are now progressing so rapidly that even during the months since the first draft of this book went to the printers there have been significant new developments both with observations of solar neutrinos and with theories to explain why so few of these neutrinos are observed. The weight of this new evidence has tipped the balance of expert opinion away from the WIMP model (as of early 1991) and in favor of a variation of the MSW process, described in Chapter 4. Appropriately, this variation on the MSW theme depends on something known as the "seesaw process" to provide neutrinos with a tiny amount of mass.

By the time you read these words, there will surely be further changes in the scientific story, and I have no intention of trying to provide a definitive "answer" to the solar neutrino problem here, but rather intend simply to give you as much up-to-date information as possible so that you can make sense out of the stories that are bound to emerge, in 1991 and beyond, in the press and on TV. But one underlying theme remains constant throughout all of this. Although the WIMP theory may no longer be front-runner to explain the puzzles posed by solar neutrino measurements, it is still clear that there is a connection between what is going on inside the Sun and the nature of the Universe at large—and it may even be that solar studies are giving us a clue to the right way to develop a unified theory of physics, touched on briefly in Chapter 8.'

○ **DAVIS WAS RIGHT**

Without the new observations, of course, there would be no foundation on which new theories could be built. The dramatic development in the solar neutrino story during 1990 was that, after two decades depending on data from just one experiment, theorists were suddenly provided with observations from four solar neutrino detectors. The bottom line from these new observations is that Ray Davis was right all along—there really are too few neutrinos coming from the Sun, and it is not due to a fault with his detector that he doesn't see more of them. But, in line with the whole saga of solar studies, the new observations do not simply confirm the measurements made by Davis, they throw up more complications for the theorists to debate. As John Bahcall said at a conference in December 1990, "This subject would be a lot simpler if there were no experiments to worry about."

Two of the new detectors use the gallium technique described in Chapter 4. One of these detectors, called SAGE (Soviet-American Gallium Experiment) is based in the Caucasus; the other, known as GALLEX (from "Gallium Experiment"), is a European venture based in the Gran Sasso Tunnel under the Alps. According to the twin standard model (standard astrophysics plus standard nuclear physics), these experiments should detect a few low-energy solar neutrinos. By the end of 1990, there was no evidence that either experiment had detected any solar neutrinos at all. This total absence of low-energy solar neutrinos came as a surprise and cannot be explained simply by adjusting the astrophysical models. As Bahcall puts it, either the standard model of physics is wrong, or the gallium experiments simply do not work.

The other "new" detector is the Kamiokande experiment, which I have already discussed. It began monitoring solar neutrinos in 1988, and by 1990 had built up enough data to provide a basis for statistical comparisons with the measurements from the fourth experiment, Davis's old faithful in the Homestake Mine in South Dakota. The comparison provides plenty of scope for theorists to use their imaginations.

The good news, of course, is that the Kamiokande detector not only records a low number of neutrinos but also tells us which direction the neutrinos it detects are coming from, confirming that they are indeed solar neutrinos. More mixed news is that after more than a thousand days of operation, right through the peak of the latest solar cycle of activity, the number of neutrinos detected at Kamiokande has stayed steady, with no trace of the correlation with sunspots seen in the data from South Dakota. Bahcall, the theorist who has spent a lifetime puzzling over solar neutrinos, is convinced that the apparent correlation between the neutrinos detected by Davis and sunspots is just a coincidence. But, as I shall explain shortly, other theorists are still using this correlation, which they think is real, to refine their versions of the MSW process—and Davis himself has not yet admitted defeat and paid up on his bet with Bahcall!

The most important conclusion drawn from the comparison between Kamiokande data and data from the Davis experiment is, however, clear-cut. The Kamiokande detector chiefly records the arrival of neutrinos produced in the boron-8 process. Interpreting the number of these neutrinos to tell us, according to standard physics theory, how many neutrinos the Sun should be producing by the various different processes going on in its heart, Bahcall can calculate how many neutrinos ought to be detected by the Davis experiment, assuming that standard nuclear theory is correct. Even this figure turns out to be twice as high as the number of solar neutrinos actually detected by the Davis experiment—but the calculation involves no assumptions about astrophysics at all. So the combination of data from South Dakota and Kamiokande unambiguously tells us that the standard theory of nuclear physics—the so-called electroweak theory—is wrong. Of course, the standard model of astrophysics might be wrong as well, but we can at least hope that all of the puzzle might be resolved simply by finding a better theory of nuclear interactions. This is where the seesaw mechanism comes in.

○ THE THEORISTS' FIELD DAY

The new Kamiokande data severely restrict the range of possible MSW variations that could resolve the shortfall of solar neutrinos detected on Earth. The basic MSW process, remember, involves one kind of neutrino, produced in the heart of the Sun, changing into another kind of neutrino ("oscillating") on its way out through the Sun. Both the Davis detector and the Kamiokande detector only detect the kind of neutrinos associated with electrons, and these are indeed the kind of neutrinos being produced by the nuclear reactions that keep the Sun hot. But the family of particles to which the electron belongs, the leptons, also has two other members, the tau and mu particles. Any electron neutrinos that are converted into tau or mu neutrinos en route to us will not be noticed by the detectors, even though the total number of neutrinos has stayed the same.

In the Kamiokande detector, the incoming solar neutrinos are recorded when they interact with electrons in the tank of water that makes up the bulk of the detector. There are no tau or mu particles in ordinary matter, so there is nothing in the water for tau or mu neutrinos to interact with, and they pass right through the detector as if it were not there. When electron neutrinos interact with electrons, however, the electrons recoil from the blow, and both the direction and energy of the fast-moving electrons that result can be measured by detectors that line the walls of the tank of water. The direction of the recoil, as I have already mentioned, tells us that the neutrinos that hit the electrons are coming from the Sun. And the energy measurements tell us how much energy those neutrinos carried with them from the heart of the Sun and out across space to Earth. It is the energy information that severely constrains the possibilities allowed for the MSW model.

In particular, the latest observations show that the flux of neutrinos from the Sun is evenly suppressed at all energies that have so far been measured. Neutrinos can only oscillate in the required way at all provided that they have mass, and the nature of the oscillation process depends on the difference in mass between the two neutrino types involved in the oscillation. The theory says that if this mass difference is relatively large, high-energy neutrinos will be preferentially converted, while lower-energy neutrinos will be unchanged. However, if the mass difference is very small, then only low-energy neutrinos will be converted, while higher-energy neutrinos remain unchanged. The energy "spectrum" of electron neutrinos arriving at Kamiokande rules out the first possibility. More subtle analysis of the measurements rules out a whole slew of other possibilities, leaving just one tiny range of neutrino properties that could allow the MSW oscillations to affect electron neutrinos leaving the heart of the Sun in just the right way to account for both the Kamiokande data and the Homestake results.

According to this variation on the MSW theme, the suppression of electron neutrinos occurs mainly at low energies, below the thresholds for detection at both the Kamiokande and Homestake detectors, while the suppression actually being measured is only a minor part of what is going on. This means that the difference in mass between the electron neutrino and the other type involved in the oscillation is tiny—about one thousandth of an electron volt. The electron neutrino itself would then, according to the theory, also have a mass of less than one thousandth of an electron volt, which is less than one billionth of the mass of an electron.

The reason theorists got so excited about this is that they already had a theory that predicted neutrino masses just about in this range. This seesaw mechanism was proposed back in 1979 by several theorists, including the Nobel Prize winner Murray Gell-Mann. It is part of one of the many attempts to develop a grand unified theory, one set of mathematical equations to describe the behavior of the three forces that operate on the scale of subatomic particles, electromagnetism and the strong and weak nuclear forces. According to all these theories of grand unification, the three forces become equivalent to one another at very high energies, and the critical energy at which this occurs can be expressed as a mass. The seesaw formula gives the mass of a particular type of neutrino in terms of the mass of the associated lepton divided by the grand unification mass.

The grand unification mass is enormous. Different theories come up with slightly different estimates, but it must be around 10^{15} billion electron volts, which is 10^{15} times the mass of a proton. The neutrino masses that come out of the seesaw equation for the two lightest types of neutrino are around a thousandth of an electron volt and less than a millionth of an electron volt. So the difference in their masses is also about a thousandth of an electron volt, just right to fit the only bit of the MSW theory that is still viable in the light of the Kamiokande data. And this raises the exciting prospect of measuring the neutrino masses accurately from studies of the Sun and using these astrophysical observations, plugged back in to the seesaw equation, to find out exactly what the grand unified mass is and how a definitive grand unified theory can be put together.

○ COSMIC CONNECTIONS— AND A WORD OF CAUTION

This flurry of excitement about the MSW process has even revived the notion that neutrinos might provide the dark matter needed to hold the Universe together. Dennis Sciama, a British astrophysicist based in

Trieste, Italy, made some calculations in 1990 linking the MSW effect, the seesaw process, and a long-standing puzzle about the nature of hydrogen clouds in the Universe. The puzzle is that the hydrogen atoms in these clouds have been energized, so that they emit what is known as Lyman-alpha radiation. It is easy to energize hydrogen in this way, using ultraviolet light; but where does the ultraviolet light come from?

Sciama has suggested that the radiation could come from the death of heavy neutrinos that were created in the Big Bang, decaying as they age. Tau neutrinos could do the job, says Sciama, if they have a mass of about 29 electron volts and an average lifetime of about 10^{16} years. By pinning down the mass of one neutrino, he is able to calculate the masses of the other two neutrinos from the seesaw equations. In Sciama's version, this comes up with a value of just over one thousandth of an electron volt, exactly in line with the calculations based on the MSW theory of solar neutrino oscillations, but for the mu neutrino, not the electron variety. In this view, the electron neutrino has an even smaller mass, about one hundred millionth of an electron volt. And there are so many tau neutrinos around, it is thought, that even if they each have a mass of only 29 eV, that is well on the way to accounting for the dark matter discussed in Chapter 5.

Sciama himself points out that his idea "ties together three unproven hypotheses: the seesaw mechanism, the MSW effect and the decaying neutrino hypothesis," but that when he does so he comes up with "a consistent pattern." If the three components of the scheme continue to hang together as more evidence comes in, this will be an exciting development indeed.

But maybe the excitement is premature. After all, as yet this all rests upon *negative* evidence. Nobody has actually made a positive observation of the MSW effect at work. Instead, the experiments actually *rule out* most of the range of predicted MSW effects. No doubt enthusiasts for the theory would say that by eliminating the impossible, what they are left with must be correct; an alternative view might be that they are clinging to a tiny loophole left to them by existing experiments and might well find the last vestige of MSW theory swept away when new observations come in.

It's worth remembering that accepting MSW theory and the seesaw mechanism means abandoning, for example, the interpretation of neutrino masses suggested by Cowsik's analysis of the supernova neutrinos. And if you make measurements that show, as they do, that the energy spectrum of solar neutrinos has not been distorted, it is all very well arguing that the distortion must be going on at lower energies where it cannot yet be seen, but just suppose we take the actual measurements at face value. If the shape of the neutrino energy spectrum really is undistorted, this is exactly what you would expect if the neutrino deficiency is actually a result of imperfections in the standard model of astrophysics and has nothing to do with neutrino oscillations at all!

The picture is far from clear-cut and is bound to change again as the new experiments produce more data. There are other theories that attempt to resolve the puzzle with nonstandard physics (for example, the possibility of oscillations linked with hypothetical magnetic properties of neutrinos), and there are still many more or less crazy variations on the astrophysical theme waiting in the wings. According to one interpretation of the latest solar sound wave data, there may even be two separate processes at work inside the Sun, interfering with the outward flow of neutrinos from the core.

○ HELIOSEISMOLOGY, SUNSPOTS, AND OSCILLATIONS

As expected, the new technique of probing the solar interior by studying the way its surface moves in and out is providing new insights into how the Sun works. It seems that the pattern of the Sun's vibrations varies over the roughly 11-year-long cycle of solar activity, and astronomers are hopeful that over the next few years this may reveal the fundamental causes of this cycle.

Vibrations involving the whole surface of the Sun, caused by sound waves bouncing around inside it, were first identified just one solar cycle ago, in 1979. Studies carried out by a group of researchers from the University of Birmingham and from Sheffield Polytechnic and reported in 1990 show variations in the detailed behavior of some of these solar sound waves that correlate with the changes in solar activity as measured by sunspot number. The newly discovered changes in the sound waves correspond to a change in the time it takes them to traverse the Sun. The variation over the solar cycle is about one second; according to the researchers, this could be produced by a change in the size of the layer of the Sun that the waves move through, or by a change in the speed of sound (possibly caused by a change in temperature) in the relevant part of the Sun.

But which part of the Sun is being affected in this way? Although these observations cover an entire sunspot cycle, this particular study does not provide information about the depth to which these waves penetrate the Sun. However, in another study reported in the same year, researchers from the Big Bear Solar Observatory in California described measurements of a slightly different family of solar oscillations that do provide information about depth of penetration.

Changes in the behavior of these waves also correlate with sunspot number, although the data only span the period from 1986 to 1988. These measurements suggest that the changes are occurring in a thin layer of the Sun's surface, covering no more than 1 percent of the solar radius.

Commenting on these new discoveries, Douglas Gough of the University of Cambridge said that although, strictly speaking, the two reports deal with different kinds of waves, "it is extremely likely that the frequency variations have a common origin." The changes in the behavior of solar sound waves over the sunspot cycle are closely associated with the changing magnetic activity of the Sun, and according to Gough, more subtle analysis may soon provide information about the more deeply seated dynamical processes that are responsible for the entire solar cycle of activity. Meanwhile, the theorists have been quick to attempt to tie this newly discovered variation of solar sound waves over the sunspot cycle with the evidence from the Homestake detector that the number of solar neutrinos reaching the Earth also varies over the solar cycle. Bahcall may be convinced that the correlation between sunspots and solar neutrinos is spurious, but other theorists, like Ray Davis, are not so sure.

Late in 1990, researchers from the University of Delaware and from Ohio State University presented their analysis, which suggests that there is indeed a strong correlation between the number of neutrinos and the sunspot number. Their analysis goes beyond earlier studies, however, in finding that the correlation is more clear-cut when they include an allowance for a seasonal variation—and they can explain how this might arise, in terms of the nature of the Earth's orbit around the Sun.

If there is a relationship between sunspot number and the neutrino flux, this must be because both the neutrinos and the spots are affected by changes going on below the solar surface. The most likely candidate to affect both of them is the changing solar magnetic field, which itself varies over the roughly 11-year cycle of activity. Then the neutrino effect can be explained in terms of a magnetic influence on neutrinos. As long as neutrinos have a small amount of magnetism (which is a pure guess and has never been measured), then oscillations very similar to those of the MSW process can be caused by the magnetic field inside the Sun as the neutrinos move out through it. As the strength of the magnetic field varies over the solar cycle, so will the strength of the oscillation and therefore the number of electron neutrinos surviving to reach the Homestake detector. But this is only part of the story.

Astronomers have good evidence that the Sun's magnetic field is wrapped around in a toroidal shape, like a doughnut, just below the surface of the Sun. The rotation of the Sun has the effect of twisting this magnetic field around and making it stronger at higher latitudes, away from the equator. So according to this theory the oscillation effect should be *less* for neutrinos traveling straight out from the core through the equator of the Sun and slightly more for neutrinos that come out from the core at an angle to the solar equator and emerge north or south of it.

The Earth itself is not always at the same distance from the Sun, and it also rises both above and below the plane of the solar equator as it travels around its orbit. This arises because the Earth's orbit is elliptical, not perfectly circular, and slightly tilted. It happens that we are slightly closer to the Sun in December than in June, but we are crossing the plane of the solar equator both in June and December, and these are indeed the months in which the Homestake detector records the most neutrinos. The Earth reaches its greatest distance above and below the solar equator in September and March, and these are exactly the months in which the flux of neutrinos is least. The team also points out that according to the MSW theory, there should actually be *more* electron neutrinos reaching the Earth when it is closest to the Sun, in December and January; this is actually the opposite of the small effect the Homestake team has measured. Taken at face value, the sunspot-neutrino correlation *rules out* the MSW process as an explanation for the scarcity of solar neutrinos!

The link with helioseismology comes from a study carried out by Lawrence Krauss of Yale University. He finds what he calls "tantalizing" hints that the neutrino variations and the sound wave variations are actually closely in step with each other, which would mean that they are each being directly affected by the same deep-seated solar variations. The variation over the solar cycle in the time it takes for sound waves to cross the Sun could be explained if the speed of sound inside the Sun changes, and one way to achieve this would be to have a large toroidal magnetic field deep inside the Sun, varying in strength over the solar cycle and affecting both neutrinos and sound waves. Such a magnetic field would affect sound waves because the electrically charged particles in the solar interior would experience an extra magnetic "pressure," as well as the weight of the outer layers of the Sun. The strong, deep-seated magnetic field would also, in fact, be an even more efficient way of making magnetic neutrinos oscillate than a magnetic field near the surface, and could flip electron neutrinos into some other variety even if they had a much smaller magnetism than the alternative version of this theory requires.

○ BACK TO THE FUTURE

It is far too soon to tell whether this line of approach to the problem will yield new insights into the secrets of the Sun. But one intriguing hint dropped by the Delaware/Ohio team, in a paper published in *Nature* in November 1990, may point to a fruitful approach for the 1990s. They point out that the magnetic influence they describe is not strong enough, in any case, to explain the overall low level of solar neutrinos reaching the Earth. It can very nicely explain why there are more neutrinos detected at certain times of the year and at certain times during the solar cycle—but only if something else has already reduced the flux of neutrinos to less than half the amount predicted by the twin standard model. "A full solution of the solar neutrino puzzle requires something in addition to the hypothesis of neutrino magnetic moments," they say, and this something may "manifest itself as a change to the standard solar model, or perhaps a combination of the magnetic moment hypothesis with the MSW effect."

The plot could hardly be thicker. The MSW effect may be close to the truth, or it may be ruled out by the next generation of detectors. The WIMP theory has faded from its position as front-runner, but still has perhaps a fifty-fifty chance (the odds were quoted by Jim Rich of Saclay in France at an astronomy meeting in December 1990) of providing part of the answer. There may or may not be a correlation between the neutrino flux and sunspot number, and if there is, this may or may not be telling us that neutrinos are magnetic.

Don't be disheartened by the confusion, though. It has always been like this in astronomy. When new observations are first made, there is a wealth of confusing and often conflicting ideas put forward to explain them. It happened with quasars and pulsars, even with the discovery of other galaxies beyond the Milky Way. The confusion is best seen as a sign that the study of what goes on *inside* the Sun, not just on its surface, really is becoming a real branch of science, fed by observations and experiments. My own feeling, at the end of 1990, is that none of the current crop of ideas is likely to prove the sole solution to the solar neutrino problem. There is still no direct observation of any effect of the MSW process at work which cannot be explained in some other way; there is still no positive detection of a WIMP in an experiment on Earth. It may be, after all, that we need *both* new physics and a better solar model to explain all the puzzles. Perhaps some combination of existing ideas, with separate processes at work suppressing the neutrino flux from the core of the Sun and modulating it in the outer layers, will indeed prove successful in the long run; or perhaps, in many ways the most exciting prospect of all, the new detectors now coming into operation will lead us to a completely new theory to resolve the problem.

Whatever happens over the next ten years, however, one thing seems certain. The more physicists study the secrets of the Sun, and especially the scarcity of solar neutrinos, the more it seems clear that the solution to these puzzles will involve both the world of the very small and the world of the very large. Insights into both the laws that govern sub-nuclear particles and the material that holds the Universe together have already emerged from studies of one ordinary, middle-sized star, and if physicists are ever to come up with their long-sought "theory of everything" it will certainly have to fit the wealth of information now coming in about the behavior of the Sun and its neutrinos. When John Bahcall and Ray Davis first proposed an experiment to monitor solar neutrinos back in 1964, it never entered their heads, says Bahcall, that you could use the Sun to discover new things about particle physics. But that may well turn out to be the most important and lasting legacy of the decades spent by Davis and his colleagues counting argon atoms in a tank full of cleaning fluid down a gold mine in South Dakota.

FURTHER READING

If you want to know more about the secrets of the Sun, the following books will provide more detailed information on some of the topics I have discussed.

Peter Atkins, *The Second Law* (New York: Scientific American/Freeman, 1984). An accessible, nonmathematical account of the importance of thermodynamics to our understanding of the world.

Peter Brent, *Charles Darwin* (London: Heinemann, 1981). A good "popular" biography that makes clear the debt Darwin owed to Lyell.

Joe Burchfield, *Lord Kelvin and the Age of the Earth* (London & New York: Macmillan, 1975). The definitive history of Kelvin's contribution to the debate about the ages of both the Earth *and* the Sun. Mainly for the specialists, or anyone with a passion for the story of how science developed in the nineteenth century.

Subrahmanyan Chandrasekhar, *Eddington* (New York: Cambridge University Press, 1983). A tiny little monograph, based on lectures given by Chandrasekhar in Cambridge to mark the centenary of the birth of Eddington. The best instant insight into the man described as "the most distinguished astrophysicist of his time."

Frank Close, *The Cosmic Onion* (London: Heinemann Educational Books, 1983). Don't be put off by the "Educational" in the publisher's name. This is one of the best and most accessible quick guides to the particle world, and will in particular put the neutrino in its place for you.

Frank Close, Michael Marten, and Christine Sutton, *The Particle Explosion* (New York: Oxford University Press, 1987). A wonderful illustrated history of all the known particles, from the electron to the W and Z. Particle physicist Close, picture researcher Marten, and science writer Sutton combine their talents to produce a book that is both informative and an attractive addition to any coffee table. Unfortunately, they stop short of any serious discussion of particles that haven't yet been detected, but might be soon— such as axions and WIMPs. Very good on neutrinos, though they don't really give Ray Davis his due.

Charles Darwin, *The Origin of Species by Means of Natural Selection* (London: Pelican, 1968). An accessible version of the great work, in a reprint that includes some later material as well but is essentially the first edition of 1859. Darwin showed from the outset that the time required for evolution to do its work was far more than a few thousand years, and he also appreciated how long it must have taken for natural forces to have molded the landscape.

Arthur Eddington, *The Internal Constitution of the Stars* (New York: Dover, 1959). This is the edition you are most likely to find around today; the original was published in 1926 by Cambridge University Press, and the Dover text is virtually the same. A textbook for astrophysicists, not something to dip into for light reading, but a classic well worth seeking out if you have the necessary scientific background.

Kendrick Frazier, *Our Turbulent Sun* (Englewood Cliffs, New Jersey: Prentice-Hall, 1982). A journalist's view of puzzles such as the dearth of solar neutrinos, the sunspot cycle, and links between solar activity and terrestrial climate. Fun, but slightly breathless; a good light read.

Herbert Friedman, *Sun and Earth* (New York: Scientific American/Freeman, 1986). A well-illustrated layman's guide to established current knowledge of the Sun and its influence on the Earth, with more emphasis on the traditional observational side of astronomy than I give here.

George Gamow, *A Star Called the Sun* (New York: Viking Press, 1964). Now out of print, but worth seeking in the secondhand shops or libraries. Like all Gamow's popularizations it is easy to read, full of anecdotal examples, and scientifically accurate. This one is particularly interesting, since it was Gamow's work on alpha decay that led to an understanding of how nuclear fusion can occur inside the Sun at a temperature of "only" 15 million degrees. Slightly outdated but still worth reading.

John Gribbin, *In Search of Schrödinger's Cat* (London: Corgi, and New York: Bantam, 1984). The story of the quantum revolution, which transformed physics in the first third of the twentieth century.

John Gribbin, *In Search of the Big Bang* (London: Heinemann, and New York: Bantam, 1986). More about the relationship between particle physics and cosmology.

John Gribbin, *The Omega Point* (London: Heinemann, and New York: Bantam, 1987). A book about the ultimate fate of the Universe, which includes a discussion of thermodynamics and the nature of time.

John Gribbin and Martin Rees, *Cosmic Coincidences* (New York: Bantam, 1989; published in the UK by Heinemann under the title *The Stuff of the Universe*). More about the variety of candidates for the dark matter in the Universe.

Fred Hoyle, *The Nature of the Universe* (Oxford: Blackwell, 1950). A short book, based on a series of talks on BBC radio, which includes a chapter on the Sun. Historically interesting—Hoyle went on, among other things, to make the key contribution that unlocked the secret of how elements are made inside stars—and full of powerful analogies and examples. But long out of print and not really worth spending much effort to track down if you cannot find it easily.

Mick Kelly and John Gribbin, *Winds of Change* (London: Headway, 1989). More about the greenhouse effect, mentioned briefly here in Chapter 6, which may be the most pressing problem facing humankind in the twenty-first century.

Clive Kilmister, *Sir Arthur Eddington* (Oxford and New York: Pergamon, 1966). A book about Eddington's work and his place in science, which includes extensive quotations from his key publications, including his book *The Internal Constitution of the Stars*. Mainly for students of the history of science.

Rudolf Kippenhahn, *100 Billion Suns* (London: Weidenfeld and Nicolson, 1983). A highly readable account of how stars work, from a leading German astrophysicist.

Hubert Lamb, *Climate, History and the Modern World* (London and New York: Methuen, 1982). The best single-volume guide to the changing climate of historical times and the impact of climatic change on human affairs. Includes a brief mention of sunspots and a great deal on the little ice age.

Kenneth Lang and Owen Gingerich, *A Source Book in Astronomy and Astrophysics, 1900–1975* (Cambridge, Mass.: Harvard University Press, 1979). A wonderful treasure trove of historic scientific papers, far too big and expensive to buy for yourself but well worth seeking out in a library.

Robert Noyes, *The Sun, Our Star* (Cambridge, Mass.: Harvard University Press, 1982). The best nonspecialist description of the Sun and its workings at the time it was written, but now being overtaken somewhat by new events. Noyes, professor of astronomy at Harvard University, includes only a brief mention of the neutrino problem and solar oscillations, and nothing at all, of course, on WIMPs, but is authoritative on topics such as solar spots and flares, the changing face of the Sun, and energy production in stars.

Abraham Pais, *Inward Bound* (New York: Oxford University Press, 1986). An astonishing book, a genuine tour de force, in which the author covers the history of particle physics from the discovery of X rays in 1895 up to atomic fission in the late 1930s in great detail but also with great clarity. This part of the book comes to 444 pages; in a mere 182 further pages Pais skips lightly over the postwar years to end with the discovery of the W and Z particles, seen by many as indicating that physicists are on the right track to a grand unified theory of all the particles and all the forces of nature.

Although full of scrupulously accurate science, the book essentially tells a story about physics and the people involved in these great years of discovery. The price, rather than any impenetrability of the contents, might put you off buying it, but it is well worth digging out of any library that has it on its shelves, or that can be persuaded to put it on its shelves. If you *are* intimidated, either by the price or the size of the volume, try Frank Close's books, mentioned earlier.

Claus Rolfs and William Rodney, *Cauldrons in the Cosmos* (Chicago: University of Chicago Press, 1988). For anyone with a serious interest in stellar astrophysics and not afraid of a few equations, this is the place to find out more about how stars live and die.

INDEX